A Mountain *of* EVIDENCE

PASTOR RANDY FRENCH

Copyright © 2020 Pastor Randy French.

All rights reserved. No part of this book may be used or reproduced by any means, graphic, electronic, or mechanical, including photocopying, recording, taping or by any information storage retrieval system without the written permission of the author except in the case of brief quotations embodied in critical articles and reviews.

WestBow Press books may be ordered through booksellers or by contacting:

WestBow Press
A Division of Thomas Nelson & Zondervan
1663 Liberty Drive
Bloomington, IN 47403
www.westbowpress.com
1 (866) 928-1240

Because of the dynamic nature of the Internet, any web addresses or links contained in this book may have changed since publication and may no longer be valid. The views expressed in this work are solely those of the author and do not necessarily reflect the views of the publisher, and the publisher hereby disclaims any responsibility for them.

Any people depicted in stock imagery provided by Getty Images are models, and such images are being used for illustrative purposes only.
Certain stock imagery © Getty Images.

Scripture quotations taken from The Holy Bible, New International Version® NIV® Copyright © 1973 1978 1984 2011 by Biblica, Inc. TM. Used by permission. All rights reserved worldwide.

ISBN: 978-1-9736-9769-5 (sc)
ISBN: 978-1-9736-9770-1 (hc)
ISBN: 978-1-9736-9768-8 (e)

Library of Congress Control Number: 2020913043

Print information available on the last page.

WestBow Press rev. date: 07/25/2020

CONTENTS

PREFACE

The very heart of moral training and sharing of Christian faith is brought to believers and nonbelievers alike through the preaching of a sermon, that is a talk or lesson which addresses a religious topic based on scripture. Early in His ministry, Jesus preached what is commonly referred to as The Sermon on the Mount. In this book, A Mountain of Evidence, Pastor Randy French takes the Sermon on the Mount and from its contents discusses how Jesus used His sermon to reveal the evidence of how a Christian can be identified as a follower of Christ. And just as Christ did, the author here also teaches the follower of Christ how the Christian life must reflect the attitude and behavior of Christ, the Son of God.

Beginning with the fifth chapter of the Gospel according to Matthew and continuing to the end of chapter seven, Jesus lays before us the basic principles of Christian attitude and behavior. As a pastor, Randy does a unique job of bringing that well-known sermon down from the mountain side and into the heart of the Christian and helps that believer discover the principles on which to build a rock-solid foundation for living the life of a Christian in the modern world. He reveals how that foundation, so vividly described by Christ, has been the same foundation that has stood firm through more than 2,000 years since Christ preached it, and how it is still God's plan by which His children can live victorious and effective lives reflecting Christ today.

As a pastor with a strong heart for children and for young families rearing small children, Pastor Randy has designed A Mountain of Evidence to also serve as a manual or guide for applying the biblical principles recorded in the Sermon on the Mount to the teaching or training of children. Those principles are explained and illustrated to ensure that the timelessness of Jesus' teaching and preaching is evident in all its content.

It is the coverage of the entire Sermon on the Mount, rather than just a few issues, that helps makes this book outstanding.

Come and sit at the feet of Jesus there on that mountain side and hear again the Sermon preached by the Savior of the World as Pastor Randy French paints the word picture of what Jesus teaches that it means to be a follower of Christ.

Vernell W. Posey

INTRODUCTION

In January 2016, I began a twenty-seven week-long sermon series on the Sermon on the Mount. I have always believed that this most famous sermon was nothing more than a step-by-step instruction booklet on what a true disciple of Christ looks like, acts like, talks like, and believes like. After the service on January 3rd, I made my way to the front entrance of the sanctuary to wish the congregation well and hug on their necks (as is the custom in our small country church). One of my most beloved congregants, dear friend and major encourager, Vernell Posey, approached me and after her customary encouraging words which always put a little more spring in my step, she told me that I needed to write a book using all of my research that I would inevitably face before the long series was through. I just sort of laughed it off at the time, mainly because I kept telling myself, "What could I possibly contribute that hasn't already been written on this subject?" After all, I suppose thousands of books have been written on the world's greatest sermon.

A few months later, my wife (Nan) and I were honored with receiving the blessing of a six-week sabbatical from our church and since Nan has always wanted to go to the northeast in the winter time, we excitedly started looking for a cabin we could rent for just the six of us (oh, did I tell you that we are also lovers of little dogs?). We found our dream cabin complete with large fireplace and an unlimited supply of firewood about 30 minutes northwest of Bangor, Maine. I know what you're thinking; Maine in the winter? Are you nuts? One thing I learned as a pastor several years ago is that I have two wives and if my first wife (to whom I have been happily married for thirty-two years and would really like to continue that track record) isn't happy, then not a single member of my church (my second wife) will be happy either. For that reason, I gave Nan complete authority and freedom in determining where we took our sabbatical, which believe it or not, leads back to why I am writing this book.

As we began making plans for what we would do while on this long sabbatical, it suddenly occurred to me why she chose Maine as the location; THERE IS NOTHING TO DO IN MAINE IN THE WINTER TIME! With an expected snowfall of several feet while we were there, we would no doubt be spending a lot of time indoors by the fireplace and Nan has given me strict instructions that I am not to do any work, including writing new sermons, while on sabbatical. Just then, Vernell's words came back to me and I decided that it would be a fun challenge and so here I am, writing away while watching the snow fall outside as the fireplace sputters and spatters on the inside.

In honor of the bug she put in my ear, I have asked Vernell to write the Preface to my book. As I already stated, I believe Jesus, the Master Preacher, gives us as disciples a literal handbook on what it means to be a disciple, and before I go any further, let me explain that I do not believe there is a difference between a "disciple" and a "Christian." I think the term "Christian" is tossed around so much that it has almost become meaningless in our society and culture. In fact, in a recent Gallup poll, 75% of all Americans surveyed, identified themselves as Christian [1](Newport, 2015). If it were true that four out of every five people were Christian, I am thinking that this world would be just a little nicer place than it is; what do you think?

In his book, Think Like Jesus, George Barna, founder and president of Barna Research Group, stated that "only about 14% of those who profess to be born-again Christians even rely on the Bible as their moral compass and believe that moral truth is absolute." He continues that saying:

> ...two out of ten born-again adults do whatever feels right or comfortable in a given situation; one out of ten born-again individuals do whatever they believe will make the most people happy or will create the least amount of conflict with others; and about one out of ten believers

[1] Newport, Frank. 2015. *Percentage of Christians in U.S. Drifting Down, but Still High*. December 24, 2015. https://news.gallup.com/poll/187955/percentage-christians-drifting-down-high.aspx December 24, 2015

> make their moral choices on the basis of whatever they think will produce the most personally beneficial outcome, whatever they believe their family or friends would expect them to do in the same situation.[2](Barna, 2005, 20-21)

As a "follower" (a.k.a. Christian) of Jesus Christ, we are, by definition, disciples. In fact, the Greek word for disciple, *mathatais,* simply means learner, student or follower. Given that basis, are we not all called to be disciples? Are we not all learners, students and followers of our Lord and Rabbi, Jesus Christ? Throughout the gospels, Jesus makes it clear that a true disciple is one who loves Him and that love is manifested by obedience to his Word. In John 8:31, Jesus says, "If you hold to my teaching, you are really my disciples." In fact, throughout the gospels, Jesus makes that exact point no less than eight separate times.

It seems pretty clear, even to this hard head, that Jesus is making a clear connection between our calling ourselves Christians and being obedient to His Word. This point marks the whole premise and purpose for my sermon series and writing this book, and in the opening verses of Jesus' sermon, we find the premise and purpose for His sermon. In Matt. 5:20, Jesus says, "For I tell you that unless your righteousness surpasses that of the Pharisees and the teachers of the law, you will certainly not enter the kingdom of heaven." I remember the first time I ever read that verse, I was like, "ok, if they can't make it, I stand more of a chance of finding a palm tree in Maine than I do of getting into heaven." The Pharisees lived for and prided themselves on their obedience to God's Word—and they won't get into heaven? But that is, I believe, the very essence of Jesus' sermon as well as the message of His gospel, that no one will enter heaven on their own merit or position. They will enter only through faith in the blood of our Lord Jesus Christ. And so once again, here lies the reason for my writing this book.

As already stated, thousands of books have been written on this most famous sermon and I would suggest that it has inspired more sermons than any other single discourse in the entire Bible as well. So, it would be a bit presumptuous of me to think that I can add anything to the discussion

---

[2] Barna, George. 2005. *Think Like Jesus: Make the Right Decision Every Time.* Nashville: Thomas Nelson

that has not already been written or said. But I also firmly believe that each sermon that I have ever preached was inspired by God to help the audience that He gave me at that time in their personal pursuit of Christlikeness. So, it is my prayer that you also are challenged in some small way to heed the words of our Master Preacher to become more like Him. With that said, may you be blessed in your reading and may we all endeavor to become more like Jesus.

SECTION ONE

THE KINGDOM AND THE BELIEVERS

In order to fully understand the Sermon on the Mount and its intended impact, not only in the days of Jesus' disciples, but also the applicability in our own time, let's look at the background, the audience, and most importantly, the Messenger of this sermon.

Over 2,000 years ago, before Jesus began His earthly ministry, He had a scheduled encounter with His nemesis the devil in the wilderness. He was tempted three times to set aside His preordained ministry to the world, by taking the "easy way out" and by-passing all of the hatred and suffering He would have to endure over the next three plus years. Satan's tactic was simple: appeal to His flesh, to His self-preservation, and to His self-exaltation, the very same tactic he used on Eve (and by virtue of their "oneness" in marriage, on Adam as well) in the Garden of Eden.

Satan's temptation:

Look carefully at those temptations. Look at how the temptation of Adam and Eve and the temptation of Jesus in the wilderness are similar.

<u>Adam and Eve</u>

> **Appeal to the flesh** (Lust of the flesh): "Did God really say, 'You must not eat from any tree in the garden'?" (Gen. 3:1)

Self-preservation (Lust of the eyes): "You will not certainly die." (Gen. 3:4)

Self-exaltation (Pride of life): "For God knows that when you eat from it your eyes will be opened and you will be like God knowing good and evil." (Gen. 3:5)

Jesus Christ

Appeal to the flesh (Lust of the flesh): "If you are the Son of God, tell these stones to become bread." (Matt. 4:3)

Self-preservation (Lust of the eyes): "'If you are the Son of God,' he said, 'throw yourself down. For it is written: "'He will command his angels concerning you, and they will lift you up in their hands, so that you will not strike your foot against a stone.'" (Matt. 4:6)

Self-exaltation (Pride of life): "'All this I will give you,' he said, 'if you will bow down and worship me.'" (Matt. 4:9)

We know how things turned out for our first parents in the garden, which in turn, affected all of humankind for evermore, but we also know the victory that Jesus experienced in the desert. He gave Satan His first black eye after which Satan left, but this would not be the final battle.

ONE

The Background of the Sermon on the Mount

The Setting

Fulfilling the earlier prophecy of His "preparer," John the Baptist, Jesus came from His victory over Satan in the wilderness and began traveling the countryside, preaching "Repent for the kingdom of heaven has come near" (Matt. 4:17). He traveled from His home region of Galilee and established His new headquarters in Capernaum. After assembling His team of disciples, He officially kicked off His three-year ministry. In the recorded Sermon on the Mount, Jesus refers to *The Kingdom of Heaven* no less than eight times, making it clear that His teachings point directly to the Messianic Kingdom taught by the Scribes and Pharisees.

Professor W. D. Davies of Union Theological Seminary, in speaking about Jesus' sermon, said that "two elements in rabbinic Judaism were particularly important in shaping the writings of Matthew: the *Halakhah*, or the Law, and the idea of Messianic fulfillment." [3](Davies, 2017)

The point he was making was that the religious leadership taught about the coming of the Messianic Kingdom but they stopped short of teaching the fulfillment of that kingdom. Jesus said Himself that He had not come to abolish the Law of Moses, but that He came to fulfill it, to give it hands, feet and a heartbeat. Even Pope Benedict stated, "The Sermon on

---

[3] Davies, W.D. 2017. *The Sermon on the Mount: The Setting of the Sermon on the Mount.* June 26, 2017. https://www.com/commentarymagazine.com/article/the_setting_of_the_sermon_on_the_mount

the Mount is the new Torah brought by Jesus... as the new Moses whose words constitute the definitive Torah." [4](Benedict, 2016)

In other words, Moses came down from the mountain with the written Word of God and Jesus went back up the mountain to give the Word life. Let's look at the audience to whom He was speaking.

The Audience

Matt. 4:25-5:2: "Large crowds from Galilee, the Decapolis, Jerusalem, Judea and the region across the Jordan followed him. Now when Jesus saw the crowds, he went up on a mountainside and sat down. His disciples came to him, and he began to teach them."

In these verses, Matthew speaks of a smorgasbord of people all assembling on this single mountainside to hear Jesus explain this "new kingdom." First of all, there were people from Galilee. We know that Jesus was a Galilean having grown up in Nazareth, so we can assume that there were family members and neighbors of Jesus present. And given the fact that the Sea of Galilee was a major fishing industry, we can also safely assume that his disciples weren't the only hard-working, blue-collared workers present. These were unlearned people who probably lacked higher religious education, just simple family men who tried their best to provide for their families and teach them to follow God.

Secondly, there were people there from a city called Decapolis, a Greek compound word meaning ten (deca) cities (polis). This "city" was actually a region consisting of ten cities populated primarily by Greeks and Romans. Being the major Greek cultural center of Palestine, there were many museums, libraries and galleries. And because of its worldly importance to the Roman Empire, it was also saturated with military detachments positioned to safeguard the empire's interests there.

Thirdly, the passage tells us there were those who had come up from Jerusalem. It is clear throughout the New Testament that when writers

---

[4] Benedict, Pope. 2016. *On the Sermon on the Mount.* June 26, 2016 http://www.ncregister.com/.../pope_benedict_on_the_sermon_on_the_mount June 26, 2016

speak of those coming out from Jerusalem, they are speaking about the religious leadership who would very soon conspire to rid the world of Jesus.

Fourthly, the Judeans represent the whole of Israel, people from all over Palestine. This was a conglomerate of folks from the entire region who had come out to hear what Christ had to say. These were people from all walks and trades who either witnessed first-hand all of the miracles at the end of Matt. 4, or were the hearers of such stories that came out of those regions in which Jesus performed the miracles.

Finally, Matthew mentions those who had come from the "region across the Jordan," meaning Arabs. As I stated, this was a smorgasbord of people: family, friends, learned, unlearned, cultural, military, religious elite, Israelites, Gentiles and Arabs. Jesus attracted people from nearly every nation to this single mountain in Palestine. He did not reject anyone because of their race, sex, past, religion, or profession. He did not single out anyone and tell them they were not welcome, even those who didn't like Him, because He knew that God loved them also and that they needed a Savior. God told Abraham that He would make him a father of many nations, Jews and Gentiles, stating that whoever obeys His Word is a child of the promise (John 14:21).

W. D. Davies, in the same article on the setting of the Sermon on the Mount quoted Justin Martyr, a second century disciple who said, "Those who have followed and will follow Christ are the true Israel, the children of the Promise, the true successors of those Jews who found justification in times past."[5](Davies, 2017)

The Purpose

In Matt. 4:17, Matthew stated that from that point on, Jesus went about the countryside preaching that the kingdom of heaven was near and that the time was now to repent. As stated, no less than eight times, Jesus speaks about the kingdom of heaven in His sermon. So, the theme or purpose of Jesus' sermon can only be simply defined as *The Kingdom of Heaven vs. The Kingdom of Self.*

---

[5] Davies, W.D.. 2017. *The Sermon on the Mount: The Setting of the Sermon on the Mount.* June 26, 2017. https://www.com/commentarymagazine.com/article/the_setting_of_the_sermon_on_the_mount.

In speaking of the format of Jesus' sermon, it is clear that being a good Nazarene, He outlined His message in <u>three major points:</u>

1. In Matt. 5, He put the doctrinal foundation of the "kingdom of self" that the religious leaders had invented against the doctrinal foundation of the "kingdom of heaven." He drew sharp contrasts between the traditional Jewish moral teaching of the Torah with the moral principles that God actually intended. Throughout this first chapter, we read the same prefacing statement of the law, *You have heard that it was said…*, followed by His prefacing statement of intention, *But I tell you...* But Jesus was not only making a contrast between the Pharisees' teaching and God's original intent. He was also giving supporting evidence to His claim in v.17 that He had *not come to abolish them* [the Law], *but to fulfill them*. More on that in Chapter five.
2. In Matt. 6, Jesus shares practical applications on being righteous. He teaches how to be compassionate toward the needy, how to pray and fast, and how not to worry. Simply put, He explained how a true member of the kingdom of heaven should behave.
3. Finally, in Matt. 7, Jesus lays out what that true righteousness looks like in the kingdom of heaven. He speaks about how true disciples aren't judgmental, receive what they ask for from God and exercise the golden rule. He draws a picture of what the kingdom of heaven here on earth looks like when its members are practicing what He preaches. Pope Benedict called this, "a preview of Christian living within the kingdom of God."

It is very important to understand and keep in mind that the Sermon on the Mount was not a new message, but just as a doctor uses defibrillator paddles to restart a human heart, Jesus uses this message to restart the spiritual heart, and what is that message? The very commandment that God gave to the Israelites from Sinai when He said, "Now if you obey me fully and keep my covenant, then out of all nations you will be my treasured possession. Although the whole earth is mine, you will be for me a kingdom of priests and a holy nation." (Exod. 19:5-6). This was known as the Sinai Covenant that God made with the Israelites. It simply stated that if they obeyed His commandments, He would separate them from the rest of the world. That is what the word *holy* means in its purest form, to be separate.

But the Israelites didn't keep the law, did they? In fact, by the time Moses had come down from the mountain with the written Law in his hand, they had already rejected God and there began a 1,500-year long track record of seeking salvation through their own self-righteous works.

If you recall, the introduction stated that the premise and purpose of Jesus' sermon can be found in Matt. 5:20 when He warns us, His disciples, that, "…unless your righteousness surpasses that of the Pharisees and teachers of the law, you will certainly not enter the kingdom of heaven." Jesus' sermon is an unveiling of what the true relationship of Christians to God must look like, in contrast to the ways in which the Pharisees and teachers behaved in their feeble attempt to keep the Law. Someone once said that the Old Testament is the New Testament concealed and the New Testament is the Old Testament revealed. There is a curtain of mystery between the Old and New Testament. Daniel said to God after receiving revelation of the end times, "I heard, but I did not understand." (Dan. 12:8*)*. This sermon unveils that mystery allowing everyone to know what true righteousness in God looks like.

Paul said in Rom. 1:17 that, "in the gospel the righteousness of God is revealed—a righteousness that is by faith from first to last, just as it is written: 'The righteous will live by faith.'" And in Rom. 3:22, he explains that "This righteousness is given through faith in Jesus Christ to all who believe." As Christians, we are cloaked with Christ's righteousness, not by our feats, but by our faith. In Rom. 13:14, he says, "clothe yourselves with the Lord Jesus Christ and do not think about how to gratify the desires of the flesh." We are to clothe ourselves with Christ because our cloaks and the cloaks of self-righteousness of the religious leaders are as "filthy rags" (Isa. 64:6) and will always "fall short of the glory of God." (Rom. 3:23)

Therefore, the purpose of the sermon was not to bring on anything new, but only to reveal what God had originally intended from before creation. Jesus was sent to shepherd us back into His eternal fold.

Preparation

Before we actually delve into the meat of Jesus' sermon, it is important that we first prepare ourselves for what God has to say to us. Jeremiah said, "Hear the word of the Lord, you kings of Judah and people of Jerusalem. This is what the Lord Almighty, the God of Israel says: Listen! I am going to bring a disaster on this place that will make the ears of everyone who hears of it tingle." (Jer. 19:3) Let us prepare ourselves to hear the Word of the Lord and pray that He give us ears to hear and eyes to see that His word is truth.

I would like to open this section with an excerpt from an article by Professor Virginia Stem Owens, of Texas A&M, in which she captures the very essence of the manner in which it is received (or more appropriately, rejected) today, as it was over 2,000 years ago. Professor Owens assigned her freshman English class with assessing Jesus' The Sermon on the Mount in current time. Here is some of the feedback that she received from her students:

> "In my opinion religion is one big hoax."
>
> "There is an old saying that 'you shouldn't believe everything you read' and it applies in this case."
>
> "It is hard to believe something that was written down thousands of years ago."

Professor Owens was bewildered at why the students were so angry and dismissive about the sermon. The negative feedback kept pouring in. Professor Owens stated in her summary of the article, "I find it strangely heartening that... the Bible remains offensive to honest, ignorant ears, just as it was in the first century.[6](Owens, 2017)

I shared that excerpt because it sums up the true motivation behind my preaching through the Sermon on the Mount and the writing of this

[6] Owens, Virginia Stem. 2017. *Why People Hate the Sermon on the Mount.* October 10, 2017. https://sharedveracity.net/2017/10/10/why-people-hate-the-sermon-on-the-mount-virginia-stem-owens/

book. The United States of America was founded on Judeo-Christian principles, but at lightning speed, is becoming the New Roman Empire that celebrates self-indulgence, self-preservation and self-service. We have lost that faith-based uniqueness that set us apart from the rest of the world. We are no longer a country of virtues, but a country of vices. We are no longer a country of piety, but a country of paganism. We are no longer a country of Bible-believers, but a country of Bible-bashers.

A couple of years ago, I preached a message about the direction that America is taking, in that it is following in the exact same footsteps that Israel took before God finally rejected them. It was to serve as a wake-up call to the moral decay of our country. I wrote this book on the Sermon on the Mount, not as a wake-up call to the moral decay of a country, but as a wake-up call to the moral decay of Christians.

As absurd as some of the comments made on those term papers by Professor Owens' students were, I have heard many of the same arguments in my own church and others. *The Bible doesn't really apply anymore, it's not relevant, it's too strict, it keeps us from having any fun, it's been written by so many people that it can't be trusted to be the actual word of God.* Does any of this sound familiar to you? As a body of believers, we have become weaklings in our faith, adamant in our defiance and ignorant in our understanding of what God desires for us, expects from us and requires of us. And you want to know something? We ARE following in the exact footsteps of Israel and we, not America, but we who call ourselves Christians, will be rejected by God-Almighty, unless we open our eyes to the commandment that God has called each and every one of us to: that of personal holiness.

Many people in the church today are in danger of facing eternal hell because we want to live our lives for today without any regard for tomorrow and as an ordained pastor in Christ's Church, it is my job to bring that to our attention. Ezekiel 33:6 says, "But if the watchman sees the sword coming and does not blow the trumpet to warn the people and the sword comes and takes someone's life, that person's life will be taken because of their sin, but I will hold the watchman accountable for their blood."

I was not called as a pastor to be anyone's friend, nose-wiper, placater, pacifier or enabler. I was called to be a watchman and until God calls me home, I am going to blow my trumpet to us all that the sword is coming.

God has laid this on my heart because He is telling me to tell us all to get ready. We have become a lazy bunch of luke-warm, self-serving self-seekers who believe ourselves to be Christian, but when we stand before the Holy Judge, He will reject many of us and declare that He never knew us.

Some of you are probably sitting here reading this and thinking to yourselves, *Man, this dude has lost it, talk about a wet spot.* I realize that some of my readers are seekers and even new believers. But many more of my readers are well-seasoned and spiritually-mature Christians, who believe they have a grasp on truth. Paul said, "follow me as I follow Christ." (1 Cor. 11:1 MEV) Let me tell you, if I am one of those seekers or new believers and I am trying to make positive change in my life, I would not want to follow many "so-called" Christians because frankly, they are not going anywhere nice.

Jesus delivered The Sermon on the Mount because He expects more from us His disciples than what the Jews of the day were interested in giving. God wanted devotion and they gave Him duty. God wanted love and they gave Him laws. God wanted worship and they gave Him works. Keep in mind that, in leading up to His sermon, Jesus said, "From that time on Jesus began to preach, Repent, for the kingdom of heaven has come near." (Matt. 4:17)

There are very few times that Jesus ever opened His mouth when self-righteous religious people were not in ear-shot. When He preached, "Repent, for the kingdom of heaven has come near," He wasn't speaking to those down at the beer joints, school yards or back yards, the hospitals or hoods, or the courthouses or the white house. He was speaking to believers and His message to believers is simple, "Repent, for the kingdom of heaven has come near."

I am not a prophet and so I will not tell you that I know He is coming back today because I do not. But I will tell you this: there are many more in the Church who aren't ready for Him to come back today, than are. God said, "if my people, who are called by my name, will humble themselves and pray and seek my face and turn from their wicked ways, then I will hear from heaven, and I will forgive their sin and will heal their land." (2 Chron. 7:14)

In speaking about this "kingdom of heaven," Jesus says that unless our righteousness surpasses that of the Pharisees, we will never see heaven.

I want you to know that I am sharing my heart with you because I love each and every one of you, even though I have never met most of you. If it were discovered during a medical examination that you had cancer, who here would want your doctor to send you home insisting that you simply had a nasty cold out of fear of hurting your feelings? Every person reading this is precious to God and just as you would want your doctor to shoot straight with you, it is my desire and my duty to shoot straight with you. I realize that some of you may be offended in this reading and might even be motivated to put this book up on your bookshelf and wait for the next book-burning to come along. It is my prayer that you fight that urge and read on.

I also want you to understand that if you are offended today, it is not I who offends you, but Jesus Himself. In John 6, referring to His teaching, some of His disciples said, "'This is a hard teaching. Who can accept it?' Aware that his disciples were grumbling about this, Jesus said to them, 'Does this offend you? Then what if you see the Son of Man ascend to where He was before! The Spirit gives life; the flesh counts for nothing. The words I have spoken to you—they are full of the Spirit and life. Yet there are some of you who do not believe.'" (John 6:60-64a) If you are offended, it is Christ's own words that offend you. God has called me to preach truth, even when it involves hard teaching and until God removes me and frees me from this old (and getting older) corrupt body, I have an audience of One and I must seek to please Him.

Before you read any further to see who else I offend in the following chapters, I pray that you will have a private altar moment. Maybe you have been carrying guilt so much so that even your posture is reflecting it and you are removing yourself from fellowship with other believers because the guilt is so great. Maybe you have just been plain lazy and all you think about is yourself and no one else. You are living in the here-and-now with no regard for the life that awaits you both in the here-and-now and beyond. God has not called you to be a pew potato but a crusader for the King.

Maybe you have been living a lie for so long now that even you don't know what is truth anymore. You claim to be covered by the blood of Christ and have assurance of your salvation, but every day, you are plagued by doubt because you know that He wants much more from you.

Today, this moment and in this reading, is a day of personal preparation.

Today is a day of personal revival. Today is a day of cleansing. It's a new beginning for you with new challenges, new hopes and new trials. Today is your day of reckoning, a day to make things right before God, to forgive people of their trespasses, to let go of anger, unforgiveness, guilt, jealousy and sin. The next 25 chapters will mean absolutely nothing to those who live on the church fence, neither being offended by sin nor sensitive to it. Your new beginning must begin at the altar of the Almighty where you and you alone can offer yourself a living sacrifice, holy and pleasing to your God and your Maker.

Professor Owens stated that she would rather people be angered by Jesus' words than to haphazardly dismiss them. If you are angry right now, then I have done my job because now you are forced to face that anger and either run to God or run away from Him. If you dismiss Jesus' words, then you have already run away and desperately need revival of your heart before you meet your Maker.

Jesus sacrificed Himself at God's altar, which, on the darkest day in human history, took the form of a Roman cross. Before He bowed His head and gave up His Spirit, He uttered those most beautiful words in the English language, "It is finished." (John 19:30) Not that He was finished, not that His ministry was finished, or even that the judgment of His killers was yet sealed, but that God's greatest work, the redemption of the world was finished. God does His greatest work at His altar. Won't you stop and kneel before God in a spirit of humility, seek revival, and allow God to perform His greatest work in you? My prayer is that you will.

TWO

The Beatitudes (Part 1)

Blessed are the poor in spirit, for theirs is the kingdom of heaven. Blessed are those who mourn, for they will be comforted. Blessed are the meek, for they will inherit the earth. Blessed are those who hunger and thirst for righteousness, for they will be filled (Matt. 5:3-6)

Jesus began His sermon with a set of rules called *the Beatitudes,* a set of rules which no carnal person can follow. The Sermon on the Mount is not about *what we must do to be a Christian,* it is about *what a Christian looks like, thinks like, and acts like.* Nowhere in Jesus' sermon does He share His Gospel of what is required to be saved. That, I believe, was not the point of His sermon, but rather, His point was to give His disciples a standard of measurement by which they ought to *measure* themselves. Many times, Jesus has been called a great Teacher. In fact, most, if not all, other world religions confess Jesus to be a great Teacher. But being a Christian is not about *doing*; it is about *being* and we cannot *be* who Jesus describes throughout His sermon unless we are first born again. Jesus was not giving us a set of rules by which we must live in order to be Christian; rather He was giving us a description of who He is, and as Christians, are we not all called to be *Christ-like*? Only through the Person and the power of the Holy Spirit are we able to live up to Jesus' teachings here and throughout the gospels.

That is the single-greatest struggle of Christians today. We are all about *doing* because many of us have not grasped the understanding that we cannot *do.* Jesus was not introducing the world to a new set of rules.

That had already been done on Mt Sinai. Jesus was introducing us to a relationship with the Father through Him, (I have not come to abolish the Law, but to fulfill. Matt. 5:17): and that without His presence in our lives through the Person of the Holy Spirit, no one will see the *kingdom of heaven.*

As Jesus began, the first word out of His mouth was *blessed.* The word blessed means happy, and so the disciples are listening intently to just who are the happy ones. Maybe He is going to talk about a Jewish aristocrat who owns nearly half of the Jewish shops, or maybe He is going to talk about the Jewish tax collector who lined his pockets every day with the hard earnings of his fellow countrymen. Everyone is on the edge of their seat waiting to find out who Jesus says are the happiest people on earth. But what comes next comes as a great surprise. He says the happy are the poor, the mournful, the meek, the hungry, thirsty, merciful, pure, peacemakers and the persecuted, to which the disciples most definitely responded, *Huh? Run that by us one more time?* It is clear that they had never heard anything like this; this was something new!

Blessed are the poor in spirit for theirs is the kingdom of heaven (Matt. 5:7)

Jesus begins His sermon with "Blessed are the poor in spirit for theirs is the kingdom of heaven," I do not believe this list to be in random order, because nothing after this verse makes any sense unless the listener first has a crisis moment where he realizes he is spiritually bankrupt.

We often hear of people filing bankruptcy when they get into trouble financially. They have come to a point where they recognize that they have a debt they cannot pay. The two most common types of bankruptcy are Chapter 7 and Chapter 11. Under Chapter 11, one's debts are restructured under more manageable terms. But under the more popular Chapter 7, the debts are forgiven entirely. While this may seem like a great deal, the moral truth is that, although the responsible party is freed of the debt, someone has to pay and it is the creditors to whom the money is owed. But since creditors are not going to take a loss, the debt is paid by other consumers through higher prices and interest rates.

When Jesus says, "Blessed are the poor in spirit," He is in effect saying, blessed are those who are spiritually bankrupt. Blessed are those who are in over their heads in debt because they know they cannot pay for it, they cannot earn it and they certainly do not deserve it. We must in fact take on the role of a beggar to get into heaven. But here is the most important part to remember; grace is free to us but grace is not free. Like financial bankruptcy, someone must pay the debt and that someone is Jesus Christ. Oswald Chambers explains it this way:

> As long as we have a conceited, self-righteous idea that we can do the thing if God will help us, God has to allow us to go on until we break the neck of our ignorance over some obstacle, then we will be willing to come and receive from Him. [7](Chambers, 1932, 12)

The kind of poverty that Jesus described here is not one of possessions but of person. In order to be a disciple, one has to be emptied of self and be replaced with the Person of the Holy Spirit. He or she must lose the carnal need for self-rule and replace it with the need to be God-ruled. Try explaining to the carnal person what it means to be happy in the midst of being persecuted, or to love their enemy. None of what Jesus teaches makes any sense to the person who is governed by and lives in the *kingdom of self.*

The Apostle Paul described this being *emptied of himself* best when in the opening verses of Philippians 3, he shares his resume of all his accomplishments and qualifications and sums them all up in v.8 saying, "What is more, I consider everything a loss because of the surpassing worth of knowing Christ Jesus my Lord, for whose sake I have lost all things. I consider them garbage, that I may gain Christ." In Romans 7, Paul acknowledges his own spiritual bankruptcy saying, "For I know that good itself does not dwell in me, that is, in my sinful nature. For I have the desire to do what is good, but I cannot carry it out. For I do not do the good I want to do, but the evil I do not want to do—this I keep on doing." (vv.18-19) The point that Jesus and Paul make here is that until we recognize our subordinate position with God and our need for God, *we will not see the kingdom of God.* King David explains our relationship to God this way, "Know that the LORD is God. It is he who made us, and we are his; we are his people, the sheep of his pasture." (Ps. 100:3)

---

[7] Chambers, Oswald. 1932. *Studies in the Sermon on the Mount.* London: Marshall

The world is full of people who believe that who we are is defined by what we do and what we have. Unfortunately, that belief has permeated Christ's Church as well. We are all about *doing good* and Jesus wants us to understand that it is not enough to do good; we must be Christ-like and the only way to obtain that godly character is to come to a point where we realize that without the Holy Spirit dwelling in us, we are as Paul says, *garbage.*

What keeps us from acknowledging our position under God? Pride! Pride is the greatest of all evils. It was pride that cast Lucifer, the most beautiful of all of God's angels, out of heaven. Pride is what lured Adam and Eve into believing that they could be *like God.* And it has been pride that has destroyed lives throughout the centuries since. One can never come to a saving understanding of Christ from a position of pride. A person must first humble himself before God before he can possibly recognize his abject spiritual poverty.

One of Christ's greatest examples of humility took place upon His entering the upper room to enjoy the Passover meal with His disciples. No servant was present to greet the disciples to wash the dust from their feet, so Jesus, without saying a word, grabbed a bowl of water, wrapped a towel around His waist and proceeded to wash the feet of each disciple. In Matthew 23:11, Jesus explains that, "The greatest among you will be your servant." What Christians need is less focus on who we are in the world and more focus on who we are in God—His slaves with only one goal, to carry out His will here *on earth as it is in heaven.* The only way we will accomplish that is by being emptied of ourselves first and filled with His Spirit. When we understand this, it naturally leads us to a spirit of mourning.

Blessed are those who mourn, for they will be comforted. (Matt. 5:4)

In the Greek, the word *mourn* means to have a deep inner pain which occurs when something tragic happens, such as a death of a loved one. Every one of us at some point will lose loved ones very close to us and will experience that deep inner pain. I met a lady in her fifties at the bank sometime back who had lost her husband just two years before and in our short conversation, she began to cry at the memory of her loss. I mentioned that the word *blessed* actually means happiness. And so, as in the case of the bank manager, it really does not make sense that Jesus would use such a jubilant word when speaking about grieving. After all, even Jesus cried when He lost his dear friend Lazarus.

This passage does not make sense to us unless it is interpreted in spiritual concert with the previous verse. Jesus had just made the statement that those who realize their fallen condition are blessed because they will then be motivated to do something about it. So, once we realize our fallen state, the next natural heart condition that follows is grief over what we have done, grief over how we have spent our lives, and grief over how we have rejected God over and over again in our lives. King David found comfort in the everlasting arms of the Lord after mourning over his sin against God. In his song of repentance, he said, "Against you, you only, have I sinned and done what is evil in your sight; so you are right in your verdict and justified when you judge. Create in me a pure heart, O God, and renew a steadfast spirit within me. Do not cast me from your presence or take your Holy Spirit from me. Restore to me the joy of your salvation and grant me a willing spirit, to sustain me." (Ps. 51:4, 10-12)

True godly sorrow is not, *I'm sorry I got caught and now I have to pay the price for my sin!* This sorrow focuses on self and simply regrets the personal consequences of our actions. It is total self-centeredness that has no consideration for the heart of God. I know this has never happened to you, but sometimes my kids would do mean things to each other and because they got caught, they would say, *I'm* sorry—all the while still having a handful of their sibling's hair in their hands. In our fallen prideful state, we sometimes forget just how our sin affects others, but more importantly, how our sin affects the heart of God. To mourn means to have a broken heart over the condition of the heart.

Mike Bickle, in his study *Pursuing a Kingdom Lifestyle* said, "Being poor in spirit speaks of how we see ourselves; spiritual mourning refers to how we feel about what we see. When we see differently, then we feel differently." [8](Bickle, 2012)

Part of our problem in the body of Christ is that we have forgotten the part of mourning that goes with sin and confession. Too often we

---

[8] Bickle, Mike. 2012. *Pursuing a Kingdom Lifestyle.* https://www.mikebickle.org/watch/mb_3247

simply say, like my kids, *God forgive me* and we think we have repented. Confession without repentance does not lead us to change, it only leads to death.

Micah gives us insight into how our poverty-stricken spirits ought to leave us broken-hearted: "What misery is mine! I am like one who gathers summer fruit at the gleaning of the vineyard; there is no cluster of grapes to eat, none of the early figs that I crave." (Mic. 7:1) He goes on to describe the broken condition of his heart and ends his thought saying, "Who is a God like you, who pardons sin and forgives the transgression of the remnant of his inheritance? You do not stay angry forever but delight to show mercy. You will again have compassion on us; you will tread our sins underfoot and hurl all our iniquities into the depths of the sea." (vv.18-19)

But now, while this beatitude speaks about our brokenness over how we have sinned against God and broken His heart, I also believe that through our healed relationship with Him, He provides tremendous comfort to those who mourn the loss of loved ones as well. Jesus says that those who grieve will be comforted. Those who truly understand this comfort are those who have gone through pain, loss and suffering in their lives. *It's one thing to say, I have heard about what the Lord can do*, but it is something altogether different when you can say, *let me tell you how the Lord brought me through this challenge in my life.*

I want to close this portion with a great illustration of what it means to be blessed in mourning:

> Legend has it that a German baron made a great Aeolian harp by stretching wires from tower to tower of his castle. When the harp was ready, he eagerly listened for the music. But it was the calm of summer and in the still air, the wires hung silent. Autumn came with its gentle breezes and there were faint whispers of song. At length, the winter winds swept over the castle and now the harp answered in majestic music.[9](Miller, 1905)

---

[9] Miller, J.R.. 1905. *The Master's Blesseds.* http://www.sermonindex.net/modules/articles/index.php?view=article&aid=32461

What a beautiful illustration of what it means to be blessed in the midst of mourning. The Christian is defined by joy, but when life is good and trouble-free, even unbelievers are filled with a sense of happiness that can be misconstrued as joy. What defines the Christian distinctly is that even in the midst of the pains of winter the Christian's song is heard. My bank friend understood what is was like to mourn, but in her testimony, she also understood the joy that comes in the morning as she sang of the tremendous strength and comfort she has found in Christ.

Blessed are the meek for they will inherit the earth (Matt 5:5)

Super Bowl Coach Tony Dungy describes meekness in the title of his book as a *Quiet Strength.* [10](Dungy, 2011) The Greek word actually describes an animal which has been trained by its master. A wild stallion is a very strong and beautiful animal, but it is useless to its master until it has become trained to bring its strength under control. The original meaning of our word *gentleman* actually comes from this word. It is understanding that although we may have a right to something, we instead extend grace to those who we may be in conflict with and place their wishes before our own. In marriage counseling, I call it *giving up the right to be right in order to be reconciled.* It is a determination to follow the commands of Christ and bear fruit for the kingdom of heaven, regardless of our circumstances.

One of the earliest biblical examples of meekness is found in the attitude of Abraham. He was a person God had called and promised that if he were faithful, God would make him wealthy. Abraham obeyed and God blessed him greatly. His nephew Lot was also blessed since he was with Abraham. But after some time had passed, their blessings of herds and flocks became so great that they needed to part ways. Abraham had every right to take the choicest land and send Lot on his way. Instead, Abraham gave Lot the pick of the land saying, "Let's not have any quarreling between you and me, or between your herders and mine, for we are close relatives. Is not the whole land before you? Let's part company. If you go to the left, I'll go to the right; if you go to the right, I'll go to the left." (Gen.13:8-9) Meekness is not weakness. It is putting another's desires and needs before our own.

[10] Dungy, Tony. 2011. *Quiet Strength.* Carol Stream. Tyndale House Publishers, Inc.

It is said that in countries where mango trees grow, the fruit of the tree is often harvested by beating on its branches. With each blow to the tree, it responds by dropping its sweet fruit to the ground and the following year, it produces even more. This is meekness at its best. I know that everyone reading this has been stepped on, trampled on, walked-over, run-over, or passed-over and you have every right to respond in-kind, but Jesus is telling us to play by a new rule. He is telling us to give up our right to be right and instead, seek to be reconciled. He is telling us to bear sweet fruit in the midst of adverse circumstances, not in the absence of them.

It really comes down to ownership. The unbeliever sees all he has as being the fruit of his own labor. His money, his possessions and even his position in life are all the *fruit* of his hard work. The Christian, on the other hand, sees all he has as a blessing from God and owned by God. Meekness is that godly characteristic needed to defeat our selfishness. Our carnal nature tells us that we deserve better than we have—whether that be a better home, a better job, a better car, or even a better spouse. As long as we allow our carnality to rule (self-rule), we will never be content, let alone grateful for what God has blessed us with.

I mentioned that pride is the greatest of all evils. Pride places the focus of everything we do and everything we have on us. It places the focus of the gift on the receiver instead of the giver and as long as one's focus is on being the receiver rather than the giver, there will always be a sense of entitlement, or expectation—and as long as there is a sense of entitlement, one will never be content. Paul stated it this way, "For who makes you different from anyone else? What do you have that you did not receive? And if you did receive it, why do you boast as though you did not?" (1 Cor. 4:7)

I have a dear friend and mentor whose name is Herb McMillian. With over fifty years in ministry, Herb has the distinction in our denomination of being the longest-tenured pastor at a single church. Herb recently retired, but continues to minister to folks as though he never stopped. Herb described humility this way; "Humility is not thinking lowly of oneself, rather it is not thinking of oneself at all." If our focus is on Jesus instead of ourselves, there is no place for pride to creep into our lives.

Those who are meek allow God to keep them under His control. We say, *Lord I do not know why this trial has come, but I thank you for the opportunity to get closer to you.* In so doing, we take the wild animal inside of each of us and begin to tame it so that we can become useful to our Master. Paul said about Jesus, "And being found in appearance as a man, he humbled himself by becoming obedient to death—even death on a cross." (Phil. 2:8) Jesus came for one purpose: to accomplish His Father's will, (John 6:38) and as Christians, that is His expectation of us.

Blessed are those who hunger and thirst for righteousness, for they will be filled (Matt. 5:6)

For a parent, one of the worst things to experience is when a child is sick. There is a sense of total helplessness that comes over a parent when the child is feeling ill, and when we have pumped him or her full of medicines and fluids, the very next thing we try to get that child to do, is eat something—anything! When a person is sick, one of the first things to go is the appetite even though it is often the only thing that can make that person feel better again. Hunger is life and *where there is no hunger, there is no life.*

Jesus chose *hunger* and *thirst,* because they are common needs to all of us. A man cannot satisfy his hunger for food for his entire life by eating just one meal. Neither can the human soul be satisfied by feeding on God's righteousness just one time. To be totally satisfied physically, man must feed himself daily. Likewise, to be satisfied spiritually, man must feed himself on God's Word daily. When we lack a hunger and thirst for God's righteousness, we are not just idle, we are dying. When a church is not growing and is just maintaining its own, it is said to be *plateaued,* but that is just a nice way of saying that it is dead and just does not notice the absence of a heartbeat yet. So it is with the human soul. If it is not hungering and thirsting for God and His Word, then it is already in a state of dying and it is only a matter of time before the person's heart flat-lines!

I am sure you have heard people make the observation that they were not fed at church, and by that they mean that they did not learn anything useful or that they did not feel the presence of God. You have probably also heard things like, *I don't like worshipping this way* or *I don't like that Bible version.* I liken that to my son Austin complaining that there is nothing to eat in the house, and when his mom points out to him all of the food that we have in the cupboards and refrigerator, he responds, *I don't like that.* Her response is usually something like, *then you really aren't that hungry, are you?*

The only people who do not like to feast on what is on God's table are those who are not really hungry. They are the ones seeking self-satisfaction and they are not really hungry because they are full of themselves. John Piper stated it this way, "The weakness of our hunger for God is not because he is unsavory, but because we keep ourselves stuffed with other things."[11] (Piper, 1960, 10) Jesus wants us to come to God's table hungry for righteousness so that when we go out into our homes and the world, His righteousness is escaping out of our pores and into the lives around us.

Every day, advertising companies spend millions of dollars insisting that we desperately need this particular pair of jeans, or that particular car in order to be happy, or content. If that is true, why do these same companies only two months later, spend millions more trying to entice us to purchase something else to finally be happy in life? Back in the 50's, the magazine *Life* came out, then *People,* then *Us* and most recently *Self.* What Piper was saying was that some of us are so full of *self* that we really are not hungry for God. It is not necessarily the *sinful* things in life that fill us, just the everyday ordinary things that we find to fill all those 1,440 minutes we have in each day. Even as I am writing this, I mentioned in my introduction that Nan and I are stowed away in a cabin, deep in the snow-filled woods of Maine. We have no TV, no video games, and given the fact that it is winter time with 4 feet of snow on the ground, there is not a whole lot to do outside either other than watch our dogs chase deer. It truly is amazing (and sad) to realize just how many of those 1,440 minutes are actually wasted, never to be returned to us.

The truth is that although we search insatiably for things with which to fill our lives, nothing of this world will ever bring true fulfillment. We will always be a slave to the next thing just over the fence. Do you realize how much more we could do for the kingdom of heaven if we just stopped trying to satisfy the kingdom of self? The joy in our homes will never be dependent on the size of our plasma TV's, or whether we have a swimming pool in the back yard. Happiness is not found in the pursuit of happiness,

---

[11] Piper, John. 1960. *A Hunger for God: Desiring God through Fasting and Prayer.* Peabody. Crossway

happiness is only found in the pursuit of God. Happiness is also not found in the absence of conflict. Conflicts are going to happen, even between loved ones. They happen in my home, especially when I finally talk Nan into playing *Monopoly.* She has this belief that just because I am a pastor, I should be kind and merciful when playing a game, but isn't the object of the game to beat your opponent into oblivion by taking everything they have? When I sit down to play a game, I hunger and thirst to win! But I digress. Jesus is telling us that we would be happy in our lives if we were only to hunger and thirst for righteousness and that means every aspect of our lives, our relationships, our careers and even our interests. When we surrender our lives to Christ, we surrender our whole lives. We don't pick and choose which parts of our lives we will surrender and which parts we will not.

Let me close by sharing an analogy that Dr. Tony Evans made to my favorite pastime in the whole world, football. The average game takes over 3 hours to play 60 minutes, but of that 60 minutes, only about 11 minutes is actually spent playing. The other 49 minutes is spent in the huddle strategizing. Now, the audience doesn't mind sitting through that 49 minutes of inactivity, because they know their team needs that time to win the game.

Church is the Christian's huddle, but all too often we give each other high-fives celebrating our huddle. We gather together and go nuts over the huddle! We say, *Boy, we sure had an awesome huddle this morning and our quarterback is one of the best in the league.* But what people do not seem to understand is that the huddle is not playing the game; it only helps us to be effective in playing the game. Our effectiveness cannot be measured by how well we do in the Sunday morning huddle. The test of the Christian is what we do once we leave the huddle and Jesus gave us this unique set of ground rules to make us distinctive—not weird, but distinctive. When we come into church with poor contrite hearts and a hunger for God's righteousness, the natural result is that righteousness spills out into our homes, neighborhoods and workplaces. It comes down to this: the quality of our worship is a reflection of how well we play the game and how well we play the game is a reflection of the quality of our worship.[14]

THREE

The Beatitudes (Part 2)

Blessed are the merciful, for they will be shown mercy. Blessed are the pure in heart, for they will see God. Blessed are the peacemakers, for they will be called children of God. Blessed are those who are persecuted because of righteousness, for theirs is the kingdom of heaven (Matt. 5:7-10)

In the previous chapter, we started looking at the list of characteristics that Jesus used to describe the attitude of the believer, since they also describe His own attitude. In His sermon in general and in these eight beatitudes specifically, Jesus provides for us a manifest or mandate that draws a parallel between how He lived and how He expects us to *be of the same attitude.*

The first four beatitudes are seen as negative characteristics by the world's standards. Poverty is seen as a great social injustice in the world, not unlike hunger and thirst. Likewise, to be meek is to be weak and to mourn is to be at a loss. But while these are seen as negative in the world, these last four characteristics of the Christian are recognized by the world for their positive characteristics: mercy, purity, peacemaking, and enduring persecution. Look again at understanding what it means to be Christ-like.

Blessed are the merciful, for they will be shown mercy (Matt. 5:7)

In WWII, a group of German soldiers doused a synagogue with gasoline. They then rounded up a group of Jews from the nearby village and stuffed as many of them in the building as possible. There were men, women, and children hoarded into the building, the doors were locked and the order was given to set the building on fire. The soldiers had orders to shoot anyone attempting to escape from the building. A few years later at the height of the war, a Jewish inmate named Simon Wiesenthal was brought out of the concentration camp called Bergen Belsen and into a German field hospital. The inmate was taken to the bed of a German soldier named Karl, who was mortally wounded. The young soldier confessed to the inmate that he had taken part in the burning of the Jews in the building. He was haunted every moment by the look of horror on their faces as he forced them into the gas-soaked synagogue. He wanted to ask a Jew for forgiveness before he died. The Jewish inmate took a look at him, turned, walked away and was escorted back to his camp quarters. Simon wrote of this account in his book, The Sunflower, and ended it with this thought, "You, who have just read this sad and tragic episode in my life, can mentally change places with me and ask yourself the crucial question, 'What would I have done.'" [12](Wisenthal, 1976, 98) What would you have done? What would you have said? Could you have offered the forgiveness that was so desperately sought by Karl, or would you have simply returned to the concentration camp and your bondage?

In v.7, Jesus says, "Blessed are the merciful, for they will be shown mercy," but what does it mean to be merciful? What does mercy look like? The Greek word (Eleemon) that is used here for mercy is found only here and in Heb. 2:17. It is different from the word pity in that it demands action. Mercy means discovering a need and having the ability to do something about it. In order to be merciful, we must be actively involved in the lives of other people. It is not enough to have pity and say, *I'll pray for you,* or *I feel really bad for you.* Encouraging words are important to be sure, but Christians need to follow those words with *now, how can I help?* We have plenty of people willing to show pity; what we need is for more people to show mercy. Pity evokes a feeling, but *mercy invokes an action.*

How do you think Jesus would have responded to that German soldier? Do you think He would have told the soldier, *you should have thought about mercy before you set the fire*? And how would Jesus have responded to the Jewish prisoner? Would He have said to him, *it's your duty to forgive those who ask for it?* I am not sure He would have taken either approach. I think instead, He would have shown mercy in both cases. He would have led the

[12] Wisenthal, Simon. 1976. *The Sunflower.* New York: Schocken Books

young soldier to a spirit of mourning and then placed His arm around the prisoner as he was walking back to the camp asking him, *aren't you tired of being in bondage to your unforgiveness?*

Mercy given is the product of mercy received. Only when we can humble ourselves to understand how God has shown us mercy and shows us mercy each day of our lives, can we truly begin to show mercy to others. And to that we must also conclude that the level of mercy we might obtain from God is directly contingent upon the level of mercy that we show others. In Matthew 6, we find this very truth when Jesus explains, "For if you forgive other people when they sin against you, your heavenly Father will also forgive you. But if you do not forgive others their sins, your Father will not forgive your sins." (v.v. 14-15) Here Jesus commands us to forgive those who have wronged us, because not to do so forfeits our own salvation. The author of Hebrews writes this same truth stating, "once made perfect, he became the source of eternal salvation for all who obey him." (Heb. 5:9) As a pastor, I have come across many suffering people as I am sure you have. I cannot help but believe that God has placed them in my path, not so much as a test, but as an opportunity for me to show the kind of mercy that He has shown me. Paul says,

> Therefore, I urge you, brothers and sisters, in view of God's mercy, to offer your bodies as a living sacrifice, holy and pleasing to God—this is your true and proper worship. Do not conform to the pattern of this world, but be transformed by the renewing of your mind. Then you will be able to test and approve what God's will is—his good, pleasing and perfect will. (Rom. 12:1-2)
>
> Paul says that in light of the mercy God has shown us; we are to be a people different from the rest of the world.

Jesus also expresses this point in the parable of the Good Samaritan (Luke10:30-37). In that story, two religious Jews came upon a suffering fellow Jew (we presume) on the side of the road and both ignored him. Quite possibly, they were on their way to perform their religious duties at the temple; we are not told. But what is clear is that they both lacked any compassion at all for the suffering man. Yet a Samaritan came upon the same man and had compassion that moved the man to action. Here was a man (the Samaritan) who was despised by the Jews yet through the mercy that flowed out of his heart, had such compassion on his enemy that he took from his own means (not to mention his precious time) to help him.

John asks the question, "If anyone has material possessions and sees a brother or sister in need but has no pity on them, how can the love of God be in that person?" (1 John 3:17) In all of these passages, God is telling us that in light of the mercy that He has shown us, our hearts ought to be so filled with love (mercy), that we show mercy to others. Years ago, the WWJD (What Would Jesus Do) bracelets were all the craze. People wore them as daily reminders of how Jesus would react in a given situation. They are not as popular today and maybe that is because we do not wish to be reminded of the example He gave us to follow. Maybe we have counted the cost of discipleship, and like the rich ruler in Luke 18, we have decided that the price tag is just too steep.

Blessed are the pure in heart for they shall see God (Matt 5:8)

What does it mean to be pure in heart? A pure heart is something that comes only after salvation by the continuous washing of God's Word as Paul says in Eph. 5. When we hunger for and feast on God's Word daily, God fills our hearts with His righteousness and all of the impurities rise to the surface and then through sincere confession and repentance, the dross is removed and the heart is purified.

Being pure in heart means that we are single-minded in our thinking and our actions. The heart is where all kinds of things, both good and bad originate. No matter how quick we are to lie to someone, it was in our heart long before it ever reached our lips. Our level of worship is not some manufactured exercise, but rather, something that resides deep within the heart long before it reaches the altar on Sunday morning. When we choose to do the right thing in a given circumstance, it is not because we were just lucky enough to choose right, but because it was in our heart long before the circumstance arose.

If you want to know what a pure heart looks like, become a friend with someone who is mentally challenged. I have such a friend. Her name is Jessica and although Jessica is now in her forties, she will never have the capacity to learn beyond the age of six. While her capacity to learn is severely limited, her capacity to love is not. Every time I have seen Jessica at the church or in the community, she will do two things: first, she will hug me as I have never been hugged before, and secondly and without any announcement that she is about to do so, she will pray for me as I have never been prayed for before. There are many things that Jessica is unable to do that you and I might take for granted. But there is one thing that Jessica does extremely well that you and I probably struggle with more times than we care to admit. Jessica can love with a pure heart because she does not know what it is to hate, and I know that Jessica holds a very special place in God's heart for her capacity to love.

C. S. Lewis said, "It is safe to tell the pure in heart that they shall see God, for only the pure in heart want to." [13](Lewis, 2001, 93) We live in an age in which we are told that everybody is okay no matter what they do or believe. Every road leads to God and it does not matter what god you believe in so long as you are true to that god. What you do and what you believe really does not matter. That is the thought that has plagued our world for centuries, but Jesus would beg to differ. Jesus will hold each of us accountable for what we do AND for what we believe.

Everything that is evil comes from the heart. Jesus says in Matt.15:19, "For out of the heart come evil thoughts—murder, adultery, sexual immorality, theft, false testimony, slander." When our kids misbehave, they don't need a therapist or a counselor to help them change that behavior; *they need a change of heart.* When we truly accept Christ, there is a change in our hearts. Jesus said in Matt. 18:3 that unless we "change and become like little children, [we] will never enter the kingdom of heaven." When that change in our heart takes place, the change in our behavior follows. I saw a great sign recently that nails it, *when nothing changes, nothing changes.*

Right now, you might be saying to yourself, *I don't have an impure heart. I have never murdered anyone, I don't sleep around, or even sit in front of my computer and view pornography. In fact, I go to church three times a week and even give ten percent of my hard-earned money to make sure my church doors stay open.* If that is you, let me ask you a couple of questions. Have you forgiven that person who has hurt you? Have you

[13] Lewis, C.S.. 2001. *The Problem of Pain.* San Francisco: Harper

sought forgiveness for getting angry at that person who nearly ran you off the road? When is the last time you gossiped about someone at church and disguised your gossip as a prayer concern? When was the last time you allowed your thought life about that girl or that guy to get away from you? Do you believe that those feelings and thoughts do not matter to God?

We do not experience new life because we compromise with doing (and thinking) wrong and try to pretend it does not matter to God. God is not so desperate that He will put up with our shenanigans simply to have us follow Him a little. How many of you would be content with a spouse who promised to love you dearly, but for six days out of the week, wanted to live as though he or she were single? Why then would we think that God would be willing to enter into such a covenant with us? When the Bible tells us what we are to do and we are not doing it, why would we expect God's blessings or favor?

New life is rooted in repentance. David said, "When I kept silent, my bones wasted away through my groaning all day long." (Ps 32:3) Do you remember when as a kid you knew you had done wrong and you knew your parents knew you had done wrong, but you didn't want to bring up the subject, so you tried to be nice and have casual conversation, but it was very awkward? Deep down inside you wished all the beans were suddenly spilt out so you could get it over with. Like David, you were wasting away inside because of your sin.

But David also said, "Then I acknowledged my sin to you and did not cover up my iniquity. I said, 'I will confess my transgressions to the Lord.' And you forgave the guilt of my sin." (Ps 32:5) Confession, coupled with true repentance, brings cleansing and purity.

John says,

> This is the message we have heard from him and declare to you: God is light; in him there is no darkness at all. If we claim to have fellowship with him and yet walk in the darkness, we lie and do not live out the truth. But if we walk in the light, as he is in the light, we have fellowship with one another, and the blood of Jesus, his Son, purifies us from all sin. If we claim to be without sin, we deceive

> ourselves and the truth is not in us. If we confess our sins, he is faithful and just and will forgive us our sins and purify us from all unrighteousness. (1 Jn 1:5-9)

As long as we live, we will always have to contend with our flesh, for as John says, we deceive ourselves if we think otherwise. But John also says that the true Christian will strive to purify his heart from ALL unrighteousness and as Jesus promises, those who do *will see God.* I believe that is just as much a promise for this lifetime as in the next. As we seek to live our lives allowing God to purify our hearts through the washing of His Word, we will see more and more of the glory of God and what He is doing around us in our day to day lives. The Patriarch Job said, "My ears had heard of you but now my eyes have seen you." (Job 42:5) Can you think of a greater reward here on this earth than to see God?

Blessed are the Peacemakers for they will be called children of God (Matt. 5:9)

The United Nations was established more than 70 years ago on Oct. 24, 1945, only two months after the end of World War II with one purpose, to prevent World War III. Unfortunately, it has not been successful in accomplishing what it had set out to do. In fact, since 1945, the most peaceful year was 1952 with only six wars and 1990 is the most war-torn year with fifty-two wars. The military element of the UN is the peacekeeping force made up of many countries, and is deployed all over the world to keep the peace. These units are placed in the middle of growing hostility to keep that hostility from escalating.

Jesus does not say blessed are the peacekeepers, but blessed are the peacemakers. The difference is a peacemaker actively seeks to overcome evil with good. Some people are never happy unless they are fighting with someone (we all know people like that) and we often avoid them at all cost. A peacemaker, on the other hand, finds great satisfaction in removing hostilities and working to bring reconciliation between enemies.

True peace is not just an absence of conflict; that is just a truce. The Cold War was a great example of that. True peace is an absence of conflict in which opposite sides are brought together in righteousness, resulting in reconciliation. John MacArthur said, "A truce just says you don't shoot for a while. Peace comes when the truth is known, the issue is settled, and the parties embrace each other." [14](MacArthur, 1998, 169)

Peacemakers are those disciples who not only seek to cease hostilities, they consider it their mission to seek peace. They use their influence to reconcile opposition among individuals, families, churches, and the community. They change hostile attitudes to attitudes that seek the best interests of everyone. Most of us probably have a peacemaker in the family, that person who is not comfortable when there is tension between family members and so, they seek to find common ground and bring reconciliation. In our family, that is Austin. Someone once referred to the local church as being the spiritual Rolaids® of their community. Rolaids are advertised as bringing soothing comfort to stomach ailments, and our role as peacemaker serves to do just that!

Obviously, the greatest peacemaker is Jesus Himself who came to bring peace between God and man. We were all once enemies of God and Jesus came, not just to make a treaty to cease hostilities and stop the shooting, but to declare a permanent end to the war and to be reconciliation…the issue is settled!

We can only be truly comfortable with ourselves when we are at peace with Jesus. This is because peace with God changes our perspective from being self-centered to being God-centered. It changes our world view because we are forced to look at ourselves as God looks at us. More and more people seem to have identity crises these days. Many people suffer because they see themselves as the world sees them instead of how God sees them. We were created in His image, formed by His hand, and only when we come to a right relationship with God can we begin to see ourselves as He sees us. The question is not *Do you promote strife or discord?* The question is *Are you a spiritual Rolaid?*

Blessed are those who are persecuted because of righteousness for theirs is the kingdom of heaven (Matt. 5:10)

When we think about countries where Christians are being persecuted,

---

[14] MacArthur, John. 1998. *The Only Way to Happiness: The Beatitudes.* Chicago: Moody Publishers

most of us probably think of Iraq and Syria because they are in the news every day lately. Christians are being beheaded, shot, crucified and butchered, all because they refuse to deny to their faith in Christ in the face of certain and immediate death.

But you might be surprised to know that according to an organization called *Open Doors,* a group devoted to the ministry of persecuted Christians, North Korea has been the world's leader in persecuting Christians for the past 14 years and holds the infamous title of being *The Worst Country on Earth to be a Christian*. President Kim Jong-Un demands god-like worship for himself and leaves no room for any other religions. Christians meeting with other Christians is virtually impossible. Anyone discovered engaging in unauthorized religious activity is subject to arrest, imprisonment, disappearance, torture, or even execution. A recent deserter from the North Korean Army shared testimony of the demolishing of a vacant home at a new construction site. According to the web site opendoorsusa.org, in the basement, two bricks were removed revealing a Bible and a notebook. The notebook contained twenty-five names from a local church congregation, a pastor, four assistant pastors and twenty lay people. The soldiers turned the Bible and notebook over to Party officials who investigated the matter. All twenty-five were tracked down, brought to a road construction site and the five leaders were tied up and laid in the path of a steamroller while the other twenty were forced to watch. They were accused of being Christian spies and conspiring to engage in subversive activities. Nevertheless, they were told, *If you abandon religion and serve only Kim Jong, you will not be killed.* None of the five said a word. Some of the church members cried, screamed out and fainted when the skulls popped as they were crushed beneath the steamroller. Then the twenty were led away by the soldiers to a hard-labor prison camp for an undetermined number of years.

The Bible is clear that as true Christians, we will be persecuted. We are fortunate enough to live in a country where that persecution is usually no more severe than to be told when we can or cannot pray, or if as a small business owner, being forced to perform some duty that is contrary to our Christian beliefs. But even as our Christian liberties continue to erode, Jesus Himself reminds us that because of Him, we are going to face troubles (John 16:33). Paul says the same thing in 2 Tim. 3:12, "In fact, everyone who wants to live a godly life in Christ Jesus will be persecuted."

And Peter further warns us not to be surprised when we are persecuted (1 Pet. 4:12). It is not a matter of *if* but *when* and Peter goes on to say that we ought to consider it a joy when we are persecuted, for to do so, we are participating *in the sufferings of Christ* (1 Pet. 4:13).

As stated in the previous chapter, I believe the poor in spirit was first of the group for a reason. None of these other *ground rules* make any sense without our sense of indebtedness to God. Likewise, I believe this beatitude is last for a reason. By obeying the principles laid down in these other beatitudes, we are going to look and live differently than others and as a result, we will be persecuted. Jesus said that because He lives in us, we are a light that will shine in a dark world. The Bible says that the light shines in the darkness and the darkness has not understood it (John 1:5). You and I are persecuted because we are not understood. People do not understand the light of life that Jesus gives. It is foreign to them and so they persecute people who have a light.

God is not looking for spiritual giants. He wants plain ordinary people who are willing to admit they have blown it, but they will always be open to His correction and hunger and thirst for His righteousness. Are you a merciful person today? Does your heart lead you, not to simply say, *I will pray for you,* but *now how can I help you?* Can you say you have a pure heart before the Lord that is being purified daily through the washing of His Word? Jesus calls us to follow in His footsteps. There is not anywhere we can go that He has not been. You can make a difference in your life and in the lives of others simply by following in the steps of our Lord and Savior Jesus Christ.

Before you progress to the next chapter in this book, ask yourself, do these eight *Christian attitudes* describe me? If not, this would be a great time to bow your head and get right with God. As already stated, Jesus' sermon will make absolutely no sense to the unregenerate heart. You must be born-again if you are to see the kingdom of heaven (John 3:3). It is as simple as confessing to God that you are a sinner and in need of forgiveness offered through the blood of His Son Jesus Christ. Ask His Spirit to come into your life today and replace your heart with His heart, a new heart, a heart that is born-again and we will see you again in the next chapter.

FOUR

Salt and Light

You are the salt of the earth. But if the salt loses its saltiness, how can it be made salty again? It is no longer good for anything, except to be thrown out and trampled underfoot. "You are the light of the world. A town built on a hill cannot be hidden. Neither do people light a lamp and put it under a bowl. Instead they put it on its stand, and it gives light to everyone in the house. In the same way, let your light shine before others, that they may see your good deeds and glorify your Father in heaven (Matt. 5:13-16)

This is the final chapter in this first segment titled, *The Kingdom and the Believers,* and I called it that because as of yet, Jesus has not given one commandment, only a series of statements about what traits a true believer must possess. As stated in the previous chapter, none of the lessons here in this sermon will make any sense to anyone, nor will anyone have any success in following them, unless he/she is a true born-again believer.

In this chapter, we will look at these two declarations which Jesus makes to every believer, that we are both salt and light. Again, notice that Jesus does not command us to be salt and light, or that we should be, could be, might be or may be—but that as believers, we are the salt of the earth and the light of the world. Let's dig in!

You are the salt of the earth

We have probably all heard of the different uses of salt in both ancient and present days. Dietrich Bonhoeffer calls it "the most indispensable necessity of life."[15](Bonhoeffer, 2012, 115) Salt is a known preservative, a flavor enhancer, and it is known for its healing powers. Even I can figure out how those qualities apply to the Christian life. The salt of a Christian life allows us to live contented lives, not being driven by the cares of this world. And because we are not caught up in those cares, we are separated, or preserved to focus on doing God's will and allowing Him to care for those things we need in life. The salt of the Christian life also enhances our lives. Jesus said in John 10:10, "I have come that they may have life, and have it to the full." And finally, there is tremendous healing power in salt.

But in most regions of the ancient world, salt was also a form of money. In fact, the English word *salary* is derived from the Latin word *Salarium* which refers to the payments made to Roman soldiers with salt.

However, did you know that salt was also a symbol of dedication? In Ezekiel 16:4, we see where Ezekiel, in speaking a parable about unfaithful Israel as a child who has been cast-off, says, "On the day you were born your cord was not cut, nor were you washed with water to make you clean, nor were you rubbed with salt or wrapped in cloths." In ancient days and even today in the Roman Catholic Church, it was a custom to rub newborn children with salt to signify their being dedicated to God. So, just as circumcision was a sign of belonging to the Israelites and baptism is a sign of belonging to the Christian faith, salt is also used to signify ownership. But unlike circumcision and baptism, salt is a sign, not to other believers, but to unbelievers. It is that silent witness that every true believer possesses that draws people, not to self, but to God by how one lives life.

Jesus says that we are the salt of the earth. He is making a declaration that as His representative here on earth, we are to draw people to Him through how we live our lives, namely, by way of the eight beatitudes that we just examined.

Nan has some black bear salt and pepper shakers which were given to her as a gift a few years ago. They are proudly displayed on our dining table. There is only one problem—they are empty! When we have people over for dinner, guests frequently shake and they shake and nothing ever comes out and we explain that they are only there for show.

---

[15] Bonhoeffer, Dietrich. 2012. *The Cost of Discipleship*. New York: Simon and Schuster

Some professing Christians are like that. They claim to represent Christ in the world, but they are really only for show. They claim to be Christian and even join local churches, but that is the extent of their Christian influence. They are not really useful in that they do not draw people to God through the living of their lives. *I do not want people to want to be who I am; I want them to want who I have* and who I aspire to be like.

I like a lot of salt on my food. Nan tries to keep me in check on my salt intake, but that ship sailed a long time ago. But now, because I like a lot of salt, I also get very thirsty. That is exactly the effect that we as Christians should have on the world around us—we want our salty witness to make others thirsty for the living water of Jesus Christ. Jesus declared us as *salt* because it is our job to permeate this evil world. Everything else that is bad in the world can be redeemed through salt, but if salt loses its saltiness, what can make it good again? As Jesus said, it is good for nothing else but to be tossed out and trampled on.

What kind of influence do you have on the world around you? What kind of influence do you have in your home? Do you leave a thirst in your family's mouths wanting more of what you have? If you have an unbelieving spouse, are you a stronger influence in his or her life than he or she is in yours? Do you live out your Christian principles in your home or do you leave them on your pew at church alongside your Bible and tush-pillow? Are you raising your children with a thirst to live out those Christian principles in their lives or, by your actions, are you teaching them that those principles only really apply at church?

Many years ago, I had an opportunity to see my beloved *Tampa Bay Buccaneers* live at *Raymond James Stadium.* A neighbor of ours whose name is Troy, became a good friend and brother in the Lord. Troy knew how much I loved my Bucs and that I had never had the opportunity to see them play live. One day, he approached me with a ticket to Sunday's big game and asked if I would like to go with him. His family was season ticket-holders, but was unable to attend that particular game, so Troy offered the free seat to me. I was in a quagmire, because although I wanted to attend the game more than you could possibly know, I also wanted my son Austin, who was six-years-old at the time, to know how important church was to me. I wasn't a pastor at that time yet and so, I didn't really have any responsibilities at church for which I couldn't find a replacement; after all it was only one Sunday and it was the TAMPA BAY BUCCANEERS! But after giving the idea thought, I turned Troy's offer down. Now, I know what some of you are thinking right now, *that sounds awfully legalistic Randy,* but that was not my heart. I saw this as a teaching lesson for my son. I could very well have attended the game and had the time of my life and no one would have thought bad of me, but imagine the thirst that I left in my son's mouth to have what I have! I am sure I made the right decision and as God would have it, the very next season, I was invited by another friend to attend another Buccaneer game… on *Monday Night Football!*

J. Vernon McGee, in his commentary Through the Bible, points out that the Scots translate *saltiness* with the word *tang.* He rightly states that, "The problem today is that most church members have not only lost their tang as salt, but as pepper they have lost their pep also." [16](McGee, 1995, 36) I like that translation because, like Nan's prized salt and pepper shakers, if our shakers have no *tang* and *pep,* we really are not much good to a world that is dire need of Jesus.

But now, while living the silent witness is a good thing, it is not everything. There are times when you must tell others the truth of Scripture. That takes me to Jesus' second declaration:

You are the light of the world

Once, I had a dear sister in Christ challenge me about being so brazen in telling people the truth of God's Word. She said that she does not believe in that *in-your-face evangelism, but* rather, she believes in *loving* them into the kingdom. She said that getting in people's faces and confronting them with truth *is no longer useful in society today.* Now, I understand that whole *catching more bees with honey than vinegar* thing, but if my child is about to run into the road, *loving him and living out my silent witness is not going to save him* from being killed by a car. There comes a time when Christ calls us to stand up for the truth of His Word. Every one of us have family, friends and neighbors who are running into the road to hell, all because we do not want to hurt their feelings by telling them truth.

Martin Luther rightly said,

---

[16] McGee, Vernon. 1995. *Through the Bible: Commentary.* Nashville: Thomas Nelson

> For Christ did not institute and appoint the office of the ministry that it might serve to gain money, possession, favor, honor, friendship, or that one may seek his own advantage through it, but that one should openly, freely proclaim the truth, rebuke evil, and publish what belongs to the advantage, safety and salvation of souls. [17](Luther, 1892, 17)

We are all called to minister. We are all called to preach, teach and proclaim the truth of Scripture and sometimes that truth hurts, but that fact does not lessen our need or our call to do it.

One night, I was making my way back from taking the garbage to the road when I got a text message on my phone. I started walking up the ramp that led to my carport while reading the text and walked right off the ramp and fell onto an iron smoker about four feet below me. Instead of reading a text, I should have shined the light on where I was walking. I dragged myself up the ramp and crawled into the living room on my hands and knees and in all humility and embarrassment, told Nan that we might want to consider getting more exterior illumination. Jesus tells us that we are the light of the world and light has one purpose, to dispel darkness. Psalm 119:105 says, "Your word is a lamp for my feet, a light on my path." Without the light, we are lost to the path we ought to be walking. Darkness hides us from the truth. The world is becoming more and more darkened every day from the effects of sin and so people are living in more and more fear. These are scary days and they are only getting more scary, but we have an incredible opportunity here to shine our light into the darkness so that people out there will not be afraid, and we do that by helping them to see that there is hope in the light of Jesus Christ.

The Apostle John, in speaking about John the Baptist, said, "There was a man sent from God whose name was John. He came as a witness to testify concerning that light, so that through him all might believe. He himself was not the light; he came only as a witness to the light. The true light that gives light to everyone was coming into the world." (John 1:6-9)

---

[17] Luther, Martin. 1892. *Commentary on The Sermon on the Mount.* Galesburg: Lutheran Publication Society

Just as the light of the moon is simply a reflection of the sun, we are only a reflection of the true light, the Son of God and we are to mirror His life with ours. That is the whole purpose of Jesus' sermon! *By insisting that telling people truth is no longer effective simply insists that Jesus Himself was ineffective.* Jesus never shied away from shining His light on the hypocrisy of His day and neither should we.

Have you ever sat down to read and while you were reading, it started getting dark out but you had not really noticed until someone came in and turned on the light? That is how it is for people who live in darkness. They do not know they are in darkness until someone turns on the light in their life. Matthew said, "the people living in darkness have seen a great light; on those living in the land of the shadow of death a light has dawned." (Matt. 4:16) But now, look at the very next verse in which Matthew says, "From that time on Jesus began to preach, 'Repent, for the kingdom of heaven has come near'" (v.17). Our purpose for sharing truth with people is so that they might be brought to a spirit of repentance through the power of the Holy Spirit. Understand, it is not our job to bring about that spirit, but how can it possibly happen if we are keeping the truth to ourselves, hiding it in the closet, or even sadder, sharing it only with those who already have the truth. That kind of witnessing encourages believers, but does absolutely nothing to save people from an eternal hell.

Palestinian homes were generally small dark single-rooms, usually having only one small window and the only light consisted of a single oil lamp. When people needed light, the lamp was placed on a lamp stand. The most difficult thing about having this light in the house was lighting the lamp. There were no matches or lighters, so they tried to keep the lamp lit at all times. But when they would leave their house, it was dangerous to leave the fire out in the open, so they would place it under a clay pot where it could continue to burn without any danger. As soon as they returned home, they would put the lamp back onto the stand.

Jesus said,

> You are the light of the world. A town built on a hill cannot be hidden. Neither do people light a lamp and put it under a bowl. Instead they put it on its stand, and it gives light to everyone in the house. In the same way, let

> your light shine before others, that they may see your good deeds and glorify your Father in heaven. (Matt. 5:14-16)

There is a story of a man whose job it was to be on the railroad tracks and warn coming trains when the bridge is raised, making it impassable. That night, as the train came, the man showed his lamp, but the train went right past him and into the ravine. The man was questioned in court so they could figure out why the train paid no attention to him in warning about the danger ahead. The man was asked, *were you on duty on the night the train had the accident?* The judge asked. The man replied, *yes sir. Did you have your lamp with you,* the judge asked, to which the man replied, *yes sir.* And finally, the judge asked, *did you wave your lamp to the train?* The man replied, *Yes sir,* and so the man was not held responsible for the accident. On his way out of the courtroom, he turned to his friend and said, *I sure am glad the judge didn't ask me if my lamp was lit!* (origin unknown)

The problem for many Christians is that, although they are given the responsibility of shining their lights in this dark world, their lamps are not lit. As a result, there are people all around them who are in danger of crashing into a ravine called hell. As Christians, our lights are to be seen. Light shines not so much that people may see the light as that they may see other things because of the light. The light reveals areas of our lives that need to be changed, not our light, but His Light who dwells in us. Will people who choose to live in darkness run from the light? You betcha! Will you be persecuted because of the light? You betcha! But neither of those reasons should motivate us to place our light under a bowl until such time it is safe to bring it out.

In my hometown of Bradenton Florida, Tampa Bay separates us from St Petersburg, but there is a bridge that spans the gap between the two lands. On the morning of May 7, 1980, a dense fog and rain covered the entire bay area. Just before sunrise, the 580' cargo ship *Summit Venture* attempted to enter the bay, but collided with one of the four main support structures bringing the entire southbound bridge crashing down into the water. Because there was no light, six cars, a pickup truck and a Greyhound bus carrying twenty-five passengers drove over the edge of the bridge falling more than 400 feet to their deaths, never knowing the danger that lay ahead of them.

People are driving off the edge of life every day all around us-completely unaware of the dangers that lie ahead of them and you and I possess the only light that can save them.

The prophet Isaiah said it best saying,

> Arise, shine, for your light has come, and the glory of the LORD rises upon you. See, darkness covers the earth and thick darkness is over the peoples, but the LORD rises upon you and his glory appears over you. Nations will come to your light, and kings to the brightness of your dawn. (Isa. 60:1-3)

In these two short declarations, Jesus explains to us that we are to be two different types of witness, the salt of the silent witness who draws people to the Lord by the way we live our lives, and the bold and illuminating witness of the light of Christ that He has charged each of us with to dispel this present darkness. It is not an either/or proposition, but both. Everyone reading this knows someone who is driving off the edge of this existence and into the sea of eternal hopelessness. We have been given the awesome responsibility of saving them. We may lose their friendship, or we may even be ostracized and mocked, but you and I have one Person to whom we must give account and He is the one who declared that we are both salt and light.

SECTION TWO

THE KINGDOM AND THE LAW

Have you ever heard anyone say, *I'm not under the law, I'm under grace?* How about, *I'm a New Testament Christian?* We seem to think that Jesus came to earth with the tablets in hand and as Moses did when he came down from Sinai, smashed them to pieces. We have drawn the faulty conclusion that the Old Testament no longer matters, that it no longer applies, that it is just a collection of history books. But in truth, the Old Testament points forward to Jesus Christ and Jesus Christ fulfills that which was written about Him. St Augustine is credited as having once said *The New* [Testament] *is in the old* [Testament] *concealed; The Old* [Testament] *is in the new* [Testament] *revealed.* One cannot be a *New Testament Christian* without understanding that it is the Old Testament which Christ reveals (and fulfills) not in His teaching but in His presence.

The title of this segment is *The Kingdom and the Law* because Jesus makes it clear throughout these next seven chapters that the law was important, because it was God's Word! We live in the age of grace, but as Paul states in Romans 6:1-15, we are not to use that grace as an opportunity to live as we please. Rather, Grace came to earth in order to fulfill that which we were unable to fulfill in our own power—the keeping of the law! Throughout this portion of Jesus' sermon, over and over, we see the phrase, *You have heard it was said…,* followed by His explanation of His original intent. Nowhere in this sermon, does Jesus command us, or even hint to us that we should ignore His law. Instead, He gives us commandments that are not only to be followed, but He gives a *higher law* that is to be written on our hearts.

FIVE

A New Righteousness

Do not think that I have come to abolish the Law or the Prophets; I have not come to abolish them but to fulfill them. For truly I tell you, until heaven and earth disappear, not the smallest letter, not the least stroke of a pen, will by any means disappear from the Law until everything is accomplished. Therefore anyone who sets aside one of the least of these commands and teaches others accordingly will be called least in the kingdom of heaven, but whoever practices and teaches these commands will be called great in the kingdom of heaven. For I tell you that unless your righteousness surpasses that of the Pharisees and the teachers of the law, you will certainly not enter the kingdom of heaven. (Matt. 5:17-20)

In his book, The Pilgrim's Progress, John Bunyan describes a house in which the main character of the story (Christian) entered on his journey toward the Celestial City. The parlor of the house was completely covered with dust, and when a man began to sweep it, everyone in the house began to cough and gasp for air, because the man had kicked up the dust into a great cloud. Then the character known as Interpreter (a.k.a. Holy Spirit) orders a handmaiden to sprinkle the room with water and as she did, the dust quickly washed away. Interpreter explained to Christian that the parlor represented the heart of an unsaved man, the dust was original sin, the man with the broom was the law, and the maid with the water was the gospel of Jesus Christ. His point was that all the law can do with sin is to stir it up and make us conscious of it, while only the gospel of Jesus Christ can wash it away. [18](Bunyan, 2009,145146)

In the opening verse of this passage, Jesus said, "I have not come to abolish the law, but to fulfill it." Then He doubles down saying, "not a single little mark of the law will pass away before heaven and earth pass away." Yet Paul, considered to be the New Testament theologian, says in Romans 10:4 that "Christ is the culmination of the law." How can we have such a disparity between these two thoughts?

Jesus is known for His many *hard sayings* (difficult to understand) and Matthew 5:17, when placed beside those like Paul's statement In Romans 10, only add to their difficulty. Another of those *hard sayings* is Matthew 5:20, which many new believers struggle with. The Pharisees and teachers prided themselves on how well they could keep the law. The law was everything to them. It was their life and they knew it inside and out, forward and back. How could you and I possibly beat that? These religious men memorized the Law and the Prophets by the time they were fourteen years of age. How can we possibly outdo that; yet *that is exactly what Jesus tells us that we must do.*

Let's set the stage by looking at just how successful we are at keeping the law, since that seems to be Jesus' emphasis here. In all of Jesus' teachings, there is probably no topic that He teaches more in regards to the law than the keeping of the Sabbath, so let us start with that one. In the Ten Commandments, God commands us to "Remember the Sabbath day by keeping it holy." (Exod. 20:8) Being a former military man, I like to see things as black and white and this one seems pretty black and white to me. So, if not a single mark will be lost from the law, that means that we are to keep the Sabbath, right? Well, remember that the Sabbath was to be observed on the seventh day, but do most Christians not observe it on the first day of the week as commanded by both Paul and Luke? Is this not already a violation the law? But maybe that is just a technicality and not really an *important* part of the law. So, how well do we keep the more *important* part, the part that *really* matters?

Exodus 35:3 says that we are not to light a fire in the home on the Sabbath. Does that include electric stoves or just gas stoves? Does that include electric heating or just fireplaces? And if we cannot light a fire,

---

[18] Bunyan, John. 2009. *The Pilgrim's Progress.* Wheaton: Crossway Books

then that means we cannot cook those incredible Sunday dinners that we love to cook, or at least go to grandma's house to eat. And even while I am up here in Maine writing this, while it is -1 degree outside, does that mean that I cannot use this beautiful fireplace on the Sabbath as well? Aren't we being just a bit extreme to suggest that we cannot eat or heat? What about when you trip trying to get out of your lazy-boy on the Sabbath and must be rushed to the ER because you broke your leg? Would you be very upset if when you got to the hospital, there was no one there to treat you? Should not the nurses and doctors also observe the Sabbath and keep it holy? And let's say that you left the house in such a hurry that you forgot your dinner on the stove and your house caught on fire. When you got home, your house is a blaze, but because it is the Sabbath, there is no sign of firefighters. You tried calling the police to complain, but they are not answering their phones either. Well, it has been such an ordeal of a day, you decided to go to evening church to receive your daily bread and receive a little encouragement, but since it is the Sabbath, there is no pastor or preacher to proclaim the good news to you. So, you just throw your arms up and tell the family, *we're going to McDonalds*, oh yeah—never mind!

Hmm, we are not doing so well are we? If you are keeping score, I think you must agree that none of us do a very good job of keeping the law, do we? Let us try another: what about all those dietary laws that we find in Leviticus 11? How well are we keeping those laws? Verse 4 says that I am not allowed to eat camel. Ok, I have never had much of a stomach for camel anyway, so I am good with that. But v. 6 says that I am not to eat rabbit either. Now, if you have never had my friend Denny's rabbit stew, that might not be a big deal for you either, but ok, I want to be a good Christian so I will cut Denny's stew out of my diet as well. In v. 7, it says that I cannot even eat pig, WHAT? No ham? No sausage? No pork chops? No BACON? Are you out of your mind? Bacon is a staple food around my house! In fact, if I could, I would have bacon-salt and bacon-pepper shakers to replace Nan's bears! Yet, if I am to keep the law, doesn't that rule that out as well? This is getting very personal isn't it? Like the man who encourages the preacher to *Preach it brother* as the preacher delivers his message—right up to the point where he hits very close to home and the man says, *Now, you're just meddling!*

In another passage, Jesus gives the Pharisees a Bible study lesson on the law and in Mark 7:9, He says to them, "You have a fine way of setting aside the commands of God in order to observe your own traditions." He rebuked them for choosing to ignore the laws of God and instead, focusing on, and forcing on others, man's laws. Then in v.v. 18-19, Jesus says, "'Are you so dull?' he asked. 'Don't you see that nothing that enters a person from the outside can defile them? For it doesn't go into their heart but into their stomach, and then out of the body.'" But it is Matthew's explanation that I want you to take note of, "(In saying this, Jesus declared all foods clean.)" In the Greek, it literally reads, *Jesus cleaning all foods.* So, did Jesus just contradict Himself then when He said that not a single mark would be removed from the law, yet what He states here seems to be a direct contradiction of Leviticus 11? Isn't Jesus in fact changing the law here in Mark 7?

Well, let us look at a few more verses to see if we can get some clarity. "He went on: 'What comes out of a person is what defiles them. For it is from within, out of a person's heart, that evil thoughts come—sexual immorality, theft, murder, adultery, greed, malice, deceit, lewdness, envy, slander, arrogance and folly. All these evils come from inside and defile a person.'" (Mark 7:20-23) So, Jesus was not changing the law, but rather, He was explaining the law and revealing to them and to us, the original intent of the law, not to forbid us from eating Denny's rabbit stew, ham hocks, or even camel roasts (if that's your thing). Rather, He was telling us to be clean! He was, in fact, not abolishing the law, but fulfilling it just as He declared in Matthew 5:17!

What then does that say about the law? Was it incomplete? Was it inadequate for its purposes? Not at all. Paul said in Romans 5:13, "To be sure, sin was in the world before the law was given, but sin is not charged against anyone's account where there is no law." Translated: the law's purpose was to help the Israelites and us to understand what sin is, so that we become *conscious of our sin* (Romans 3:20). But what the law was never meant to do was to fulfill righteousness, because only Jesus could do that. The purpose of the law was to point us to Jesus. When Jesus arrived on the scene, He was simply declaring that, "Today this scripture is fulfilled in your hearing." (Luke 4:21)

In Deuteronomy 9, Moses gives the Israelites a little pep talk, before they move in to take possession of the land that God had promised them, a land *flowing with milk and honey.* They had been wandering aimlessly in the desert for some thirty-eight years and it was finally time for them to go in and take possession of their inheritance. Then Moses said:

> After the LORD your God has driven them out before you, do not say to yourself, 'The LORD has brought me here to take possession of this land because of my righteousness.' No, it is on account of the wickedness of these nations that the LORD is going to drive them out before you. It is not because of your righteousness or your integrity that you are going in to take possession of their land; but on account of the wickedness of these nations, the LORD your God will drive them out before you, to accomplish what he swore to your fathers, to Abraham, Isaac and Jacob. Understand, then, that it is not because of your righteousness that the LORD your God is giving you this good land to possess, for you are a stiff-necked people. (v.v. 4-6)

It appears that even among this new generation of Israelites which had been born in the desert, there was still a sense that this is their reward for all of their goodness and so Moses sets them straight, saying *Look, this is not of your doing, but of God's doing.* This is the exact same righteousness that the Pharisees and teachers of the law possessed, their self-righteousness and it is this self-righteousness that Jesus explains that we must exceed in Matt. 5:20. When Jesus said that He had come to *fulfill the law,* He did so in the way that only He could, a true righteousness—a holy and sinless righteousness—the very same righteousness that Moses spoke about, God's righteousness. This was in fact a *new righteousness,* because *God's Righteousness had not walked the earth since the garden.* The writer of Hebrews says, "The law is only a shadow of the good things that are coming—not the realities themselves. For this reason it can never, by the same sacrifices repeated endlessly year after year, make perfect those who draw near to worship," (10:1) The law was simply a precursor to a *new* law, a *new* covenant, a *new* righteousness—Jesus Christ!

In Luke 24, Jesus talks about the prophets writing about Him and we see that in passages like Jeremiah 31:31-33 where he says,

> 'The days are coming,' declares the LORD, 'when I will make a new covenant with the people of Israel and with the people of Judah. It will not be like the covenant I made with their ancestors when I took them by the hand to lead them out of Egypt, because they broke my covenant, though I was a husband to them,' declares the LORD. 'This is the covenant I will make with the people of Israel after that time,' declares the LORD. 'I will put my law in their minds and write it on their hearts. I will be their God, and they will be my people.'

Jesus was not bringing with Him a revised copy of the old covenant that God made with Israel some 1,500 years earlier, He was bringing a new covenant, a new righteousness that did not abolish the law, but fulfilled it. The Greek word here for *fulfill* is found throughout the New Testament translated as, completed, accomplished, finished, proclaimed, summed up, produced and satisfied. Jesus *satisfied* the law to its perfect intent. *Christ is the culmination* [completion] *of the law* (Romans 10:4).

As the writer of Hebrews said, the law was only a shadow of what was to come. It is like a birthday party invitation. The invitation is not the party, but only an invitation. The party has not yet arrived and when it does, then we go to the party and enjoy it. And so, looking back to the dietary laws of Leviticus 11, they were only invitations to prepare us for the holiness that was yet to come. They were only *shadows* of the One who would come and command us to, "Be perfect" (a.k.a. holy, a.k.a. righteous) "therefore, as your heavenly Father is perfect." (Matt. 5:48)

Yes, I have thrown a lot of Scripture out there, but what does all of this mean for us? Jesus came to perfect what Heb. 8:6 calls an imperfect law. The old covenant focused on the outside like tattoos, body piercings and spiked hair, but Jesus focused on the inside. The law says, *Do not murder.* It is obvious even to a blockhead like myself that when someone dies at the hand of another, that law is broken. But Jesus goes deep inside the heart and asks, *What are you thinking about?* Because whatever is in your heart, that is what makes you unclean, not the ham and eggs you had for breakfast.

Jesus was not about making us more theological. That is not what it means to be a Christian. We see over and over where people ask Jesus into their hearts, get baptized and join churches and then get frustrated because nothing has changed for them. Nan had a conversation with a lady sometime back who struggled over and over with trying to *keep the law* in order to be a good Christian and each time she failed, she got frustrated, and when she got frustrated, she gave up. Sound familiar to anyone? Being a Christian is far more than just believing a set of theological truths, it is about being born-again. It is about allowing the Holy Spirit to send His handmaiden into every room in the heart and clean house (with holy water) and have such a way in our lives that no one can deny His presence. It is about giving control of one's life over to the One who knows the plans and allow Him to work in, on, and through every part of life. But it all begins in the heart. That is what Jeremiah meant when He said that Jesus would come and write His law on our hearts and change us. And just as I have stated already (and will remind us again), the carrying out Christ's commandments in His sermon is impossible until one has received Him who is the fulfillment of the law. Oswald Chambers puts it this way:

> Our Lord goes behind the old law to the disposition. Everything He teaches is impossible unless He can put into us His Spirit and remake us from within. The Sermon on the Mount is quite unlike the Ten Commandments in the sense of its being absolutely unworkable unless Jesus Christ can remake us.[19](Chambers, 1915, 21)

David rightly said, "The law of the Lord is perfect" (Ps. 19:7), but the writer of Hebrews also rightly said that "the law made nothing perfect." (7:19) The law is perfect because it reveals the will of God (Deut. 29:29), but what the law could not do is give us life (Rom. 8:2). Paul stated in Rom. 3:20 that no one will be declared righteous according to the law, but that this *new righteousness* only comes by faith through Jesus Christ, APART

---

[19] Chambers, Oswald. 1915. *Studies in the Sermon on the Mount.* Cincinnati: God's Revivalist Press

from the law (Rom. 3:21-22)! Jesus is the fulfillment of the law because He is the true Righteousness of the law and the only way that anyone will *surpass* the righteousness of the Pharisees is by being one with the Person called Righteous!

One of my favorite Bill Murray movies is *Groundhog Day*. In the movie, Bill is a self-serving, self-preserving and self-promoting TV reporter who travels to Punxsutawney PA for the annual Groundhog Festival. Something very strange happens when he awakens the day after Groundhog Day and is forced to relive the same day over and over, because he has not learned what is truly important in life. I guess that many of us feel like that sometimes in trying to do good and do the right things—go to church—love our spouses—raise our kids, and we do ok for a few days, maybe even a few weeks, but then we mess up just once and we have to relive that same guilt trip over and over again. It is possible that many of you have even thrown your hands up and given up trying to live as a Christian is *supposed* to live.

Jesus Christ came to fulfill the requirements of the law on our behalf, not to place the burden of the law around our necks to fill us with guilt every time we mess up, but *to free us from that burden so that we could live wholly and holy for Him.* Jesus fulfilled the law so that we do not have to. All that we need to do is to place our faith in Him and strive to be like Him, because in doing so, we uphold the law which He perfectly fulfilled (Rom. 3:31). Jesus said that unless your righteousness surpasses that of the Pharisees, you will never see heaven. It is not enough to be in the law, reading, studying, or even memorizing the law; the law must be written on our hearts. I wonder how many people reading this have been frustrated with trying to keep the law, without realizing that what you really need is to give yourself over to Jesus!

SIX

The Danger of Anger

You have heard that it was said to the people long ago, 'You shall not murder, and anyone who murders will be subject to judgment.' But I tell you that anyone who is angry with a brother or sister will be subject to judgment. Again, anyone who says to a brother or sister, 'Raca,' is answerable to the court. And anyone who says, 'You fool!' will be in danger of the fire of hell. "Therefore, if you are offering your gift at the altar and there remember that your brother or sister has something against you, leave your gift there in front of the altar. First go and be reconciled to them; then come and offer your gift. "Settle matters quickly with your adversary who is taking you to court. Do it while you are still together on the way, or your adversary may hand you over to the judge, and the judge may hand you over to the officer, and you may be thrown into prison. Truly I tell you, you will not get out until you have paid the last penny (Matt. 5:21-26)

I drove to Nashville once to pick up my oldest daughter Tiffani and our granddaughters at the airport. I had left in ample time to get them at the airport, had it not been rush hour. I found myself on Interstate 65 huffing and puffing, looking at my watch and having this imaginary conversation with the people in front of me. I was so animated that I could have probably moved over into the HOV lane designed for multiple occupants only and no one would have known the difference. I was plagued with a slight case of road rage. For me at least, I think God has a way of slowing me down because I seem to only get behind slow drivers when I am running late for an appointment.

One of the most common places where this feeling of anger occurs is while driving a motor vehicle. Someone rightly said, *Anger is just one letter short of danger.* Here are some interesting statistics regarding road rage according to one website:

> 19.3% of respondents reported feeling anger and intense aggression while driving in the past year, while 5.5% said they experienced those same feelings weekly
>
> The most common act of road rage witnessed by American drivers was another driver honking their car horns in anger (48.3%). However, 41.1% (almost half of the respondents) witnessed drivers giving rude hand gestures to the person of their aggression. 35.8% saw other drivers yell at another driver, while 6.2% actually witnessed drivers get out of their car and fight in a physical altercation
>
> Distracted driving, tailgating, and being cut off in traffic are the most enraging behaviors, according to the survey (respondents reporting 27.7%, 21.4%, and 15.6% respectively).[20(]Taylor, 2002[)]

Most of us have probably been the victim of road rage at some point. People make mistakes while they are driving, no matter how *gifted* a driver your husband or wife claims to be! The problem begins when a driver is trying to correct a mistake and it occurs at the expense of another driver, and that other driver takes the situation personally, *The nerve of that guy!*

I know this statement to be true because when I am running late for that appointment, I think that people can see that and they purposely pass me and then slow down and I begin that imaginary conversation with them that I am certain I would not have face to face, especially given the possibly that they may be packing a gun, at least back home on Alabama and Tennessee roads.

---

[20] Covington, Taylor. 2020. *Road Rage Statistics. https://www.thezebra.com/research/road-rage-statistics/.* June 2, 2020

So, what gets you angry? More importantly, how do you deal with anger? Here are just some of the ways that people deal with anger:

- They suppress it. They hide their anger until their faces turn red and their veins start bulging from their collar. Suppressed anger is like a really bad migraine that you medicate yourself to the point of passing out, but you never really get any relief.
- Some people spiritualize their anger saying they are only righteously outraged, insisting that they have a God-given right to be angry.
- Some people garner support groups for their anger. They work very hard to get people to come over to their side called camp pity.
- Still, others have superiority complexes. They are proud of their anger. *This is the way God made me, and I can't help it. If you push me too far, I turn green and my clothes start ripping at the seams.*

Children learn at a very young age how to use anger to their advantage, throwing their strained vegetables against the wall over and over until mommy finally gives them the strained pears. If you are a parent, you can relate! The real problem is that the kid grows up believing that is how they act to get what they want.

You've heard that it was said... This is the first of several statements Jesus makes in drawing a comparison between something that the listener already knows from the law and that which is required of born-again Christians. In this case, it is the sixth commandment not to murder. But as stated in the introduction, Jesus does not introduce a new thought to counter *the Law*, but rather He explains the original intent behind God's law. He says, "I tell you that anyone who is angry with a brother or sister will be subject to judgment." That word *judgment* does not mean earthly consequences, like we unfortunately see in road rage sometimes, but rather it means burning in hell, so when someone makes you angry and you say, *he really burns me up,* you may be closer to being right than you know.

Now, I am not going to delve into forgiveness too deeply at this point since we will be looking at that in much greater detail later. But forgiveness is certainly the key ingredient that buys us that fire insurance we all need to have. Instead, what I really wanted to discuss in this chapter is 1) the heart of the law and 2) how the condition of the heart affects our worship.

We all understand the sixth commandment, *do not kill.* Once again, this seems fairly black and white to me. If you are responsible for stopping another person's heart, you have broken the sixth commandment. But what about the executioner dolling out capital punishment to a convicted murderer? What about the soldier, sailor, airman, or marine killing in the defense our great nation? Are they also guilty of breaking the sixth commandment? There are nine different Hebrew words used in the Old Testament for the word *kill,* but only one word that is actually translated *murder.* That is the word used in Exod. 20:13. It is the only word used that carries with it an *evil intent.* Webster's Dictionary defines *murder* as *the crime of unlawfully killing a person especially with malice.* Likewise, there are five words used for *kill* in the Greek New Testament, but only one translated as *murder* and that is the word used by Jesus here in v. 21.

According to Jesus, getting un-righteously angry with another is no less punishable (in God's eyes) than if you were to murder them. The understanding behind this statement is only found in our understanding of His sermon's theme: the kingdom of heaven vs. the kingdom of self. In Matthew 23, Jesus calls out the Pharisees for their hypocrisy saying,

> Woe to you, teachers of the law and Pharisees, you hypocrites! You clean the outside of the cup and dish, but inside they are full of greed and self-indulgence. Blind Pharisee! First clean the inside of the cup and dish, and then the outside also will be clean. "Woe to you, teachers of the law and Pharisees, you hypocrites! You are like whitewashed tombs, which look beautiful on the outside but on the inside are full of the bones of the dead and everything unclean. In the same way, on the outside you appear to people as righteous but on the inside you are full of hypocrisy and wickedness. (v.v. 25-28)

The purpose of Jesus' sermon is to draw the disciples back to God's original intent of His law, the heart! Murder begins in the heart, not in the hands. Jesus said that what comes out of the heart is that which makes a person unclean (Matt. 15:18). Ralph Earl writes, "The anger and intention that have led up to the act are more serious than the act, for without the bad temper the act would never have been committed." [21](Earl, 1954,84) The origin of murder is unrighteous anger and so Jesus' only concern here is what is in the heart, for what comes out of the heart (anger) is the only heart condition that can lead to murder.

I also want to look at Jesus' other concern: how the condition of the heart affects our worship. See if you can relate to this scenario: You walk into church on a Sunday morning to worship and you are all ready to worship. You have had your morning prayer time asking God to open your heart to what He has in store, you enjoy the fellowship of other believers in Sunday school and you finally make your way to the pew that bears your name (some of you will laugh, others, not so much). You sit down, open your Bible, ready to praise and worship, and then he walks in, or she walks in. You know who I am talking about—that person who has done you wrong—that person who gossiped about you, who cheated you, who took advantage of you, or that person who just keeps rubbing you the wrong way. Maybe, it is even that same person who ran you off the road this morning and for the record, it was not me. I have been here at my desk all morning. How does that affect your ability to worship? It does nothing to get you into that spiritual zone right?

Nineteenth-century British Theologian Adam Clarke stated, "God will not accept any act of religious worship from us, while any enmity subsists in our hearts towards any soul of man." [22](Clark, 1972, 70-71) Given the fact that Jesus was 100% human, I am pretty sure Jesus understands the emotional response expressed in that previous scenario and you might even sense Him sitting on your little shoulder saying, *you have a right to be angry, after all, I got righteously angry a time or two also.* But that is not how Jesus tells us to respond is it? He says, "Therefore, if you are offering your gift at the altar and there remember that your brother or sister has something against you, leave your gift there in front of the altar. First go and be reconciled to them; then come and offer your gift." (v.v. 23-24) He is telling us that when we come to church to worship and there remember that someone has something against us, we are to stop worshiping and go and make things right with that person. Jesus is telling us here in regards

[21] Earle. Ralph. 1955. *Exploring the New Testament.* Kansas City: Beacon Hill Press

[22] Clark, Adam. 1972. *The Holy Bible Containing the Old and New Testaments with Commentary and Critical Notes. Vol.5.* New York: Abington Press

to people who have wronged you, that you are to go and reconcile with them, YOU are to go and reconcile, not the person who has something against you, but YOU. Clarke makes this point in his commentary adding, "or while any [enmity] subsists in our neighbor's hearts towards us, which we have not used the proper means to remove." [23](Clark, 1972, 70-71) That has to be the biggest horse pill for anyone to have to swallow in the history of the world. You are the victim here! You have a right to be angry! Maybe so, but Jesus is asking us to give up our right to be right so that we may be reconciled. Jesus is drawing a two-edged sword here because, He is not only telling us the importance of being reconciled with that person who wronged us, but more importantly, that as long as that human relationship is broken (which we can possibly rectify), our relationship with God is broken as well and we must be reconciled to Him.

I have a dear friend and co-worker in the ministry named Marcus. Whenever I tell Marcus I love him, he always replies, *you have to if you want to go to heaven.* I am not near as spiritual as Marcus, because I always just say, *I have to love them because shooting them is frowned upon in our society.* Jesus says to *stop your worship, go reconcile, then come back and worship.* Why? Because only then is your worship meaningful and accepted. Otherwise your worship of God is tainted, fractured, divided. When you step into church on Sunday morning and you have a bitterness welling up toward another, it hinders your worship. Your broken human relationship is affecting your relationship with God and ultimately, what *Jesus wants for us is a fruitful relationship with God.*

So, this commandment that Jesus gives us to leave our worship and go make things right is not for the benefit of the other person (although it certainly does benefit them), it is for our benefit in our standing with God. It is so our praise and our worship will be fruitful, fulfilling, and most of all accepted.

How does this lesson apply to the kingdom of heaven then? We can answer that by answering this question: how effective would we be in leading to the kingdom of God, those to whom we harbor bitterness, unforgiveness, or ill feelings?

In regards to retaliation, we often hear a passage by Paul misquoted

[23] Clark, Adam. 1972. *The Holy Bible Containing the Old and New Testaments with Commentary and Critical Notes. Vol.5.* New York: Abington Press

when he says in Rom. 12:20, "If your enemy is hungry, feed him; if he is thirsty, give him something to drink. In doing this, you will heap burning coals on his head." Many believe that he is referring to making the person burn with guilt for the way they treated them and makes them have a really bad day. But that is not at all what Paul is saying. As hard as you may try, you will never guilt anyone into the kingdom by trying to make them feel bad for something they did to you. Guilt is not a gift or a tool from God; guilt comes from our mutual enemy the devil. I mentioned in a previous chapter about forcing your child to apologize to their sibling, all the while they still have a handful of their hair in their hand. That is a heart issue and if the heart is not right, all the superficial apologies and alligator tears one can muster will not change anything in the heart.

In that Romans passage, Paul is referring to a common custom of the day. In Chapter Four, I mentioned that households never let their lights go out because of the difficulty in relighting them without matches or lighters. Sometimes, the man of the house forgot to stoke the fire before going to sleep and so everyone woke up at two in the morning on a cold winter's night with icicles hanging from their nose hairs. When that happened, the custom was for the man to go to his neighbor and ask him for a couple of hot coals to relight his own fire and they would carry the coals in a basket… on their heads. Paul is actually saying that, not only should you give a few coals to your enemy, you should put a heaping amount of coals in their basket, so when that nasty neighbor walks home with more than he could possibly have imagined after treating you so badly, he is forced to consider that maybe there is something different about you!

That is what Jesus wants us to do here. He wants us to do something so incredibly outside the box, that the person who wronged us, will walk away having to deal with the fact that something is very distinctive about us, not weird, but distinctive (kingdom of heaven vs. kingdom of self); and what makes us distinctive is that we are kingdom people. We belong to the King!

Not only will this "kingdom-thinking" keep our relationship with God intact, and not only will the human relationship hopefully be restored, but in looking at the kingdom purpose, we might just help win that person over for the kingdom of Christ.

The story of Jonah is a great Old Testament illustration of what we are talking about here, albeit, not one for the kingdom of heaven. When God told Jonah to go and witness to his enemy the Ninevites, he ran the other way in defiance. Jonah would rather disobey God than to reach out to his enemy and love them into the kingdom. In other words, he would rather go to hell alone than to share heaven with his enemy. And isn't that exactly what we are saying when we say something like, *I could never do that? I could never come down from my pinnacle of pride and offer the olive branch of peace to those who have wronged me.* We are in affect saying that *we would rather go to hell alone than to share heaven with our enemy!*

In his book Wishful Thinking, Frederick Buechner writes:

> Of the seven deadly sins, anger is possibly the most fun. To lick your wounds, to smack your lips over grievances long past, to roll over your tongue the prospect of bitter confrontations still to come, to savor to the last toothsome morsel both the pain you are given and the pain you are giving back—in many ways it is a feast fit for a king. The chief drawback is that what you are wolfing down is yourself. The skeleton at the feast is you. [24](Larson, 2007, 16)

So, who here reading this today is feasting on anger, or more correctly put, who here today has anger feasting on you? Who here has some bridge-building to do? Who here has been wronged by someone else who has just gotten under your skin? Maybe you have even been wronged more than once by the same person. Let me ask you this question, how much sleep have you lost over that? How many nights have you laid awake wondering how they could have done something like that? Ok, so now what are you going to do about it? I guess it comes down to this—would you rather go to hell alone or share heaven with your enemy?

---

[24] Larson, Craig Brian Editor. 2007. 750 Engaging Illustrations for Preachers, Teachers, and Writers. Ada: Baker Books

SEVEN

The Lure of Lust

You have heard that it was said, 'You shall not commit adultery.' But I tell you that anyone who looks at a woman lustfully has already committed adultery with her in his heart. If your right eye causes you to stumble, gouge it out and throw it away. It is better for you to lose one part of your body than for your whole body to be thrown into hell. And if your right hand causes you to stumble, cut it off and throw it away. It is better for you to lose one part of your body than for your whole body to go into hell. (Matt. 5:27-30)

Back in my hometown of Bradenton, on a particularly busy street corner, there is a panhandler who always occupies the same bench at the same time and he always bears the same sign which reads, *Why lie, I just wanna beer.* I applaud him for his honesty. The topic of this chapter, The Lure of Lust, is a very sensitive subject, one which I could skirt around over and over again, maybe even teach the lesson in allegories so as to not offend anyone or make anyone uncomfortable, but like my panhandler friend says, *why lie? I just wanna talk about lust.* There, that felt good to get that off my chest. The sad part is I have a much harder time getting it out of my head, and an even harder time getting it out of my heart!

I am reminded of a marriage study by Tommy Nelson, Senior Pastor at Denton Bible Church in Denton Texas. My wife and I once worked through the study which was on *The Song of Solomon* and Pastor Tommy explained that not many pastors and preachers like to speak on this book because it is all about SEX! He jokingly portrays an elderly pastor who stands up in the pulpit with little sweat beads forming on his forehead trying to explain *The Song of Solomon* as an allegory of God's love, rather than the physical love and desire that a man and woman have for each other. [25](Nelson, 2009) I am not going to try and explain this away in allegories because the desire for sex is a very strong emotion in the human heart and that is not a bad thing; that is the way God designed us. The problem lies with when we forget that He designed us to enjoy sex only within the confines of marriage—period! It is high time that the Church stop skirting around this issue and talk about it, Amen? Oswald Chambers said, "As long as I remain under the refuge of innocence, I am living in a fool's paradise." [26](Chamber, 1915, 17)

You should know that I struggle with lust and now before you close your book and toss it into the garbage, please hear me out. I struggle with lust in that I am very well aware that it seeks to have me. A couple of years ago, Nan and I challenged ourselves with cutting out TV and the internet for a solid week. Do you understand what a sacrifice that is in the fall? That's right, no football Saturday, No football Sunday, no football Monday or Thursday…None, notta, zilch! Now for the record, the challenge had nothing to do with football, or even the subject of which I am writing about now. It had to do with understanding how much time we were spending in front of TV or *Facebook* allowing someone else to entertain us with what they thought we needed to know. But here is an unexpected revelation that came to me: after we turned the TV back on, my spiritual eyes were propped wide open to all of the sex that is being sold on TV every hour on the hour whether you are watching football, *Fox News*, or the *Hallmark Channel*. Society (a.k.a. the kingdom of self) is saturated with the subject of sex; why? Because it sells!

Here is where my confession comes into play. As I sit there looking for only wholesome things to watch on the guide channel on the TV, I pass over these shows and movies that are there just to titillate me and if Nan is in the room, I might even sigh in disgust that we have to put up with such garbage. But in my heart, when given access through my flesh, the devil is saying, *click on it, click on it, you know you want to click on it.* If you

---

[25] Nelson, Tommy. 2009. *Love Song—A Study in the Song of Solomon*. Denton: Denton Bible Church Media

[26] Chambers, Oswald. 1915. *Studies in the Sermon on the Mount.* Cincinnati: God's Revivalist Press

still wish to stop reading and toss your book out, I will understand, but I confess to you that I struggle with lust.

For those who are still reading, I wonder if I were to ask if you have ever struggled with this sin, how many confessions I would receive. This is a sin that not too many of us like to confess and yet it is a sin that is as natural to us as lying and one which few of us have not had to deal with. Let us be honest, whether male or female, most of us have struggled with and may still struggle with the sin of lust. I am asking that you be honest with yourself and with God, because He knows whether you acknowledge it or not.

What is lust anyway? In the Greek, it simply means to have an impulsive passionate desire for something. Esau and his *lust* for Jacob's stew is a great example, whereby he willingly forfeited his birthright just so he could have some stew—right now! In this chapter, I am only writing about lust in the context of Jesus' sermon, but if you think for one moment that this same allure is not applicable to shopping, eating, or any other crutch, you are mistaken. To lust in the context of this passage means to have a longing for sexual satisfaction outside of marriage. It has been described as a frightening craving, or an out of touch desire for something or someone that is not yours. It is a desire to possess, own, or consume without caring about the needs or feelings of any other being or more importantly, caring about the will of God. Some Jewish scholars call it the chief of all sins.

The same Greek root word for lust (*epithumeo*) is found in a fishing tackle box. Any guesses on what that is? Lure! Do you know why fishermen have so many lures in their tackle boxes and even more on their hats? Because each fish has its own weakness and is *drawn away* (remember *lure* is a verb as much as a noun) by whatever disguised danger that is placed before them. The other word of note that Jesus uses here is the word *stumble* (v. 29). The Greek word *skandalizo* (from which the English word *scandal is taken)* describes a trap. Most often, it is a trap which uses a stick which when the animal touches it, the trap shuts around it. What a great word illustration that describes the danger of lust. When the fish is lured away and touches the *skandalon, it does not get the lure, the lure gets it* and when the lure gets it, it never turns out good for the fish.

Lust has the exact same effect on us, male or female, where we are drawn away from the path that God has set before us, enticed by a lure that is over-powering, in spite of the fact that we know by witnessing marriage and family break-ups all around us, it can only lead to destruction.

Lust seeks to fulfil its desires without any consideration for love. As Christians, we are called to love one another. The world insists that lust and love are similar, but in truth, they are entirely different. Lust, in the absence of love, moves directly to physical passion. The Greek word for physical love is *eros,* from which the English word *erotic* is derived. *Eros* eliminates the need for relationship and turns the other person into an object or thing. The other person becomes a body to conquer. Lust is temporary and never has any lasting satisfaction whereby love never ends and never fails (1 Corinthians 13). Lust has no lasting quality. As one minister once put it, *Love is a marathon runner, whereby lust runs the 10-yard dash.*

I heard a very interesting perspective about David once and it was this: We know how when he saw Bathsheba bathing, he thought she was a beautiful woman and was filled with lust in his heart for her. But if we look closer at David's life before his fall, we can see this lust possibly forming in his heart in at least two instances. The first takes place during the time before David became king. Saul was chasing David and wanted to kill him because he was jealous of David. He asked Nabal to give some food and provisions for his men. When Nabal refused, David told his men to prepare to attack Nabal and his servants. Nabal had a wife and we are told that she was a beautiful woman. When she heard that David was about to attack, she quickly gathered some provisions and rode out to meet David without telling her husband. David accepted her gift and was convinced not to attack Nabal. When Nabal was told about this by Abigail, his heart failed him and he died. After David heard this, David sent word to Abigail to become his wife. We read that when she got the invitation, she quickly got on her donkey and became David's wife, never even grieving her husband's death. It seems that beautiful women already had an effect on David's heart and in turn, his actions. Was it her beauty that stopped him from attacking? Was he already lusting for her and waiting for the first opportunity to make her his wife?

Later we read about David dancing when the ark was brought to Jerusalem. Scripture says that David danced wearing practically nothing, right there in sight of the slave girls of his servants. Now it is possible that

I am reading into these stories more than is there, but there seems to be some evidence that David enjoyed seeing beautiful woman and enjoyed attracting them.

I am reminded of a very funny audio clip that floated around social media a few years back in which a woman called into a radio show complaining about the placement of deer crossing signs. She insisted that the local road works officials placed these signs in the most inconvenient and unsafe places such as hills, bends and busy roadways. She was concerned about all of the accidents that occur where these *crossings* exist and insisted that the signs should be placed in less-traveled places. The radio DJ's had a hard time maintaining their composure struggling to believe that the woman was serious. I am convinced that she was! But on a serious note, I have a dear friend and brother in the Lord named Jeff who manages a local auto body shop and he explains that their busiest time of year for *deer strikes* is in the fall, and it is not because the deer are being chased by guns either. It is because the bucks are in rut. Fall is their mating season and the bucks are so driven by their desire to mate that they do not give any thought to chasing a pretty doe across the road without checking to make sure the way is clear, or at least, finding a place where there is a deer-crossing sign posted!

That is the effect that lust has on the human heart. If given any access into lives, it causes people to forego all faculties of thought and cross dangerous roads that should never be crossed, and the more we cross them, the more we want to feed those thoughts. In Chuck Swindoll's Ultimate Book of Illustrations and Quotes, he shares a gruesome story by Radio commentator Paul Harvey that accurately depicts the insatiable appetite of lust. Harvey explains the process Eskimos use for killing wolves. They begin by dipping a very sharp knife in blood and then allowing the blood to freeze on the blade. He repeats this process many times until finally the blade is completely encased in the frozen blood. Then he places the blade into the ground so that the deadly *bloodcycle* is sticking up. When the wolf catches the scent of the blood, it begins licking away and the more it tastes the blood, the more it desires it. Finally, once the blade is exposed, the wolf is so lusting for more that it does not even realize that the blood it is now longing for is its own and the Eskimo finds it dead by the exposed knife having bled itself out.[27](Swindoll, 1998, 124) That is a very graphic yet accurate description of lust. Lust begins with the desire to flirt with or to focus on members of the opposite sex with the wrong thoughts. Then, if left unchecked, this *innocent* flirtation gives birth to a desire for more and more until it finally gives birth to a full-blown physical affair. The Apostle James said, "…but each person is tempted when they are dragged away by their own evil desire and enticed. Then, after desire has conceived, it gives birth to sin; and sin, when it is full-grown, gives birth to death (James 1:14-15). Jesus said, "But I tell you that anyone who looks at a woman lustfully has already committed adultery with her in his heart."(Matt. 5:28) Lustful desires are natural to the sinful man, but they prevent us from honoring God and from being satisfied with the spouse that God has given us. Wrongful desires thereby distance us from God and from our spouses. And that is why Jesus takes such a strong stance against lust.

If lust then is a natural by-product of our flesh, how can we overcome it? The opening words to Jesus' commandment are the same words that opened the previous commandment regarding murder, "You have heard that it was said…" once again eluding to their understanding of Moses' law. He goes on to say, "You shall not commit adultery. But I tell you…" Remember that Jesus declared that He was the fulfillment of the Law. You see that fulfillment here in these four little words, *But I tell you…* Jesus is rightly placing Himself above Moses and equal to the One who gave the Law, since He is One in the same. So, what advice does Jesus the Lawgiver have for us in combatting lust?

> If your right eye causes you to stumble, gouge it out and throw it away. It is better for you to lose one part of your body than for your whole body to be thrown into hell. And if your right hand causes you to stumble, cut it off and throw it away. It is better for you to lose one part of your body than for your whole body to go into hell. (Matt. 5:29-30)

---

[27] Swindoll. Charles. 1998. *The Tale of the Tidy Oxcart: Swindoll's Ultimate Book of Illustrations and Quotes: Temptation*. Nashville: Thomas Nelson Publishers

Wow! Should we take these words literally? I am thinking that if we did, we would have an awful lot of Christians who could dress up as Captain Hook every Halloween complete with eye patch and hook hand. Jesus is not telling us to mutilate ourselves for one simple reason—*a blind paraplegic can lust in his heart just as easily* as you or I can. What Jesus is telling us to do is change our ways. If you struggle with lust of any kind, it does not have to be sexual, change your habits. Change the way you do things. Change the books you read, the TV shows you watch, the websites you visit and the places you go. Whatever it is that leads you to lust, *cut it out* of your life. I have a friend whom I was counseling who struggled with an *addiction* to pornography. I asked my friend to explain to me how and when this urge got triggered in his thoughts. He said that every time he went home at night, the video store would practically take control of his steering wheel and draw him into its parking lot. He explained that the video store was only a few blocks from his house and he drove past it every time he was going home from work. I simply told him that he needed to find a different way to go home. Now, it may be easy for us to judge someone like that, or someone who goes to those kinds of clubs, but Jesus is making it clear in this passage that anyone who even thinks about it, has an issue and left unchecked, will only get worse, much worse!

I am reminded of a story I once read in which a pastor opened the altar at the conclusion of his message on lust. A man in his mid to late forties came forward and knelt at the altar asking God to remove the cobwebs of lust from his mind that were gathering there. In a very pastoral manner, the pastor knelt and prayed with the man and he hugged the pastor and thanked him. A few weeks later, the same man returned to the altar and asked God to once again clear his mind of the cobwebs. Again, the pastor prayed with him and he left. Only a few weeks after that, the Holy Spirit convicted the man yet again over this same issue but this time, the pastor placed his hand ever so gently and compassionately on the man's shoulder and yelled, *Lord, help this man kill the spider!*

Maybe you have struggled with this issue. I am pretty sure that as I stated at the beginning, if we are to be absolutely honest with ourselves, most of us have. I can tell you that for most people, there will be a hesitancy to take steps to ask God and others to help them with this issue. Do not continue to ask God to remove the cobwebs from your head; ask Him to help you kill the spider in your heart! *The cobwebs in your head are just products of the spider in your heart.* Many of us struggle every day trying to battle our way through the cobwebs that have been formed in our minds, even to the point where we cannot focus on anything else. It is not enough to just sweep out the cobwebs, we have to go after that spider that is leaving them there! If you are dealing with this issue of lust, I want you to know something: God's love for you is much bigger than your spider. Christian singer Steven Curtis Chapman said, "In the Gospel we discover we are far worse off than we thought and far more loved than we ever dreamed." [28](Chapman and Smith, 1999, 72) When Jesus talks to us about lust, He helps us to discover that we are worse off than we thought, that we really are poor in spirit, and that we even mourn over the sin in our heart. But let us never forget the rest of Jesus' message; we are more loved than we ever dreamed.

---

[28] Chapman, Steven Curtis & Smith, Scotty. 1999 *Speechless: Living in Awe of God's Disruptive Grace.* Grand Rapids: Zondervan

EIGHT

D-i-v-o-r-c-e

It has been said, 'Anyone who divorces his wife must give her a certificate of divorce.' But I tell you that anyone who divorces his wife, except for sexual immorality, makes her the victim of adultery, and anyone who marries a divorced woman commits adultery. (Matt. 5:31-32)

A troubled man contacted his lawyer seeking a divorce from his wife. The lawyer asked, *Do you have any grounds?* The man replied, *About three acres.* The lawyer tried again, *No, I mean do you have a grudge?* The man said, *No, but we have a carport.* The lawyer made one last effort: *Are you really sure you want a divorce?* The client replied, *No, I don't but my wife does. She says we can't communicate!* [29](Fehl, 1987, 37)

Jesus never shied away from speaking out on many sensitive subjects, even the one Tammy Wynette refers to as, *D-I-V-O-R-C-E.* You have heard many people say that divorce is as much a problem in the church as it is outside the church. George Barna of the Barna Research Institute states that, "Born again Christians are just as likely to get divorced as are non-born again adults. Overall, 33% of all born again individuals who have been married have gone through a divorce, which is statistically identical to the 34% incidence among non-born again adults." [30](Barna, 2001)

It seems that divorce was important enough to Jesus that He was sure

[29] Fehl, Jim Editor. 1987. *Standard Lesson Commentary.* Standard Publishing

[30] Barna, George. 2001. *Born Again Adults Less Likely to Co-Habit, Just as Likely to Divorce.* https://www.barna.com/research/born-again-adults-less-likely-to-co-habit-just-as-likely-to-divorce/. Aug 6, 2001

to include it as one of only seven specific issues that man had deviated from God's original intent of the Scriptures. And since it is important enough for Him to do that, I believe it is important enough for His Church to understand what God has to say on the subject.

Let us begin by understanding God's original intent for marriage and then focus on how we can help people who themselves may be in the midst of divorce, or have already been through it. God instituted marriage in the garden between our first mom and dad. He said in Genesis 2:20b-24,

> But for Adam no suitable helper was found. So, the LORD God caused the man to fall into a deep sleep; and while he was sleeping, he took one of the man's ribs and then closed up the place with flesh. Then the LORD God made a woman from the rib he had taken out of the man, and he brought her to the man. The man said, "This is now bone of my bones and flesh of my flesh; she shall be called 'woman,' for she was taken out of man." That is why a man leaves his father and mother and is united to his wife, and they become one flesh.

In v. 24, we see God's design for marriage where man and woman expected to leave the bond-relationship with parents, cleave to a new bond-relationship with that spouse and in the course of that cleaving, become one inseparable flesh with that spouse. It was God's intent that we become each other's helper and completer and through that process, enrich one another's lives.

Before the service started, the townspeople were sitting in their pews and talking with one another when suddenly the devil himself appeared at the front of the congregation. Everyone started screaming and running for the back door, trampling each other in an effort to get away from evil incarnate. Soon everyone had evacuated except for one elderly gentleman who sat calmly in his pew, seemingly oblivious to the enemy in front of him. The devil walked up to the man and said, *Don't you know who I am?* The man quietly replied, *Yep, sure do.* Satan asked, *Aren't you afraid of me? Nope, sure ain't,* said the man. A perturbed Satan, asked, *Why aren't you afraid of me?* The man calmly replied, *Been joined at the hip to your sister for over 46 years.*[31](Knox, 2003, 200)

I know, that is a bad joke and I will probably pay for that one when Nan reads this, but you must admit, it was funny! Besides, it provides a great light-hearted segue into introducing an element of thought into this discussion that frankly, I am very uncomfortable even mentioning, but it at least deserves to be explored. I am speaking about the blessing of suffering for Christ's sake within the marriage.

Martin Luther wrote in his Sermon on the Mount commentary:

> For trouble here is owing solely to the fact that men [and women] do not regard marriage according to God's word as His work and ordinance, do not pay regard to His will, that He has given to everyone his spouse, to keep her, and to endure for His sake the discomforts that married life brings with it; they regard it as nothing else than a mere human, secular affair, with which God has nothing to do.[32](Luther, 1892, 169)

The point that Luther was making here was that divorce has become such an interwoven part of society, because society has completely taken God out of the marriage. When my daughters were little, I was a master at braiding hair. I could braid it with the best of them. When you look at a braid done properly, you see what looks to be only two sections of hair wrapped around each other and tied off at the end. But if you actually tried doing that, the braid would come apart from bottom to top because there is nothing that keeps it bound together—you need that third section that holds the other two tightly in place. And so it is with marriage. When we see marriage as purely a secular institution without any emphasis on God, there is nothing there which holds the marriage together.

Luther goes on to say:

---

[31] Knox, Carl. 2003. *Read This: It's Funny, A Laughable Email Collection.* Our Computer Guy Inc.

[32] Luther, Martin. 1892. *Commentary on the Sermon on the Mount.* Galesburg: Lutheran Publication Society

> Therefore, one soon becomes tired of it, and if it does not go as we wish, we soon begin to separate and change… and no one wants to carry his cross, but have everything perfectly convenient and without discomfort, that he gets an exchange in which he finds twice or ten times more discomfort, not alone in this matter but in all others. For it cannot be otherwise upon the earth; there must daily much inconvenience and discomfort occur in every house, city and country; and there is no condition upon earth in which one must not have much to endure that is painful, both from those who belong to him, as wife, child, servants, subjects, and externally from neighbors and all kinds of accidental mishaps. (Luther, 1892, 169-170)

What Luther is saying then is that, when suffering within the marriage occurs and with no attention paid to the fact that marriage is solely God's ordinance, we will always look for the easy way out, with little or no effort in reconciling the marriage.

Let me take this thought then back to the Scriptures by looking at 1 Peter.

1. In 1 Peter 1, Peter reminds us of our calling to be holy, which is also the emphasis of Jesus' Sermon on the Mount, (see Matthew 5:48) saying in v.v. 15-16, "But just as he who called you is holy, so be holy in all you do; for it is written: 'Be holy, because I am holy.'"
2. In the opening verses of Chapter 2, Peter provides for us the formula needed to become holy, by growing in our spiritual maturity. He says in v. 2, "Like newborn babies, crave pure spiritual milk, so that by it you may grow up in your salvation."
3. In the second half of Chapter 2, Peter commands us to live out that spiritual maturity in our lives so people can see that we are different. He says in v. 16, "Live as free people, but do not use your freedom as a cover-up for evil; live as God's slaves."
4. Then in the opening verses of Chapter 3, he commands both the wife and the husband to live out their faith in their marriages, submitting to one another, respecting one another, etc.

5. Finally, beginning in the second half of Chapter 3, Peter speaks about suffering. I am not at all suggesting that Peter insists that suffering follows marriage, so do not go there. But he concludes this progression of thought speaking about righteous suffering in Chapters 3 and 4 and in the interest of helping us to see this thought progression in the context of our topic, I have shortened the passage to emphasize the point:

    Finally, all of you, be like-minded, be sympathetic, love one another, be compassionate and humble. Do not repay evil with evil or insult with insult. On the contrary, repay evil with blessing, because to this you were called so that you may inherit a blessing… keeping a clear conscience, so that those who speak maliciously against your good behavior in Christ may be ashamed of their slander. For it is better, if it is God's will, to suffer for doing good than for doing evil. For Christ also suffered once for sins, the righteous for the unrighteous, to bring you to God… Therefore, since Christ suffered in his body, arm yourselves also with the same attitude, because whoever suffers in the body is done with sin. As a result, they do not live the rest of their earthly lives for evil human desires, but rather for the will of God… Above all, love each other deeply, because love covers over a multitude of sins. Offer hospitality to one another without grumbling. Each of you should use whatever gift you have received to serve others, as faithful stewards of God's grace in its various forms. If anyone speaks, they should do so as one who speaks the very words of God. If anyone serves, they should do so with the strength God provides, so that in all things God may be praised through Jesus Christ… Dear friends, do not be surprised at the fiery ordeal that has come on you to test you, as though something strange were happening to you. But rejoice inasmuch as you participate in the sufferings of Christ, so that you may be overjoyed when his glory is revealed. If you are insulted because of the

> name of Christ, you are blessed, for the Spirit of glory and of God rests on you. If you suffer, it should not be as a murderer or thief or any other kind of criminal, or even as a meddler. However, if you suffer as a Christian, do not be ashamed, but praise God that you bear that name… So then, those who suffer according to God's will should commit themselves to their faithful Creator and continue to do good (1 Pet. 3:8-9; 16-18; 4:1-2; 8-16,19)

The key verse here in Peter's discourse is found in Chapter 4 v. 13, "But rejoice inasmuch as you participate in the sufferings of Christ." When two people fall in love and get married, everything is daisies and daffodils. Life is grand and there is not a problem in the world. No one seems to even notice all of the not-so-nice things that each brings into the relationship. But when the *discomforts* come (as Luther calls them), couples become disenchanted about their fairy-tale marriage and begin to see life as it truly is, with the highs as well as the lows (*for better or worse?).* Quite possibly, a couple may experience many more lows in marriage than highs. It is even possible that their marriage is completely absent of any highs whatsoever. But when one looks at the marriage from God's perspective and solely as God's ordinance, one quickly realizes that it is God's will that you hang in there and *suffer for Christ's sake.* I realize that this is another one of those horse pills we are told to swallow, but if we agree that God is sovereign, that He knows all and ordains all, and if we agree that our marriage is designed by God and for His glory, then certainly we must agree that it is God's will that we stay in our marriage and work at it with all diligence for the glory of God (Colossians 3:23, 1 Corinthians 10:31). Don't misunderstand me, I realize that some of you are probably thinking to yourself, *Well, it takes two to tango Randy and he/she just isn't pulling his/her weight.* I understand and my heart hurts for those who are caught up in a loveless and faithless marriage. But each partner must do his/her part as though doing it for the glory of God and let Him take care of the rest.

Let me move on to one place in the gospels where Jesus speaks out most loudly against divorce and more specifically, the Pharisees perversion of God's Law. In Matthew 19, the Pharisees approach Jesus with what they believe to be a contradiction between His teaching and God's Word (Deuteronomy 24:1) saying,

> "Why then," they asked, "did Moses command that a man give his wife a certificate of divorce and send her away?" Jesus replied, "Moses permitted you to divorce your wives because your hearts were hard. But it was not this way from the beginning. I tell you that anyone who divorces his wife, except for sexual immorality, and marries another woman commits adultery." (v.v. 7-9)

In the Deuteronomy passage, Moses neither encouraged nor commanded divorce. Women were being sent away from their husbands in increasing numbers for any and every reason and since they were sent away while still being married, they were being stoned to death for adultery when they were received by another man. God provided a way to protect the women from this unjust punishment, but as Jesus said, *it was not this way from the beginning.* God hates divorce and He makes no bones about it. He only allowed it as a means of protecting women from the hypocrisy of those who demanded that the law be upheld, even though they were the very same ones who were sending their wives away for *irreconcilable differences.*

In Matthew 19, Jesus attests to the fact that Moses permitted divorce because of man's hard heart, but then v. 8, states that that was not God's intent. Now, this short clause back in Matthew 5:32 has become known as the divorce clause or exception clause, that *anyone who divorces his wife, except for sexual immorality.* Let me touch on this for just a moment before moving on, because I think this too, is either often misunderstood, or probably more accurately, seen more as an *escape clause* than the manner in which Jesus said it. I have counseled with many people who have been on the victim side of this clause and they are very quick to quote this passage as their justification to leave the marriage. Jesus makes it clear here that they are in fact justified in divorce because the defilement of the marriage bed is just too great of an obstacle to overcome for many. What Jesus does not say is that divorce is His desire for them. This *divorce clause* does not negate His view on divorce (see Mal. 2:16).

But allow me to get pastoral for a moment. I do not think it is just a happenstance that Jesus speaks about divorce right after He speaks on lust and adultery in His sermon, because infidelity is devastating to marriage. Paul says in 1 Corinthians 6:16, "Do you not know that he who unites himself with a prostitute is one with her in body? For it is said, 'The two will become one flesh.'" He follows that with "All other sins a person commits are outside the body, but whoever sins sexually, sins against their own body." (v. 18). When God says in Genesis 2:24 that they *become one flesh,* He is speaking about their sexual relationship, and when one is unfaithful to the spouse, they are literally ripping away from their spouse's flesh to become one flesh with the other person. Having said that, I have witnessed many couples who have overcome the devastating issue of infidelity and have gone on to have lasting and rewarding marriages through a spirit of repentance and forgiveness.

Maybe you are in that situation today. Maybe you have been devastated by infidelity in your marriage and are contemplating your next move. Might I suggest that you and your spouse seek the counsel of a spiritually mature person, a pastor, or trusted friend. One of the sad realities of my position as pastor is that people most often do not come and talk to me until the marriage has already crossed the line of no return. Do not wait until there is absolutely no hope, get help right away and do not be deceived into thinking that you do not need help and that you can make it work alone. That is a lie of the devil who wants anything but reconciliation for your marriage.

And while I am speaking about seeking counsel, I read something somewhere that it is estimated that one in ten of the people who go for help already have a third person involved in their lives, making it difficult at best to fix the marriage. Any obstacle can be overcome, even infidelity, but it cannot be overcome if both people are not totally committed to reconciliation. One of the first ground rules that I establish with couples who come to see me is that they must be 100% committed to making the marriage work. If one member of that covenant is not committed, I excuse them and insist that to talk with me will only be a waste of their time—and mine.

I heard a story once about a man who bought the city garbage dump. He covered it with dirt and began to build houses on the land. It only took a short while for the land to start settling and the houses begin to crumble. The people who purchased the houses found out very quickly that there is no foundation over a garbage dump. God has a plan and purpose for the Church and that plan requires strong families. Marriage is the foundation of the family and the devil will do whatever is needed to make that foundation to crumble. But our nation largely has rejected God's plan turning instead to the garbage lies of the devil, and today we see the destruction of trying to build upon that garbage. Today, families that have no foundation crumble.

Finally, I want to speak to those who are reading this who have experienced the devastation and aftermath that comes from divorce. If the national statistics stand true, quite possibly half of the adults in church have experienced divorce in their lives. If you are divorced, whether it was your choice, or that it was forced upon you, you have probably experienced the stigma of being a divorcee in the church and all the biases and dejections that go along with that. You need to know that there is life after divorce, there is forgiveness after wrong-doing and there is hope and healing after despair and brokenness. Jesus came to earth just for you, the dejected, the ostracized, the singled-out. Reconciliation may not have been possible in your marriage, but there is always reconciliation at the cross.

Let me close with a statistic that I found fascinating following the attacks on 9-11. We all witnessed over and over the tragic details of these events and the aftermath as it was broadcast repeatedly, images that are likely seared into our minds for the rest of our lives. But immediately following those tragic events, many married couples withdrew their applications for divorce on file before September 11, 2001. In Houston, Texas, for example, "Dismissals in divorce cases have skyrocketed in the Harris County Family Law courts since the terrorist attacks of September 11th." Then, after the attacks and before our military troops deployed to Afghanistan and Iraq in response, many military personnel quickly made their way to the marriage altar. Why the sudden spike in divorce proceeding dismissals? Why the sudden spike in marriage licenses being issued? Why is it that in times of crisis, we place higher value on marriage and family relationships than when we are not in crisis? Michael Von Blon, a family law attorney in Texas, stated that "in times of tragedy, people stop and think about the most basic things in life: companionship, love and family." [33](Flood, 2001)

That begs a deep-thinking question for us to ponder. Why do we need a national tragedy to remind us of the importance of marriage? Apparently, those events help us realize the value of ancient divine wisdom given us thousands of years ago.

[33] Flood, Mary. 2001. *Couples Want Peace at Home.* Houston: Houston Chronicle. Sep 26, 2001

NINE

I Swear

Again, you have heard that it was said to the people long ago, 'Do not break your oath, but fulfill to the Lord the vows you have made.' [34] *But I tell you, do not swear an oath at all: either by heaven, for it is God's throne;* [35] *or by the earth, for it is his footstool; or by Jerusalem, for it is the city of the Great King.*
[36] *And do not swear by your head, for you cannot make even one hair white or black.* [37] *All you need to say is simply 'Yes' or 'No'; anything beyond this comes from the evil one.* (Matt. 5:33-37)

I remember a story from a sermon that I heard years ago about a busload of politicians who were headed to a convention, but because of highway construction, they had to take a detour down a rural road. The driver was having problems with this windy, country lane and lost control of the bus. It ran off the road and crashed into a tree in an old farmer's field. The old farmer was driving to town when he noticed that there was a gaping hole in his fence. He went to investigate and saw what had happened. He went back to his truck, got a shovel and buried all the politicians. Since the politicians never arrived at their destination, a state trooper was dispatched to locate them. He back-tracked their route, followed the country road, saw the wrecked bus in the field and looked up the old farmer that owned the property. The trooper asked the farmer where the politicians had gone. The farmer informed the trooper that he had buried all of them. The trooper said, "They were all dead?" The old farmer replied, 'Well, some of them kept saying they weren't but you know how them politicians lie!'

Every two years in America, we are faced with an incredible lack of integrity on display. The trustworthiness of campaign promises is measured by none other than the number of *Pinocchio's* that it receives from fact-checker groups, and in truth many of them would be considered as nothing short of a national joke if it were not so sad.

In order to sufficiently understand Jesus' teaching on oaths, we need to understand a little about the background behind His commandment because after all, several Old Testament patriarchs took oaths. Abraham, Isaac, Jacob and Jonathon all took oaths. In fact, even Jesus swore an oath in His trial before the high priest and the Sanhedrin. Jesus, in His teaching about oaths, was not condemning oath-taking. Rather, He was speaking out against the natural tendency in our hearts to lie. I often remind people that the one thing we never have to teach our kids is how to lie. They pick that up very easily and quickly because it is their carnal nature to do so.

In ancient Israel, the Pharisees had developed an elaborate set of rules governing when a man was bound by his word and when he was not. For example, if he swore by Jerusalem, he was bound by his words, but if he swore towards Jerusalem, he was not bound. Any promise that he made using God's name bound him, but if he could avoid using God's name when he made a promise, then he was not held to his word—or so they thought! So, they began to swear by anything that sounded like it might mean something when in fact, it meant nothing at all. In fact, a whole Jewish book of the law-code dealt with making vows and promises: which ones they had to keep, and which ones they did not.

Jump ahead 20 centuries and we find that we have also come up with our own elaborate set of oath-making rules to convince others that we are telling the truth—that we have integrity: *Cross my heart and hope to die (stick a needle in my eye); Oops, sorry, I had my fingers crossed; I swear on a stack of Bibles; If I'm lying, I'm dying; May lightning strike me if I'm not telling the truth;* and a personal favorite, *As God is my witness.*[34](Smead, 2011)

We now explore a subject that touches every one of us. We look at what Jesus has to say about integrity. I was listening to Dr. Laura Schlessinger many years ago on the radio, and in one broadcast she described integrity in a way that has stuck with me ever since. She explained (and I paraphrase),

[34] Smead, Jeffrey. 2011. *Integrity—A Christian is Faithful 100%. Sermon Central.* Sermoncentral.com. *Feb 8, 2011.*

integrity is walking up to a newspaper machine to purchase a newspaper and finding the door already open, and with no one else around, putting a quarter into the slot, taking the newspaper, and closing the door.

In our passage, Jesus says, *Let your Yes be Yes, and your No, be No; anything beyond this comes from the evil one.* Jesus, in speaking about the devil, said, "He was a murderer from the beginning, not holding to the truth, for there is no truth in him. When he lies, he speaks his native language, for he is a liar and the father of lies" (John 8:44).

There is another popular story about a wealthy businessman who lay on his deathbed. His pastor came to visit and talked about God's healing power and prayed for his parishioner. When the pastor was done, the businessman said, 'Preacher, if God heals me, I'll give the church a million dollars.' Miraculously, the businessman got better and within a few short weeks was out of the hospital. Several months had passed when the pastor bumped into this businessman on the sidewalk and said, 'You know, when you were in the hospital dying, you promised to give the church a million dollars if you got well. We have not received it as of yet.' The businessman replied, 'Wow! I guess I was sicker than I thought!'

In our world of deception today, do you find yourself longing for the day when a handshake was a man's bond? I do not know if it because I am wiser from the many times I have been duped, or simply because I am becoming more cynical in my older age (boy, I feel ancient just for saying that!), but I have a tendency to follow President Reagan's advice in regards to nuclear disarmament with the old Soviet Union, *Trust but verify.* Larry Wolters, better known as *Lawn-chair Larry* rightly stated, "A commentary of the times is that the word 'honesty' is now preceded by 'old fashioned.'"[35](Ajith, 2012, 437)

When Jesus commands us to let our yes be yes and our no be no, He is telling us that our word is our bond and not something that can be broken without critical life-long consequences. Keep in mind, the purpose of this *You have heard it was said...* portion of Jesus' sermon was to re-establish God's original standard, not the standard by which man had made it become.

Where I lived in North Alabama, there are hundreds of Amish farms

---

[35] Fernando, Ajith. 2012. *Deuteronomy: Loving Obedience to a Loving God.* Wheaton: Crossway

about thirty-five miles to the north in Ethridge, Tennessee. Even after more than ten years of living there, I am still every bit as intrigued about the Amish as when we first arrived. Every time we passed a buggy pulled by a horse galloping along the highway, I took notice and pondered their lifestyle. It dawned on me some time ago, that besides an engine and air conditioning, there is one piece of equipment you will never find on a horse buggy, a speedometer! Now why is that? Maybe it is because they will never get up to a speed where they have to wonder if the blue lights behind are directed at them. And they will never have to wonder that, because unless they are feeding the horses from my friend Charles' cabbage garden (which I am pretty sure, is because he buries nuclear waste there!), they will never get close to the speed limit. Amish never have to pay any mind to the posted speed limits.

Believers are called to live by God's standard and not man's. And if we are living by God's standards, we never have to be concerned about breaking man's standards. If we are radically devoted to God's standard, we are automatically keeping the law, because it is such a high standard that all of the law is automatically included in it. When I am driving down the road, at any point I can usually tell what the speed limit is. Why? Because I want to get right up to it and since we are speaking about truthfulness today, I find that I am not even overly concerned with going a few miles over the limit, unless I am driving through some of the well-known speed traps around my neck of the woods. I know, you have never done that. Right?

Let me illustrate this point using two of my kids. If you have more than one child, chances are, you have that *pleaser* who likes to do things just to please you. For the most part, pleasers are obedient and they are so because they have a desire to please their parents. In our home, that was our oldest daughter Tiffani. We never had to worry about Tiffani crossing the line because that would have been contrary to her character. But chances are, you also have a *tester* in your home! Our middle daughter, Emily, was that rebellious one who always liked to put her foot right up to the line and when we weren't watching her, she would even slip that big toe across, just to keep us on ours.

That is how many of us approach the law. We study it and strive to see just where that line is and we try to edge right up to it as close as we can (and yes, some of us even stick our big toe over it!) to see how much we can get away with and still be spiritually safe. When we do that, our focus is at the wrong end! If we ever find ourselves having to focus on the law to live our lives by the law, then our focus is misplaced—we are focusing on keeping the obligation to the letter of the written law rather than the law that God has written on our hearts. But if our focus is to love God and love people, then our focus to love propels us far beyond the law. Those are not my words, those are Jesus' words when He said in the Great Commandment that when we do that, we sum up the whole law.

Let me give an example of what I am talking about: the tithe. The Old Testament law according to Lev. 27:30, was that people were to give ten percent of everything they raised or grew. The tithe was for the Israelites and was connected with the temple sacrificial offerings. But since the temple was torn down and replaced with Jesus, we are no longer under the temple law. After all, as Jesus already pointed out, He was the *fulfillment of the Law.* So then, since there is no New Testament command for believers to tithe, we are told instead to give as the Lord lays on our heart to give according to 2 Cor 9:7. But, if we ever find ourselves giving less than ten percent, we can be sure that our focus is still misplaced, because we are still focusing on the law instead of reflecting on our love for God in our giving.

Jesus said in Matt. 23:23, "Woe to you, teachers of the law and Pharisees, you hypocrites! You give a tenth of your spices—mint, dill and cumin. But you have neglected the more important matters of the law—justice, mercy and faithfulness. You should have practiced the latter, without neglecting the former". Jesus is clearly not telling us that the practice of tithing is no longer important, only that our love for justice, mercy and faithfulness surpasses the law. If the practice of tithing was still important to Jesus, why on God's green earth would He ever lay it upon on our hearts to give less? It is all a matter of misplaced focus. In speaking about integrity, many people like to argue that because we are no longer *under the law,* there is no longer a command to tithe, but see, that is evidence in itself of a misplaced focus. If we are truly focused on our purpose (to glorify God), then we will give joyfully and generously. But when we have to *look it up* to see what the demands of the law are, we need to ask ourselves, *Where's my focus?*

Man's standard was to make an oath so that people know you are telling the truth. Jesus' standard was to let your yes be yes and your no be no. Anything beyond that was nothing more than a futile attempt to prove that what you are saying is the truth.

Solomon had much to say about honesty and integrity. In Prov. 10:9, he said, "Whoever walks in integrity walks securely, but whoever takes crooked paths will be found out." The first thing in this passage that jumps out at me is that he uses the word *in* and not *with.* Integrity is not something that a person possesses; it is rather something that person is. It is something that is in your being, not something that you can turn on and off as it suits you. "A person of integrity does not have to remember everything he said, but a person who is untruthful must remember everything he said." [36](Zuck, 1997, 196) Someone said, "Speaking honestly is better. It takes a lot of stress out of our lives." How true that is. If you have ever been caught in a lie, you know how it tears you up inside until you finally come clean.

I am reminded of the story of little Tommy who was playing with his slingshot outside his grandmother's house and he was shooting at his grandmother's cat. He struck the cat and killed it. Out of fear of being found out, he hid the cat in the rose bushes, but unbeknownst to him, his sister Susie was watching him from her bedroom window. She confronted her brother and told him that to buy her silence, he would have to do everything she told him. So, when it came time to clear the table and do the dishes, the grandmother told her granddaughter that it was her turn to do the dishes to which she replied, "Tommy said he will do them tonight," and Tommy did. The next morning Susie came out of her room and her grandmother asked if she had made her bed and she replied, "Tommy said he was going to do it for me," and he did. Later that day, Tommy came into the kitchen and confessed to his grandmother what he had done, to which she replied, "I know, I saw you from the kitchen window. I was wondering how long you were going to allow your sister to torture you before you confessed."

Not being truthful eats away at the soul; it consumes us and enslaves us. Jesus said that, "you will know the truth and the truth will set you free" (John 8:32). Jesus gave us the standard: not man's standard, but His

---

[36] Zuck, Roy. 1997. *The Speakers' Quote Book.* Grand Rapids: Kregel Academic & Professional

standard by which we are to live. In the Garden called Eden, there were two very special trees, the Tree of Life and the Tree of Knowledge of Good and Evil. We were free to eat from The Tree of Life, but forbidden from the other. Have you ever wondered why Adam was expressly commanded not to eat from the Tree of Knowledge of Good and Evil? It was because it was never God's intent that we choose for ourselves what is right (good) and what is wrong (evil), because *at that point, we start choosing for ourselves what the standard is.* And we have been doing just that very thing ever since!

I preached an Independence Day message once in which I shared what I believed was wrong in America. It is not that we have crime, it is not that we have drugs, or that we have poverty, homosexuality, or even abortions. It is that we have decided long ago to choose for ourselves what is right and wrong, instead of following God's standard, and the problem with choosing for ourselves is, we will always come down on the side of what we think is best for us (and easiest), instead of allowing God to guide us to what He knows is best for us. "I have the plans for your life He says and all you have to do is trust me."

My wife and I sometimes teach a parenting class called "Growing Kids God's Way." One of the principles that we teach is, since it is from God's Word that we get our values, it is from God's Word that we ought to parent to instill those same values in our children. John Wesley said, "What one generation tolerates, the next generation will embrace."[37(Wesley, 2011)]

When people speak of you, do they know that your yes is yes and your no is no? There are many things that you can give up in your life and with some effort, get them back. Your word is not one of them. It takes a lot of hard work, confession, time and humility to regain the confidence of men. But that is not the case with God. When a person genuinely repents and confesses dishonesty to Jesus and vows to Him to live to a higher standard than man can possibly offer, Jesus turns and says, *what sin?* "All you need to say is simply 'Yes' or 'No'; anything beyond this comes from the evil one." (Matt. 5:7)

---

[37] Wesley, John. 2011. *What one generation tolerates, the next will embrace.* wesley animmersion.wordpress.com/2011/05/13/what-one-generation-tolerates-the-next-generation-will-embrace-john-wesley. May 13, 2011

TEN

Eye for an Eye

You have heard that it was said, 'Eye for eye, and tooth for tooth.' But I tell you, do not resist an evil person. If anyone slaps you on the right cheek, turn to them the other cheek also. And if anyone wants to sue you and take your shirt, hand over your coat as well. If anyone forces you to go one mile, go with them two miles. Give to the one who asks you, and do not turn away from the one who wants to borrow from you. (Matt. 5:38-42)

One summer evening in Broken Bow, Nebraska, a weary truck driver pulled his rig into an all-night truck stop. He was tired and hungry. The waitress had just served his dinner when three tough-looking, leather jacketed *Hell's Angel's* motorcyclists came into the diner. They decided to give the trucker a hard time and started verbally abusing him. Then, one of them grabbed the hamburger off his plate while another took a handful of his french fries. The third biker picked up the man's coffee and began drinking it. The tired truck driver calmly rose from his stool, picked up his check, walked to the register, put the check on the register along with a tip and quietly exited the diner. The waitress watched him through the door as he and his big rig disappeared into the night. When she returned to the counter, one of the belligerent bikers said to her, *Well, he's not much of a man, is he?* To which she replied, *well, I don't know about that, but he sure isn't much of a truck driver. He just ran over three motorcycles on his way out of the parking lot!* [38]

---

[38] Jeeva Sam. 2001. *Late One Summer Evening....* https://www.sermoncentral.com/sermon-illustrations/1864/late-one-summer-evening-in-broken-bow-nebraska-by-jeeva-sam

We are looking at the passage about retaliation in this chapter and while the trucker may not have responded the way Jesus would have had him to, no one can say that he did not drive his point home, three times (pun intended)!

We have heard this *eye for an eye* passage used in the death penalty argument over and over and rightly so. In Old Testament times, before the law was given, people often took justice into their own hands and doled out the punishment as they saw fit, often taking it to the extreme and crossing that line between justice and revenge. God gave this law, at least in part, to keep them from crossing that line, but as we have stated many times, the law that Christ has written on every believer's heart was meant to be a new approach to the written law. That is what He meant when He said, *I give you a new commandment.* As mentioned in the previous chapter, when our focus is on this law written on our hearts, we never need to be concerned with the written law.

And while advocates for the death penalty cling to the *eye for an eye* passage, opponents of the death penalty stand fast to the sixth commandment, *thou shall not kill* which was addressed in Chapter six. The issue that Jesus is dealing with in this passage is retaliation. Mahatma Gandhi said *an eye for an eye makes the whole world blind.* [39](Gandhi, 1869-1948)

The story is told of the farmer who had been pestered by a carload of people who delighted in climbing his orchard fence and eating his apples without asking permission. One day, as he walked up to them, one of them smiled sheepishly and said, *we hope you don't mind that we borrowed a few of your apples. No, not at all*, said the farmer, *and I hope you don't mind that I borrowed some of the air out of your tires.*

The lesson from Jesus is about taking matters into our own hands when we are wronged. It is a very sensitive issue because, while Jesus commands us to do one thing, no one can blame us for wanting to seek revenge for wrong-doing. But before we actually delve into this, let me explain something about the teaching method He uses here. Jesus is using hyperboles to make his point. Hyperboles are *overstatements,* or *embellishments*, usually used to stress the importance of something. An

[39] Gandhi, Mahatma. 1869-1948. *The Quotations Page.* http://www.quotationspage.com/quote/30302.html.

example of a popular hyperbole used today is, *if I've told you once, I've told you a thousand times—don't exaggerate!*

Jesus said in Luke 14:26, "If anyone comes to me and does not hate father and mother… …such a person cannot be my disciple." Now, Jesus was not actually telling people that they needed to break one of the ten commandments in order to be a Christian. Otherwise, He would have contradicted Himself since He wrote the ten commandments in the first place. He was simply using a *hyperbole* to teach the importance of placing Him first and foremost in our lives.

Likewise, here in Matthew 5:38-42, Jesus is not telling us that we must not defend ourselves, become enslaved by others, or even to give away all of our possessions. He is simply wanting us to see His law from His perspective, the Author's perspective. Let us look at each of these three teachings:

Turn the other cheek:

"You have heard that it was said, 'Eye for eye, and tooth for tooth.' But I tell you, do not resist an evil person. If anyone slaps you on the right cheek, turn to them the other cheek also." (v.v. 38-39).

The title of this segment is called *The Kingdom and the Law.* The purpose of this portion of Jesus' sermon was to draw a sharp contrast between the kingdom of heaven and the kingdom of self. Verse 38 represents the law and verse 39 represents the kingdom of self.

Back in the 1940's after the introduction of nuclear weapons, a doctrine of retaliation began to develop between the United States and the Soviet Union. It came to be known as *Mutual Assured Destruction* (appropriately, MAD for short). The basic principal of this doctrine was that by building up stockpiles of weapons sufficiently enough to literally annihilate the other country, it would act as a deterrent against a first strike. It would literally be *MAD* to do such a thing! I was stationed at Barksdale Air Force Base in Louisiana when the *Strategic Arms Reduction Treaty* (START) between the United States and Soviet Union was signed between President George H.W. Bush and Soviet President Mikhail Gorbachev. Prior to that time, we had several B-52 Bombers, loaded with nuclear weapons, on *Alert* at all times, a deterrent practice that has been in place since the beginning of the Cold War. I vividly remember the order coming down from our Commander in Chief to remove the weapons from those aircraft after the START Treaty was signed as an act of good faith toward our enemy. I remember because there was such a sense of uneasiness and vulnerability that came over me and my fellow airmen.

Jesus wants us to make ourselves vulnerable to our enemies. He wants us to make the first move and act out in good faith. I mentioned in Chapter Six how murder is merely the logical conclusion of what had first begun in our hearts. The shopping day after Thanksgiving Day, known as Black Friday, is a testimony to the kingdom of self. On November 25, 2016, a person was shot and killed over a department store parking space--a parking space! But that killing was a result of an escalation of offenses committed by both sides. Had either of those men exercised Jesus' teaching in that parking lot, both of them would have gone home to their wives and children at the end of the day.

Jesus is not advocating being defenseless against aggression, but He is insisting that as Christians, we act differently from the rest of the world. He wants us to act out of our Spirit-filled hearts and not our carnal-filled hearts. He is telling us not to avoid the evil person, but rather give of ourselves to them that we might win some for the kingdom. In 1 Corinthians 9:19-23, Paul says,

> Though I am free and belong to no one, I have made myself a slave to everyone, to win as many as possible. To the Jews I became like a Jew, to win the Jews. To those under the law I became like one under the law (though I myself am not under the law), so as to win those under the law. To those not having the law I became like one not having the law (though I am not free from God's law but am under Christ's law), so as to win those not having the law. To the weak I became weak, to win the weak. I have become all things to all people so that by all possible means I might save some. I do all this for the sake of the gospel, that I may share in its blessings.

Paul is saying that he is not slave to anyone but will do whatever it takes and be whatever he needs to be in order to reach the lost for the sake of the Gospel.

Richard Weaver, a Christian worker, made his living in the mines, but had the higher goal of trying to win souls for Christ. While most of the men were indifferent to his *workplace evangelism*, one actually became offended and finally said, *'I'm sick of your constant preaching. I've a good mind to smack you in the face!' 'Go ahead if it will make you feel better,'* replied Weaver. The man immediately struck him a stinging blow. Weaver did not retaliate but literally turned the other cheek and the unbeliever struck him a second time and walked away, cursing under his breath. Weaver called after him, *'I forgive you, and still pray that the Lord will save you!'* The next morning, the unbeliever was waiting for him when he came to work, and in a voice filled with emotion said, *'Dick, did you really mean it when you said you forgave me?' 'Certainly.'* Weaver extended his hand and told him again the message of salvation, God opened his heart and he received Christ.[40](Swindoll, 1991, 102)

Give the shirt off your back:

"And if anyone wants to sue you and take your shirt, hand over your coat as well… Give to the one who asks you, and do not turn away from the one who wants to borrow from you." (v.v. 40, 42) In Jesus' time, there were two particular articles of clothing worn by men, the tunic and the cloak. The tunic was the garment worn closest to the skin like a t-shirt, while the cloak was the outer coat that was also used at night as a blanket. If a poor person was to be sued, it was acceptable practice to sue him for the tunic since that was not considered necessary for survival, but not so with the coat. Since it also was used to keep warm at night, the man usually could not be forced to give it up. In the unlikely case that he was forced to give up his cloak, Mosaic law required that it be returned to him by nightfall (see Exodus 22:26).

Jesus is not telling us that we have to turn over everything we own, leaving ourselves without a means of caring for ourselves and our families. He is telling us that we are to do whatever we are physically able to help

[40] Swindoll, Charles. 1991. *Simple Faith.* Dallas: Word Publishing

anyone who is in need. Now, can you imagine how His audience was receiving these strange commandments that absolutely flew in the face of everything they had ever been taught. Pastor Swindoll said, in speaking about His teachings, they "cut cross-grain against our human nature." (Swindoll, 1991, 102)

Go the extra mile:

"If anyone forces you to go one mile, go with them two miles. Give to the one who asks you." (v.v. 41-42). Finally, Jesus teaches us that we are to go the extra mile and do what we are not forced to do. In Jesus' time, it was permissible for Roman soldiers to require villagers to carry their heavy packs for them when they were moving from one location to another, but only for one mile. After that, the law forced the soldier to free the person from servitude and find someone else to carry the pack the next mile. What Jesus is commanding His disciples to do here is, if they are forced into servitude for one mile, to go an extra mile beyond what they were forced to do.

In all three of these teachings not to retaliate, there are two common denominators. First, they all are voluntary, and second, they all go against human nature. Human nature when we are wronged is to fight back, our nature when made to give is to get it back, and our nature when made to serve is to take back control of our lives. Christian joy does not come from retaliation, receiving, or being served. Real Christian joy comes from resisting retaliation, from giving and from serving. In those relationships closest to us, how much sweeter are they when we voluntarily seek to go the extra mile, how much sweeter is it to give than to receive and how many relationships have been reconciled when each person's focus is on loving the other person? Hudson Taylor, a missionary to China understood the sweetness in following Christ's example:

> Hudson Taylor, dressed in a Chinese costume, while waiting for a boatman to take him across the river, stood on a jetty. Presently a richly dressed Chinaman came and also stood waiting. When the boat drew near this man not seeing that Mr. Taylor was a foreigner, struck him

> on the head and knocked him over into the mud. Mr. Taylor said the feeling came to him to smite the man, but God immediately stopped him. When the boat came up, the Chinaman looked at Mr. Taylor and recognized him as a foreigner. He could hardly believe it, and said, "What! You a foreigner, and did not strike me back when I struck you like that?" Mr. Taylor said: "This boat is mine. Come in and I will take you where you want to go." On the way out, Mr. Taylor poured into that Chinaman's' ears the message of salvation. He left the man with tears running down his face. Such is the power of the Gospel of Christ. [41](Author Unk, 2007)

Dr. Benjamin Mays delivered what is considered to be one of the greatest eulogies of all time, when he spoke at the funeral of Dr. Martin Luther King, Jr. Here's a portion of what he said:

> If any man knew the meaning of suffering, King knew. House bombed; living day by day for thirteen years under constant threats of death; maliciously accused of being a communist; falsely accused of being insincere; stabbed by a member of his own race; slugged in a hotel lobby; jailed over twenty times; occasionally deeply hurt because friends betrayed him—and yet this man had no bitterness in his heart, no rancor in his soul, no revenge in his mind; and he went up and down the length and breadth of this world preaching non-violence and the redemptive power of love. [42](Daley, 2016, 168)

What tremendous blessings can be found in the second mile. The first mile is filled with those who are Christian in name only, who grumble and complain about their self-serving lives and what they must give up

[41] Author Unknown. From the King's Business. 2007. https://www.biblestudytools.com/pastor-resources/illustrations/self-control-11548576.html

[42] Daley, James, Editor. 2016. *Great Eulogies Throughout History.* Minfola: Dover Publications Inc.

to behave as a Christian. But the second mile is never crowded and for those who willingly live to the standard that Christ has laid out for them, incredible testimonies of God's grace await them in the second mile.

Maybe you have been taken advantage of. In fact, I would argue that if you are truly living by Christ's standards, being taken advantage of is a common occurrence. I would like to suggest to you that God allows that to happen for one reason, that you might seize the opportunity to *go against the grain of your nature* as Pastor Swindoll says, and in the process, build His kingdom. Peter says that we ought to rejoice in our suffering for righteousness sake. Maybe, just maybe, you were meant to endure that wrong-doing so that His message of love would overcome evil and victory in Jesus and might be experienced in their lives.

ELEVEN

Be Distinctive, Not Instinctive

You have heard that it was said, 'Love your neighbor and hate your enemy.' But I tell you, love your enemies and pray for those who persecute you, that you may be children of your Father in heaven. He causes his sun to rise on the evil and the good, and sends rain on the righteous and the unrighteous. If you love those who love you, what reward will you get? Are not even the tax collectors doing that? And if you greet only your own people, what are you doing more than others? Do not even pagans do that? Be perfect, therefore, as your heavenly Father is perfect. (Matt. 5:43-48)

We have come to the final chapter in this segment called, *The Kingdom and the Law* in which Jesus draws a distinction between how the religious teachers interpreted the law (kingdom of self) and God's original meaning behind the law (kingdom of heaven). And although we have covered much ground between these two past segments, there is really only one lesson that Jesus has been drilling into our heads (or more importantly, our hearts) thus far, and that is that we are to be distinctive, not instinctive. In this chapter, we are looking at a passage where, in the final verse, Jesus sums up this whole comparison between the believer and the law. In Matthew 5:48, Jesus says "Be perfect, therefore, as your heavenly Father is perfect.

Some time ago, Nan and I had a meal with some dear friends at *Cracker Barrel* and while waiting for the ladies to make their way through the gift shop, Farrell and I sat down outside to play a game of checkers. He started first and boldly put his piece out there daring me to take it, but I refused. I refused, because it was only going to result in a tit-for-tat.

In fact, as I studied the board looking at my possible moves, I could only see a string of *take one-give one* moves. At that rate, the winner would just be determined by who is left standing after all the blood and mayhem. So instead, I chose a different route and refused to take his bait. He got a little frustrated with me and that is pretty much the last thing I remembered as he proceeded to teach me that in checkers, it does not pay to take the high road. And because I did not quite learn my lesson after the first game, he decided to teach that lesson to me twice!

But in all of that harmless fun, he gave me a great illustration to explain my lesson from this passage and my friend Farrell plays the bad guy. Where he was playing instinctively, I was attempting to play distinctively. I was trying a different path, while he was perfectly content letting his thirst for my blood guide his every move. When it comes to dealing with conflict, the world generally likes to play checkers, trading slug for slug until the last man is standing. But God wants us to play a different kind of game. He wants us to play distinctively. Bonhoeffer calls it *peculiar, extraordinary and unusual.* [43](Bonhoeffer, 2012, 152)

In a word, Jesus wants us to play chess. You see, chess uses the exact same board as that of checkers, but to win, it is a completely different strategy. Instead of trading slugs as in checkers, in chess, you measure your response to your opponent's response. Instead of going head to head, there is a constant maneuvering and measuring to fully understand your opponent's motives. There is much patience involved in playing chess because to move too soon could certainly result in your downfall. But the biggest distinction between the two games is in chess, each move is focused on the final objective which is to get to the king.

That is how God wants us to view conflict in our own lives. He wants us to take a distinctive approach with an end-goal in mind of winning the hearts of our enemies for our King. After all, that is really *the only way to rid one's life of its enemies—to make them friends!* President Abraham Lincoln was once asked about his attitude toward his enemies, "'Why do you try to make friends of them? You should try to destroy them.' 'Am I not destroying my enemies,' Lincoln replied gently, 'when I make them my friends'?" [44](Zuck, 1997,168)

---

[43] Bonhoeffer, Dietrich. 2012. *The Cost of Discipleship.* New York: Simon and Schuster

[44] Zuck, Roy B. 1997. *The Speaker's Quote Book.* Grand Rapids: Kregel Publications

Jesus begins the passage by stating the way of the world, like Farrell the checker player, *love your friends and hate your enemies*, but then He commands us to look at our enemies differently, He commands us to love them and pray for them. Of all of Jesus' teaching, this is by far the hardest of them to accept. After all, how does a person become an enemy? Usually by hurting you, cheating you, stealing from you, lying to you, or just plain out being nasty. With that kind of history, who could blame us for wanting to retaliate? More importantly, who in their right mind could command us to love them? Yet that is precisely what Christ commands us to do. He commands us to be distinctive.

Of those of you reading this, there are those who have never told someone who has done you wrong that you love them and want the very best for them. Our instinct is to play checkers, return slug for slug, but Jesus wants us to be distinctive and play chess, go for the King! Adam Clarke calls this, "the most sublime piece of morality ever given to man. Has it appeared unreasonable and absurd to some? It has. And why? Because it is natural to men to avenge himself and plague those who plague him… Jesus Christ designs to make men happy. Now he is necessarily miserable who hates another. Our Lord prohibits that only which, from its nature, is opposed to man's happiness. This is therefore one of the most reasonable precepts in the universe."[45(Clarke, 1817, 52)] Everything that is good in the world comes from God (James 1:17) and it is not His will that we should have turmoil in our lives. As long as you have enemies who have hurt you, wronged you, etc., you will be the only one to lie in bed at night tossing and turning because the offense of the other person. The offender will be sleeping like a baby.

I read a story about a man from the state of Washington. His wife had filed for divorce and he was so furious that he went down to the courthouse and paid $11.50 for a demolition permit. Then he went home, hired a bulldozer and bulldozed their $85,000 home. He figured if she was going to divorce him, she wasn't going to have the house.[46(Maxfield, 2015)] Yeah, that will teach her, won't it? That is the game of checkers. I

---

[45] Clarke, Adam. 1817. *Clarke's Commentary.* London: J. Butterworth and Son

[46] Maxfield, Jen. 2015. *Man Bulldozes Home Without Telling Wife.* NBC New York. Jan 21, 2015 https://www.nbcnewyork.com/on-air/as-seen-on/man-rents-excavator_-bulldozes-home-without-telling-wife_new-york/2000566/

am going to hurt you because you hurt me, and I don't care how much it costs me—because I am going to win!

Jesus desires that His followers take a different approach to handling difficult people. He wants us to love them and pray for them. Why? Is it so that our standing with God will not be hindered, and that we might win them over for the King? It comes down to the question of God's love for us. Have you ever thought of yourself as being hard to love? Have you ever thought of your husband or wife as being hard to love? Be careful. Some of you wives are going to develop a case of whiplash from nodding your heads so vigorously. If you have a hard time loving your husband or your wife, how much harder do you think it is for God to love your husband or your wife? And given the many times you rejected Him and the many wrong choices you have made, how hard do you think it is for God to love you? Paul said, "once you were alienated from God and were enemies in your minds because of your evil behavior." (Colossians 1:21). Chances are pretty good that no matter what you have done in the past, you have probably never considered yourself to be an enemy of God, but that is in fact what the Bible calls those who live in the kingdom of self (1 John 2:15).

Our *Instinct* is to rebel against God and reject His Word for our lives. But God's Word says that "while we were still sinners, Christ died for us." (Romans 5:8) How many of us would like to trade slugs with God? Do you think any of us would even be able to take a step out of our corner? Let me ask another question; how many of us would like for God to treat us as we deserve? Peter wrote, "The Lord is not slow in keeping his promise, as some understand slowness. He is patient with you, not wanting anyone to perish, but everyone to come to repentance." (2 Peter 3:9)

In the Christian magazine, Voice of the Martyrs, there is the story of a young man who ignored his instincts and chose instead to be distinctive in responding to hatred. His name was Damare, a young Sudanese slave boy. He was a Christian and regularly attended church in an area that was predominantly Muslim. One day, as he was making his way back from a church service, he was met by some men who hated the fact that he was distinctive. They dragged him into the brush and beat him terribly. Before they left him to die, they nailed his knees and feet to a board. Miraculously, the boy survived and was asked how he felt toward those who had done this to him. He responded that he forgave them. But why? How could he possibly think of forgiving those who had done this to him? His answer might surprise you: Jesus was nailed and forgave them. [47](Knowname, 2011, 151)

That is what we are called to do. We are called to remember that God has forgiven us and that He paid a terrible price to purchase us for Himself. When we remember that and we try to respond to the hatred of this world with the love Jesus gave to us, then we have truly honored God. That is when we have been distinctive.

The greatest threat facing the world today is not the mutually assured destruction through the use of nuclear weapons that I spoke about in the previous chapter. It is radical Islam—a *religion* that is bent on ridding the world of all *infidels*. So, in the face of those who wish to separate our heads from our bodies and rid the world of us, how does Jesus' lesson apply to those enemies who have absolutely no regard for human life and are completely absent of any ability to love? Does Jesus give us a pass in the face of a very real evil that seeks to destroy Christianity, Judaism and our entire way of life? Surely, Jesus could not have foreseen this kind of persecution when He spoke these words from the mountainside in Palestine, could He? How are we supposed to respond to those who wish us dead and every western world country removed from the face of the earth?

As hard as it may seem to believe, the Christians of Paul's and Peter's day did face an evil that even surpassed the evil that the world is experiencing today. The Roman Emperor Nero is infamously known for committing vile and unspeakable acts of horror and terror toward Christians. He committed such horrors as having Christians eaten alive by wild beasts, torn to pieces tied between multiple horses and even dipped them in oil and set them ablaze to provide outdoor illumination for his palace garden parties. In fact, it was under Nero's reign that Paul was beheaded and Peter crucified upside down. Yet, Peter himself wrote,

> For it is commendable if someone bears up under the pain of unjust suffering because they are conscious of God. But how is it to your credit if you receive a beating for doing wrong and endure it? But if you suffer for doing

[47] Knowname, Dr. J.. 2011. *Untroubling a Troubled World.* Victoria B.C.: Trafford Publishing

> good and you endure it, this is commendable before God. To this you were called, because Christ suffered for you, leaving you an example, that you should follow in his steps. 'He committed no sin, and no deceit was found in his mouth.' When they hurled their insults at him, he did not retaliate; when he suffered, he made no threats. Instead, he entrusted himself to him who judges justly (1 Peter 2:19-23).

Be perfect:

As we conclude this chapter and segment let's speak for a moment on that last verse that really sums up this entire segment. He says, *Be perfect, therefore, as your heavenly Father is perfect.* Now we know that we cannot be perfect in that we can be sinless (1 John 1:8), but that is not what the word means. The Greek word is *teleios,* describing someone who has accomplished the intended goal. If something accomplishes what it is designed to do, it is said to be perfect, that is *teleios.* I have a favorite pen. It was given to me as a gift at my ordination. My pen is perfect, not because it is a nice pen, or because it is an expensive pen, or even because it was a gift from a dear friend and brother. My pen is perfect because it is able to perform the duties for which it was created. It writes! The word *teleios* is often translated as *mature.* Jesus is telling us to be mature in relation to our enemies, to take the distinctive path, rather than the instinctive one. And the only way we can become *mature,* that is *pure in heart,* is by faith in the One who is truly perfect in every way. Maturity does not come by way of a state of doing but by a state a *being,* like Christ. J. Vernon McGee, in his book, Through the Bible, reminds us of a popular nursery rhyme we all learned as children: *Little Jack Horner, sat in a corner Eating a Christmas pie; He put in his thumb and pulled out a plum and said, 'what a good boy am I!* We see much of that in the church today, with people trying to do good things to warrant praise. Oswald Chambers put it this way:

> Beware of walking in the spiritual life [distinctive] according to your natural affinities [instinctive]. We all have natural affinities—some people we like and others

> we do not. Never let those likes and dislikes be the rule of your Christian life. 'If we walk in the light, as He is in the light, we have fellowship with one another (1 John 1:7). [48](Chambers, 1915, 31)

We will not change the world by acting out of instinct and hating those who hate us. In the end, there is not a winner and a loser as in checkers. Christ showed His love toward us while we were still in *enemy* status with Him (Romans 5:8). His commandment to His followers is that we be like Him by showing that same love to our enemies. Clarke writes, "There is nothing greater than to imitate God in doing good to our enemies... God has no enemy which He hates but sin; we should have no other as well."[49](Clarke, 1817, 51) When we hate our enemies, there are only losers and the kingdom of heaven suffers. When we choose to be distinctive, we are all winners and God's kingdom abounds.

My wife and I watched a movie recently called, Hacksaw Ridge. It was a story about a devout Seventh Day Adventist named Desmond Doss. Desmond was the only *Conscientious Objector* in World War II to have received the nation's highest military honor, *The Medal of Honor,* for saving the lives of 75 men single-handedly during a single battle in the Pacific War—without using a weapon. Desmond was mocked, ridiculed and even beaten by his own platoon comrades for his distinctiveness. He almost never even made it into the war, having been threatened with a courts-martial by his superiors for his refusal to handle a weapon. Before the battle was over, Desmond had won the hearts of everyone in his platoon, many of which had taken part in his beating and many of which were included in those he saved. Even his own company officer who tried to get him courts-martialed sought forgiveness from Desmond, acknowledging that he had never been so wrong about someone as he was about Desmond.

When we choose to play a different game from that of the world, our distinction does not go un-noticed. Our instincts call for retaliation. Our instincts call for revenge. Our instincts call for an eye for eye and tooth for tooth, but what makes us distinctive is not retaliation trading slug for

---

[48] Chambers, Oswald.1915. *Studies in the Sermon on the Mount.* Cincinnati: God's Revivalist Press

[49] Clarke, Adam. 1817. *Clarke's Commentary.* London: J. Butterworth and Son

slug. *What makes us distinctive is allowing Christ to live through us to change from hate to love, one enemy at a time,* and in the process, we get to the King and we get to take our *enemies* with us! And when we are distinctive rather than instinctive, our reward is that we become *perfect* as our *heavenly Father is perfect.*

SECTION THREE

THE KINGDOM AND THE DISCIPLINES

Wilma Rudolph was born prematurely at 4.5 pounds on June 23, 1940 in Saint Bethlehem, Tennessee. As a result of her premature birth, she was plagued with one complication after another including double pneumonia on two occasions, scarlet fever, and the polio virus at Age 4. The polio forced her to wear a leg and foot brace for the next nine years and an orthopedic shoe for two years after that, leaving her foot twisted.

This *set-back* would have been enough to limit anyone, but not Wilma. By the time she reached 11 years of age, she had taught herself to walk without any special orthopedic equipment. Wanting to follow in her sister's footsteps, she tried out for and secured a spot on her high school basketball team. In her tenth-grade year, while playing basketball, she was *discovered* by Tennessee State track and field coach Ed Temple. He knew that he had found a lady with a special talent to run.

By the time Wilma was 16-years old, she tried out for and made the U.S. Olympic Team and competed in the 1956 summer games in Melbourne, winning the bronze medal in the 4 X 100m Relay. Four years later, she returned to the Summer Olympics in Rome and became the first woman in Olympic history to win three gold medals in track and field: the 100m dash, 200m dash and as anchor of the 400m relay.[50] Wilma's success was due to her willingness to endure discipline.

[50] Wikipedia. *Wilma Rudolph.* https://en.wikipedia.org/wiki/Wilma_Rudolph

As we begin Matthew 6, we find Jesus preparing His disciples for what is yet to come. Discipline is something that no one looks forward to, but something that is totally necessary, whether we are speaking about a world-class athlete like Wilma, or a Christian like yourself. But to be an effective servant of the kingdom, we must discipline ourselves to overcome the obstacles in life. Jesus said, "In this world you will have trouble. But take heart! I have overcome the world." (John 16:33). Jesus also knew that overcoming would not be easy and that it would take discipline on our part. In this segment, we are looking at three disciplines which Jesus addresses in His sermon: giving, praying, and fasting, along with the emphasis He places on forgiveness. Let's get to it!

TWELVE

Give in Secret

Be careful not to practice your righteousness in front of others to be seen by them. If you do, you will have no reward from your Father in heaven. "So, when you give to the needy, do not announce it with trumpets, as the hypocrites do in the synagogues and on the streets, to be honored by others. Truly I tell you, they have received their reward in full. But when you give to the needy, do not let your left hand know what your right hand is doing, so that your giving may be in secret. Then your Father, who sees what is done in secret, will reward you. (Matt. 6:1-4)

Following the attack on Pearl Harbor, Commander Joe Rochefort was assigned to break Japanese communication codes. Stationed at an intelligence base in Oahu, he predicted the Japanese would attack near the island of Midway on June 3, 1942, which they did. Because of his expertise, the United States surprised the Japanese Navy with its first defeat in 350 years with Japan losing four carriers, one cruiser, 2500 men, 322 aircraft, and their best pilots. Many say that this victory at sea began the end of the Pacific War. Surprisingly, Rochefort never received recognition for his efforts. Instead, some intelligence men in Washington, D.C., coveting the praise of their superiors, falsified reports and claimed credit for the attack date even though it was discovered later that they had predicted a date of June 10 for the attack. The intelligence men in Washington sealed the records for forty years and in his life time Rochefort was never recognized for his insight. In fact, he was actually removed from intelligence and assigned to a floating dry dock in San Francisco. Sixty years after the Battle occurred, three of his fellow seamen wrote the tell-all book, *Deceit at Pearl Harbor.* In it, they wrote about a note Rochefort kept on his desk: "WE CAN ACCOMPLISH ANYTHING PROVIDING NO ONE CARES WHO GETS THE CREDIT." They added, "That was the attitude that won the battle of Midway." [51](McDowell, 1985)

In this opening chapter of this segment, "The Kingdom and the Disciplines," we will look at the discipline called giving. I strongly believe that our giving is the true litmus test of our faith. The last bastion of control that most of us surrender to God is our money, but as the Prophet Malachi rightly states, either our money builds for us a bridge for receiving God's blessings, or our money builds a wall between us and the experiencing of mountain-moving faith. Malachi 3:10 says that we are to trust God with our finances and even test Him to see if He doesn't flood our homes with blessings. George Mueller put Malachi's promise this way: "God judges what we give by what we keep."[52](Zuck, 1997, 162) For the record, I believe not trusting God with our finances, not giving what He has laid on our hearts to give is a sin. It is neither the giving nor the not giving that is the sin, but rather the unbelief—the lack of faith—the disobedience of a command that is sin. In Matthew 6:2, Jesus does not tell us that we should consider giving, or that it would be good to give. He gives us a command of expectation. He says, *when* you give, so not to give is disobedience.

But the emphasis of Jesus' message to us goes deeper than just giving or not giving. In fact, Jesus does not condemn their giving, only the heart behind it. *Jesus' real issue is the motive, not the money.* He says that we are not to do these things to be honored by men, but that we should be seeking God's approval.

We have all probably sought the approval of people on more than one occasion in our lives. I get it; we are human. I am not speaking about that occasional needed pat on the head or multiple likes to our selfies on *Facebook.* But there are some people who live for the praise of people. That, I believe, is the motivation that Jesus is speaking against in this passage and the ones to follow pertaining to prayer and fasting. Keep in

---

[51] McDowell, Edwin. 1985. *Officer Who Broke Japanese War Codes Gets Belated Honor.* NY Times. Nov 17, 1985

[52] Zuck, Roy B.. 1997. *The Speakers' Quote Book.* Grand Rapids: Kregel Academic & Professional

mind the audience that Jesus had there on that mountainside, included the Pharisees from Jerusalem who thrived on the attention and praise of the *little people.* They were always given the place of honor at the table, given financial and tangible gifts hand over fist and for what? To be seen as admirable, important and reverent by the commoners. Their goal was to be placed upon a pedestal of prestige by those who would never hold such lofty positions.

This is the standard by which Jesus is telling us to measure ourselves. In Matthew 5:20, Jesus says that the motivation for the things that we do must exceed the praise of others if we are to get into heaven. How does this commandment to keep our deeds a secret harmonize with His earlier admonition to ensure that our good deeds are seen by men (Matthew 5:16)? How in one breath can we seek to make our righteous deeds known while in the very next, keep it strictly between ourselves and God? Is this a contradiction? Not at all. Once again, it all comes down to motivation. If what we are doing is so we can be seen and praised by others, then there is no eternal value whatsoever. We have, as Jesus said, *already received our reward.* So then, if we are to be seen by others, from whom then are we to hide our good deeds? Dietrich Bonhoeffer suggests that it is from ourselves we are to hide. He says, "We must be unaware of our own righteousness, and see it only in so far as we look unto Jesus, then it will seem not extraordinary, but quite ordinary and natural."[53](Bonhoeffer, 1983, 106)

Several years ago, I preached a message that I titled *Double-shot Christianity.* I took the name from the *Starbucks* drink that I find in my stocking every year at Christmas. They are only little four-ounce cans, but boy do they pack a punch! I explained that there were basically three kinds of people who call themselves Christians. The first is the decaffeinated Christian, who, like decaf coffee, is really a Christian in name only. There is no substance there and for you who are coffee drinkers, you know what I mean! Then there is the *regular* Christian who does its job and fills its role for which it is tasked to do. But then, there is that *Double-shot* Christian who is extraordinary and God's love oozes out of his or her pores. This is that *extraordinary* Christian, but if you want to know the truth about it, there is nothing extraordinary about that person at all. If one is truly

[53] Bonhoeffer, Dietrich. 1983. *The Cost of Discipleship.* San Francisco: Harper and Row

filled with the Spirit of Christ, then that person is only acting out of the ordinary and natural self.

I mentioned in an earlier chapter that my oldest daughter Tiffani is a people pleaser. Most of us know someone who strives to please others. In fact, most of us reading this strive to please people at least to some degree. There is nothing wrong with trying to please people as long as it is with a *pure heart*. But there are some fundamental problems that come when pleasing people is the primary motivation behind our actions:

1. The mood will look more like an EKG chart because it is determined by how others feel and think about you. People are fickle; one minute they will be applauding you and the next, they throw rotten vegetables, taking you from hero to zero in sixty seconds flat!
2. You will never please everyone. Have you ever come across that one *fun-sucker* that no matter what you do, you never seem to get on their good side? No matter what church you attend or call home, there will always be those who are determined to be unhappy. In the town of Lexington, Alabama, which I called home for ten years, they have a monthly newspaper called *Around the Town* where the editor, my good friend and sister in Christ Angie, provides to the community, free of charge, keeping us updated as to what is happening *Around the Town*. At the bottom of Page One, she has a disclaimer stating, *If you find any mistakes, I have put them there just so you have something to find of interest to you.* That just about sums up the fun-sucker, doesn't it?
3. You will grow very tired very quickly because you have a hard time saying *no*! A lot of people have a hard time saying no to others, especially when what they are saying *no* to is a good and noble cause. Compound that difficulty when the person is a people-pleaser and wants everyone to like them. Leaders of church ministries are often guilty of playing on this emotion. They see a new warm body walk through the front doors and immediately, they are trying to put them to work in ministry!
4. You will be consumed with wondering what others are thinking about you. I know some people who are eaten alive by even the

idea that someone does not like them. I used to have a sign on my office door that read, *I perform for an audience of One!*

5. Finally, most people do not really care about you anyway. Someone once said, *If you worry too much about what people think of you, you'd probably be disappointed to discover how seldom they did.*

It is human nature to be liked and appreciated. Our children desire nothing more than the approval of their moms and dads—stay-at-home moms desire the approval of their husbands and people who work outside the home desire the approval of their supervisors. But when that desire spills over into our spiritual lives, it becomes a problem.

As mentioned, it is clear that Jesus is not condemning the Pharisees' giving as a means of gaining attention or approval. He simply states in v.v. 1-2 that they will not be getting any *atta-boys* from God, since they already received their reward from men. That is what Jesus meant when He said that our righteousness must surpass theirs.

In December of 2016, it was announced that *Facebook* Founder Mark Zuckerberg and his wife Priscilla donated a whopping $45 Billion to celebrate the birth of their daughter. [54(Dolan, 2015)] For the record, I applaud their desire to help cure diseases and further education, but I wonder how big that donation would have been had we never heard about it. Would that donation have been any less if only they and their accountant were aware of the generous donation? If not for vanity sake, why else would Zuckerberg call a press conference with all of the major networks to announce their donation?

John MacArthur tells about a man who came into his office one Sunday and told him it was his first time to worship with them and that he intended to make their church his church home. He then handed John a very generous check, with the promise that he would receive one just like it every week. John told him he did not want to receive his checks personally and suggested that he should place it into the plate as does the rest of

---

[54] Dolan, Kerry. 2015. *Mark Zuckerberg Announces Birth Of Baby Girl & Plan to Donate 99% Of His Facebook Stock.* Forbes Magazine. December 1, 2015. https://www.forbes.com/sites/kerryadolan/2015/12/01/mark-zuckerberg-announces-birth-of-baby-girl-plan-to-donate-99-of-his-facebook-stock/#29eb6d5d18f5

the church family. I wonder if John never saw him again.[55](MacArthur, 1985, 356)

I have had the honor for ten years of being called Pastor at the greatest secret in the Nazarene Church, a great little country church called Mary's Chapel in Lexington, Alabama. The very first action I took as Pastor was inform my treasurer that I never wanted to see a single giving report that recorded people's names and the amounts of their giving. I understand, this might rub some of my pastoral friends the wrong way and I certainly do not begrudge them of thinking differently, but allow me to explain: I see my role as Pastor as helping my congregation understand what God requires of them, but not as an *enforcer* to make sure they are doing what God tells them to do! I try to help them understand that their obedience to God is between them and God. But now, there is also a stronger reason for my wanting their giving to be kept secret from me. I never want to have to trust my flesh not to treat others differently based on what they give—or don't give! I believe that Jesus calls all of us to show love, compassion, mercy and grace to all people, believers and unbelievers alike and this is my *checks and balance* to ensure I am doing that.

Jesus is telling us to do our good deeds in secret. When you help someone out with a bill, or take them food, Jesus is calling you to do it a manner which does not bring any attention to yourself. But now, doesn't that fly in the face of the passage we already looked at in Matthew 5:16 which says, "let your light shine before men, that they may see your good deeds and praise your Father in heaven?" The difference is in the motivation. John Ortberg said, "We'd all like to be humble, but what if nobody notices?" [56](Ortberg, 2009, 178) We must ask ourselves, *a*re we seeking to exalt Jesus, or are we seeking to be noticed?

In v. 2, Jesus calls those who do good things with selfish intentions hypocrites. According to Warren Wiersbe's Commentary of Matthew, "The Greek word translated hypocrite, originally meant an actor who

[55] MacArthur, John. 1985. *Matthew 1-7 MacArthur New Testament Commentary.* Chicago: Moody Publishers

[56] Ortberg, John. 2009. *The Life You've Always Wanted.* Grand Rapids: Zondervan Publishing House

wears a mask." [57](Wiersbe, 1989, 25) In the ancient theater, one actor could play several roles on stage and they designated the changing of the role by wearing different masks. Evidently the Pharisees who craved the praise of men, sometimes made a big show out of what they gave to the temple treasury. In the Jewish system of worship, they would line up at the treasury and give their offering very publicly. We saw that in the story of the widow with the two mites in Luke 21.

Here's how v. 2 reads in *The Message*:

> Be especially careful when you are trying to be good so that you don't make a performance out of it. It might be good theater, but the God who made you won't be applauding. When you do something for someone else, don't call attention to yourself.

It goes back to that central question of worship; *who is your audience?* If God is not your audience, that is, if what you are doing is not for Him, then He is not going to pay any mind to what you are doing and furthermore, it is not *God-worship,* but *self-worship.* If I am preaching to impress you, God is not in it. If someone sings to be adored by you, God is not interested. And if you are giving to impress your neighbor, God does not want your money, because He is not the object of your worship, your vanity is the object of your worship.

When Jesus speaks about not letting *your left hand know what your right hand is doing,* He was not speaking of literal hands. He was speaking about your best friend and we still use that term today when we speak about someone being our *right-hand man.* He is not telling us that we should not keep track of our giving for tax purposes. He is simply telling us to let our giving be our reward and not look for anything in return—give and forget!

Let us be honest with one another. When we think about our own Christian charity, our flesh seeks something in return, give and take. It is like inviting someone over to your house for dinner. You sort of expect an invite in return at some point. Jesus is telling us to quit expecting that. In

---

[57] Wiersbe, Warren W.. 1989. *The Bible Exposition Commentary: New Testament.* Colorado Springs: David C. Cook. 1989

fact, elsewhere, Jesus tells us to exercise our greatest Christian charity on those who are unable to reciprocate. That is where the real reward is. He says, for "Truly I tell you, whatever you did for one of the least of these brothers and sisters of mine, you did for me." (Matthew 25:40)

Blindside was a popular movie made about Michael Oher, right guard for the *Baltimore Ravens.* In the movie, the position of right guard is explained as the one position that literally makes or breaks the quarterback. On the neighborhood football field, everyone wants to be the quarterback, wide receiver or safety, because they get all of the glory. No one wants to be a tackle or guard, because they never get to touch the football and unless you are well-versed in football, you never remember a single one of their names. But the *Guard* is the one position on the field that makes all of the other offensive positions successful. The quarterback's opportunity to pass the ball and the receiver's opportunity to receive it, rests squarely on the shoulders of the guard who gives his all for the team's success without bringing any attention to himself. When his team goes on to the playoffs, just knowing that he helped make that happen is reward enough.

When you give to your church, I don't think it is necessarily God's intent that you wait till you get to heaven to see what your generosity has done. When your church reaches the lost—when people come to a saving and healing relationship with Jesus Christ—when people are fed, clothed and cared for, every person in church who gives faithfully to the ministry of their church, ought to take personal pride in the fact that they helped make that happen.

Jesus says, "*I seek not to please myself but Him who sent me.*" (John 5:30) That is the question that He puts to us here in these disciplines. Who are you seeking to please, God or man? Because if it is man you seek to please in your giving, you have already received your reward, but if God's pleasure is your end-game, hold on to something tight because God is going to open the floodgates of heaven's blessings on your life and your only dilemma according to God's own promise will be where to put it all!

THIRTEEN

Preparing for Prayer

And when you pray, do not be like the hypocrites, for they love to pray standing in the synagogues and on the street corners to be seen by others. Truly I tell you, they have received their reward in full. But when you pray, go into your room, close the door and pray to your Father, who is unseen. Then your Father, who sees what is done in secret, will reward you. And when you pray, do not keep on babbling like pagans, for they think they will be heard because of their many words. Do not be like them, for your Father knows what you need before you ask him. "This, then, is how you should pray: "'Our Father in heaven, hallowed be your name, your kingdom come, your will be done, on earth as it is in heaven. Give us today our daily bread. And forgive us our debts, as we also have forgiven our debtors. And lead us not into temptation, but deliver us from the evil one. (Matt. 6:5-13)

A young man went into a drugstore to buy three boxes of chocolate: small, medium, and large. When the pharmacist asked him about the three boxes, he said, '*Well, I am going over to my new girlfriend's house tonight for supper. Then we are going out for the evening. If she only lets me hold her hand, then I will give her the small box. If she lets me kiss her on the cheek, then I will give her the medium box. But if she really lets me smooch seriously, I will give her the large box.'* He made his purchase and left. That evening as he sat down for dinner with his girlfriend's family, he asked if he could say the prayer before the meal. He began to pray and he prayed a most earnest and intense prayer that lasted for almost five minutes. When he finished his new girlfriend said, *'you never told me you were such a religious person.* He responded, *and you never told me your dad was a pharmacist!'*

When a person prays selfishly, he/she may find out that God "is the pharmacist." Prayer life is a reflection of the relationship with God. When the relationship is meaningful and real, prayers are very much like a conversation with a good friend, but when one is living in the kingdom of self-rule and self-sufficiency, like that young boy, the moment trial and adversity hits, one suddenly finds religion very quickly.

In our passage about prayer, we are given what has come to be known as the Lord's Prayer. Many of you know this prayer by heart. Some of you may have grown up in a church where folks recited the prayer every Sunday. Maybe your parents taught you to pray the prayer before going to bed at night. On the Sunday morning that I preached this message, I asked a young lady named Maslynn to play the part of the person praying while her youth leader, stood out of view and played the part of God. It is a great skit that explains how many Christians view prayer. In the skit, the young girl began reciting the Lord's Prayer and after each sentence, God would respond. The girls was stunned at first that God would actually answer her while she was praying, but the "God" character would urge her to continue. Once again, after each statement, God would interrupt and ask her what that meant, to which she would respond, "I don't know, it just what I am supposed to say!"

The banter between the "God" character and Maslynn was quite comical and amusing, but in it, we are brought face to face with some of the pitfalls of the Lord's Prayer, not the least of which is that many people get caught up not even thinking about its words while they're praying it. I want to share a few points with you about this prayer. But instead of actually focusing on the prayer itself, I want to focus on Jesus' instructions leading up to the prayer where He says in v. 6, "But when you pray, go into your room, close the door and pray to your Father, who is unseen. Then your Father, who sees what is done in secret, will reward you". Three things I want to look at regarding this verse: we are to go into our rooms, we are to close the door and we are to pray to our Father. How much simpler can the instructions be?

Go into your room:

A Christian movie came out recently called War Room. The lady had a special room where she had all of her strategies laid out, what she needed to pray for, how she needed to pray and the Scriptures that would help her to do battle. That room only had one chair and was only big enough for one person. The Greek word for *room* here actually describes a room where treasure is stored. The woman in the War Room had filled walls with her treasures, promises that God makes and keeps.

Jesus wants us to go to that special place where He can remind us of who He is and what He wants to do for us, in us, and through us. Maybe it is not a physical room; maybe it is a garden, a trail, or an exercise bike. My friend Marcus has a special rock garden where each rock represents a different person or a different need and he walks around his garden praying over each rock. It doesn't have to be a room, just that special place where we can get down to business with God and the only thing we should have with us is His Word.

Close the door:

No matter whether it is a physical room or driving down the road, we need to close the door to the world around us. There are the obvious things like our phones, the TV, radio, kids, etc. When I was stationed in South Korea, I attended a three-day prayer retreat on Prayer Mountain outside of Seoul. Scattered all over this mountain were little earth-covered igloos that had a door about three feet high and two feet wide. Inside was nothing but a small mat and an altar. Once I squeezed inside and got situated on my knees, I closed the door behind me and because of the two-foot walls between each and the earth covering them, I could not hear anything but my own heartbeat. I want to tell you that God's voice becomes very loud when your ears are trained to hear Him and only Him. That is when I realized that there are not-so-obvious things that I need to shut the door to as well; things such as, distractions in my head, evil thoughts, bitterness, even worry, just to name a few. Those were the things God brought to my attention and wanted to help me deal with in that small confined cell. In a sentence, I had to shut the door to my selfishness, and we will talk more about that in the next chapter which discusses fasting. We must shut the door to our flesh because flesh only breeds flesh. Prayer is the open communication lines between our spirit and God's Spirit (John 3:6). God says that when we come to Him in quiet communion, we are to shut the door, not only to the physical around us, but also the distractions within us that drown out His small still voice.

One of my favorite stories of the Old Testament is that of Elijah being run off by Queen Jezebel. God knew he needed some encouragement and so He sent him up to the mountain to meet with Him and picking up the story in 1 Kings 19:11-12,

> The LORD said, 'Go out and stand on the mountain in the presence of the LORD, for the LORD is about to pass by.' Then a great and powerful wind tore the mountains apart and shattered the rocks before the LORD, but the LORD was not in the wind. After the wind there was an earthquake, but the LORD was not in the earthquake. After the earthquake came a fire, but the LORD was not in the fire. And after the fire came a gentle whisper.

My life verse is Psalm 46:10, "Be still and know that I am God." We need to still our hearts and our minds when we go into that special *room* of prayer.

We also need to shut the door to our feelings. Feelings can lead us to do unthought of things that are completely contrary to God's Word. I tell the folks at my church that we should never rely on our feelings because they are often all over the map; they are a moving target. Our feelings are up and down depending on our circumstances and if you ladies have ever experienced menopause, that movement looks more like an 8.6 on the Richter Scale. God's Word never changes, and it can be trusted. Finally, once we have gone into our special room and closed the door to the world around us, we need to...

Pray to the Father:

I mentioned earlier that many people know this Lord's prayer by heart, but have become so numb to it, that they could be doing virtually anything while reciting it. Muslims and Jews are often admired for their discipline in prayer, but most people do not realize that they often pray the exact same thing each time. They could be doing just about anything else while accomplishing their *requirement* to pray.

I wonder how deep and fulfilling my relationship would be with Nan if the only time I ever spoke to her, I said the exact same thing each time. It would do nothing for our relationship, so why would we expect it to be any different for God? God just wants us to get real with Him, like that special friend that we could spend hours speaking to on the phone. Jesus says in v. 7 that "we are not to keep babbling, meaning just talk to me! Do not ramble off some memorized prayer that is not coming from the heart because you are boring me."

I am reminded of the only time in the gospels where Jesus asks the disciples to pray was in the garden on the night He was arrested. Do you remember what happened? That's right, they fell asleep—more than once! How many of us do the same thing? We spend the whole day focusing and living in the kingdom of self and when we are finally weary enough to go to bed, we try to give God what ounce of energy we have left and wind up drifting off to sleep before we even get past, *Our Father in Heaven...* I make it a habit to pray in the early morning and yes, it is a preference. But as I said, when I lay my head on the pillow at night, I am ready to sleep! I pray in the morning for a couple of reasons. First, God wants my *first* fruits and shouldn't that include the first fruits of my day? He is not interested in my leftovers. He wants the choicest part of my day. But I also pray in the morning because I know that that is when I am going to need His help the most, when I walk out that door to do the things that I need to do. It does very little to pray and ask God to lead me *not into temptation* before I drift off to sleep, because frankly, I am not tempted to do anything—except sleep! I need to pray for God's armor before I go out to slay my dragons in the morning. That is when I am going to need it most. Besides, can you imagine trying to sleep wearing a suit of armor?

The Lord' Prayer should more appropriately be called the Disciple's Prayer, because Jesus modeled it just for you and me, His disciples. But the Lord's Prayer was only a model, not a step-by-step how-to instruction booklet. Prayer is not about a religion; it is about a relationship!

In these three disciplines that we are looking at (giving, praying and fasting), I mentioned in the last chapter that there was a common thread and that thread was secrecy. But in fact, there are two common threads and it is that commandment of expectation, w*hen you give, when you pray,* and *when you fast.* Notice how Jesus never addresses the question as to whether we should do these things, only with what heart we do them. And in our passage, He is telling us that when we set out to speak to Him, we are to go into that place where He wants to meet with us, close ourselves from the world around us and just talk to Him and tell Him what's on our hearts. So, before you talk to our Father, prepare for prayer!

FOURTEEN

Forgiveness

For if you forgive other people when they sin against you, your heavenly Father will also forgive you. But if you do not forgive others their sins, your Father will not forgive your sins. (Matt. 6:14-15)

The teaching of forgiveness is another one of those *hard sayings* of Jesus. In fact, if His hard sayings were measured in pill size, this one would surely reach the size of an ostrich egg. This commandment to forgive is the only part of Jesus' model prayer that He felt so strongly about, that He went back and hit it a second time. Have you ever wondered why?

I have never met a person who has never been wronged by someone else, nor have I ever met a person who has not wronged someone else. This topic is crucial to every believer, especially since the issue of unforgiveness is so corrosive to our bodies and spirits. Remember in the last chapter, I stated that many times we say the Lord's Prayer but without thinking about what we are saying? Nowhere is that fact more important than it is here. When we say, *And forgive us our debts, as we also have forgiven our debtors*, do we ever give any thought to what we are actually asking of God? We are asking God to forgive us with the same measure by which we are forgiving others. If you say to someone or about someone for something they have done, *I could never forgive you,* you are commanding God not to forgive you. Right? *Forgive us JUST AS, in the same manner, just like we forgive others!* I told you this was a dangerous prayer, didn't I? So, I want to speak about forgiveness because we all can relate, we are all guilty, and finally it really is a heaven and hell issue!

Why should we forgive?

First of all, we should answer the question, *Why should we forgive?* The most obvious reason we should forgive is so we can be forgiven. Someone once said that the issue is not that God withholds His forgiveness from those who do not forgive, but that our hearts are not in the willing position to receive His forgiveness. We can only forgive when we have experienced God's forgiveness, but we can also only truly appreciate God's forgiveness when our hearts are in a place where we can freely offer forgiveness to others. That is the point of the unmerciful servant in Matthew 18 who owed his master an insurmountable sum of money for which he had no way of paying. After his master offered him the free gift of forgiveness (by the way, the Greek word for forgiveness is actually a financial term), he demanded that a fellow servant pay him what was owed him, a much smaller sum of money. The servant could not truly appreciate the gift his master had offered since his heart was not in a place to offer the same for a much smaller offense.

General Oglethorpe once said to John Wesley, "I never forgive and I never forget. To which Wesley replied, Then, Sir, I hope you never sin."[58](Wesley, 2009) When we choose not to forgive, or insist that we are unable to forgive, we are in truth, saying that the debt owed us is much greater than the debt we owed God. Can we really stand before God and make a solid argument for why we cannot forgive someone else?

What if we do not forgive?

The second question we ought to answer is what are the results if we don't forgive? The first answer we have already covered; unless we forgive, neither can we be forgiven, which means eternal separation from God. The only option to not forgiving is to condemn ourselves to hell for all eternity. Think about that for a moment because there is a very sad irony there. The person who wronged you may very well come to their senses and reconcile their relationship with God, accept God's free gift of forgiveness, and for whatever reason, was not able to make things right with you before

[58] Wesley, John. 2009.Source Unk. Bible.org. February 2, 2009. https://bible.org/illustration/john-wesley-1

entering their heavenly home. All the while, you never forgave them and you pass on and condemn yourself to the eternal lake of fire. Where is the justice in that for you? And since we are asking that question, which is more important to you at this point, justice or mercy?

Unforgiveness also affects one physically. It causes one to have sleepless nights because some person has been wronged? If there is too much of that, one winds up with ulcers and decay. Then there is the relentless and overbearing burden of unforgiveness that one carries around. Anyone who has ever gone through dramatic weight loss knows what that extra weight did to the back. That is what the weight of unforgiveness feels like. A person is always thinking about it and every time he sees the person, drive by the house, see their name, or have a memory, that old 50 lb. weight just pushes one down closer to the ground.

Then, there are spiritual side-affects to unforgiveness, that corrosive characteristic that unforgiveness has on our souls. Left unchecked, it eats away from the inside like one has just swallowed a piranha. It eats away at us every day and makes us more poisonous to ourselves and to those around us. Other relationships begin to corrode, beginning with the closest relationships (spouse, children, etc.), and slowly creeps out into other relationships. The once friendly personality is now a vindictive spirit of hurt, hatred and regrets. In contrast, Booker T. Washington said, "I will not permit any man to narrow and degrade my soul by making me hate him." [59(Washington, Unk)]

Probably, the greatest example I can use for this issue is the popular story of a woman known only as prisoner #66730 at the German Concentration camp called Ravensbruck. Corrie Ten Boom was speaking at a church service in Munich when she came face to face with the guard who stood at the shower room door at that camp, the same camp that killed her entire family. Here is how she explained that encounter:

> It was at a church service in Munich that I saw him, a former S.S. man who had stood guard at the shower room door in the processing center at Ravensbruck. He was the first of our actual jailers that I had seen since that time.

---

[59] Washington, Booker T.. Date Unk. *Brainy Quote.* https://www.brainyquote.com/quotes/booker_t_washington_105621

> And suddenly it was all there – the roomful of mocking men, the heaps of clothing, Betsie's pain-blanched face.
>
> He came up to me as the church was emptying, beaming and bowing. "How grateful I am for your message, Fraulein." He said. "To think that, as you say, He has washed my sins away!" His hand was thrust out to shake mine. And I, who had preached so often to the people in Bloemendaal the need to forgive, kept my hand at my side.
>
> Even as the angry, vengeful thoughts boiled through me, I saw the sin of them. Jesus Christ had died for this man; was I going to ask for more? Lord Jesus, I prayed, forgive me and help me to forgive him. I tried to smile, I struggles to raise my hand. I could not. I felt nothing, not the slightest spark of warmth or charity. And so again I breathed a silent prayer. Jesus, I prayed, I cannot forgive him. Give me Your forgiveness.
>
> As I took his hand the most incredible thing happened. From my shoulder along my arm and through my hand a current seemed to pass from me to him, while into my heart sprang a love for this stranger that almost overwhelmed me. And so I discovered that it is not on our forgiveness any more than on our goodness that the world's healing hinges, but on His. When He tells us to love our enemies, He gives, along with the command, the love itself. [60](Boom, 2006, 174)

What it comes right down to is there are only two options: to forgive or not to forgive. When I counsel folks on their *options,* I tell them there are only two: one leaves them spinning circles in the cesspool of self-pity and the other one moves them on down the road. We cannot have it have both ways. We cannot say we will not forgive and expect to get ourselves out of the cesspool.

---

[60] Boom, Corrie ten. 2006. *The Hiding Place.* Grand Rapids: Chosen Books

Joseph Richardson was a millionaire who lived in New York City. He owned a narrow plot of land in the midst of a number of houses. This lot was only about five feet wide. He wanted to sell it to the people on either side of him and so he determined the selling price and offered it to each of them. Both neighbors were interested in buying the land, but not at the price that he was asking. Instead of bargaining with them, he built a house on the land instead. The house was 150' deep but only 5 feet wide. He then moved in and set up home. Because of his hatred for his neighbors, Mr. Richardson condemned himself to a life of discomfort in that house which has since been called, *The Spite House.* His intention was to be a thorn in the sides of his neighbors, but instead, the thorn was his alone to bear.[61(Architecture)]

It is said that revenge is sweet, but is it really? Revenge is like that candy-coated onion. It may taste sweet at first, but it leaves a terribly bitter taste in the mouth once it has been sucked on for a while. Does revenge ever really give the desired outcome? Does a person ever really feel satisfied by becoming as little as the person who wronged him? And finally, has there ever been a time where revenge has led to reconciliation?

But if forgiveness and revenge are not an option, one can always try and ignore it. Right? We often masquerade our hurt by insisting something like, *oh, it was no big deal, forget about it, I never even gave it a second thought.* If that is you, how is that working out for you? The deeper the hurt goes, the deeper the scars are. Forgiveness is not easy and it becomes even harder when the offender is someone very close. Acknowledge that it hurt, that it mattered, but that we choose to extend forgiveness. Forgiving is not saying, *It really didn't matter.* Forgiveness says, *it was wrong. It did matter, but I release you.* Forgiveness does not ignore the reality of an offense but, in fact, it validates that the offense occurred, but then it releases both the offender and the offended from the offense.

To forgive hurts because it costs to forgive. Forgiving means that one must forfeit justice in seeing the other person punished for the wrong committed against another. Be honest with yourself; how many of you do not secretly pray that the fleas of a thousand camels infest your enemy's armpits? Our flesh wants to hurt them equally as much as they hurt us,

---

[61] Architecture, New York. *The Spite House.* http://www.nyc-architecture.com/GON/GON005.htm

but now, just think about the sweet offering you are making to God every time you choose to act like God and forgive as He forgave you.

I usually take Mondays off from the church work, but since I live directly across from the church, I can usually see everything that goes on over there while sitting in my living room. The trash man comes every Monday morning through my street and every once in a while, I will see someone stopping by the church trash cans to dump their garbage in the cans. My immediate thought is to run outside in my pajamas and bring their offense to their attention. Luckily, my spirit quickens me and tells my flesh to shut up and think about their situation. Maybe they were running late on Monday trying to get their little ones ready for day care and forgot to put their can out. Maybe, they cannot afford to have their garbage picked up and so, have to find other ways of disposing it, or maybe they just got evicted and need to unload some things that they just do not have any other room for.

One of the best ways to find forgiveness in your heart is to try and understand the person who wronged you. I am not saying that you should find ways to justify their bad behavior, only to remind yourself that they may be lost, they may not know forgiveness themselves, they might not have ever experienced the free gift of forgiveness that you have. And then remember John 3:16; God loves them every bit as much as He loves you and He wants you to forgive that person so that they might come to God to be forgiven also.

An anonymous child once prayed, "And forgive us our trash cans as we forgive those who put trash in our cans." Is there someone you have been trashing? Or has someone been trashing you? Has someone been filling your trash can with offenses and hurt

You have probably already figured out that I am black and white, as I stated earlier. I am sure that probably comes from more than twenty years of military service where there is not a lot of room for gray area. But, as I also stated, I am pretty sure that Jesus is a black and white kind of a Guy also. He does not give us commands based upon our circumstances, but based upon His Word. Looking at this from a black and white perspective, take a look at the things that you have already tried in dealing with unforgiveness, whether it be revenge, ignoring it, or some other means of escaping the issue. Ask yourself this question; is what I am doing working? Is my way of managing hurt, pain, or disappointment achieving its intended goal? It has been said that *if you always do what you always did, you'll always get what you always got,* and isn't that Einstein's definition of insanity, to try the same things over and over and expect different results? Why not try something different? Why not try forgiving, so your Father has a chance to help you heal and those scars of hurt will stop hurting. You have nothing to lose and all of eternity to gain.

FIFTEEN

A Stomach for Fasting

When you fast, do not look somber as the hypocrites do, for they disfigure their faces to show others they are fasting. Truly I tell you, they have received their reward in full. But when you fast, put oil on your head and wash your face, so that it will not be obvious to others that you are fasting, but only to your Father, who is unseen; and your Father, who sees what is done in secret, will reward you. (Matt. 6:16-18)

The last of the disciplines that Jesus addressed in His sermon is one that is both controversial and misunderstood in the Church today. I am speaking about fasting. Fasting is defined in *Christian Apologetics & Research Ministry* as:

> The act of depriving oneself of food for a period of time for a specific purpose, often for a spiritual need. It is the 'weakening' of the body in order to 'strengthen' the spirit. It is interesting to note that sin entered the world through the disobedience of eating.[62](Slick, Unk)

Fasting is the temporary abstention of superficial earthly physical pleasures to obtain a deeper heavenly spiritual closeness and understanding of God. It is designed to bring us into a deeper sense of God's presence in our lives.

---

[62] Slick, Matt. *Christian Apologetics & Research Ministry: Fast, Fasting.* https://carm.org/dictionary-fast-fasting

I was watching a *History Channel* special recently on the period known as the Dark Ages, which shadowed all of Europe for nearly 350 years beginning in the mid-400's A.D. The Dark Ages actually began with the fall of the Roman Empire brought on by an army of disgruntled Roman barbarians forcing the great city into starvation. In the great city, things had gotten so bad that people were buying pounds of human flesh from corpses that littered the streets just trying to avoid starvation.

I share this gruesome fact because we have no understanding of what it means to have to go without food. We are the richest people in the world living in the richest nation in the world and although we all may live on different levels of means, I think I am pretty safe in saying, that if we feel like having a *Krispy Kreme* donut, we will get a *Krispy Kreme* donut. Richard Foster, in his book Celebration of Discipline, says that, "our stomach is like a spoiled child, and spoiled children do not need indulgence, they need discipline."[63](Foster, 1983, 57)

Because of our prosperity, disciplines such as fasting are not only as necessary today as they were in Jesus' time, but more so, because we have so much blessing to indulge us that we forget about the One from whom all those blessings flow. I think that was the meaning behind Jesus saying, "it is easier for a camel to go through the eye of a needle than for someone who is rich to enter the kingdom of God." (Matthew 19:24). Not that it was impossible for a rich person to get into heaven, but because there is no need to focus on God, there is a lack of urgency to hear from God.

Why has the discipline of fasting become such an archaic thing in the Church today? We often preach and teach on the discipline of prayer and giving. We talk a lot about the spiritual need to serve and to study, but if those things are important enough for Jesus to include them in His sermon, why isn't fasting still practiced today as it was in Jesus' time? One reason might be its connection to New Age thinking. New agers believe that fasting has mystical powers and so that we do not practice as the pagans do, we shy away from it. Another reason might be that we don't understand enough about fasting to practice it. We know that studying God's Word helps us to understand His will and helps us to share the gospel with others. We know that by focusing on giving and serving, not only are we fulfilling commandments of God in doing so, but so doing

[63] Foster, Richard. 1983. *Celebration of Discipline.* San Francisco: Harper and Row

also helps us to take our focus off ourselves and places that focus on to the needs of others. Do we really understand the reasons and rewards of fasting as God intended? It comes down to the issue that I already spoke about: the personal need to fast. In this chapter, we will look at the reasons we should not fast and then look at the reasons we should.

Why should we not fast?

As Jesus clearly points out here, just as He did in the previous disciplines of giving and prayer, we should not fast for the approval of men. He says in this passage that we are not to disfigure our faces so that it is obvious that we are fasting, but instead, we are to wash our faces and rub oil into the skin so that we look refreshed.

Fasting was a regularly practiced discipline of Jesus day. In fact, many of the religious people fasted twice a week. In Matthew 9:14 for example, we read where John the Baptist's disciples are asking Jesus, "How is it that we and the Pharisees fast often, but your disciples do not fast?" But while the Pharisees were champions in the practice of their spiritual disciplines, they were anything but spiritual. They had an insatiable desire, not to be drawn into God's presence and showered with His blessings, but to be in the presence of their subjects and showered with their blessings, to which Jesus says, they have succeeded! They have already received the very reward they were seeking.

When I fast, it is not something that I share with anyone other than Nan. It is kind of difficult to keep that to myself, come dinner time as the empty chair is a dead give-away. There are many things that we are called to do corporately. For example, we are called to worship corporately. Hebrews 10:25 says that we are to be in the habit of meeting together regularly for worship and for teaching. We are to study God's Word together. In Acts 2:42, we see everyone gathered together for Bible study. We are even to pray together. Acts 1:4 says that they constantly joined together in prayer. There are many other disciplines that we are to practice in the fellowship, but fasting is not one of them. There are many Old Testament examples of the entire nation of Israel being called to a corporate fast, but that does not mean that they sat around watching each other not eat. That would be kind of weird wouldn't it? They went into their own homes and devoted their personal and private time to God. Let me put this in terms that even I can understand. If my only two choices were to impress you with my piety or eat a 2" thick 16oz T-bone, you had better steer clear of my steak knife.

Secondly, we should not fast if we do not understand the discipline of fasting. I have called my church to periods of corporate fasting before, but I strongly urge them, that if they do not understand the spiritual significance of the discipline they should not participate.

Christianity is a faith-based relationship between God and His people. We are not to get caught up in doing works to warrant our salvation, because that does not work. One should never fast because people expect it, or because everyone else is doing it. That is not relationship; that is religion. Let me explain this another way. I am not a big suit-wearing kind of guy. In the winter time, I prefer sweaters. In fact, I usually only wear suits at weddings or funerals. So, if you see me in a suit, there will probably be a catering truck or a hearse parked outside the church. It is not so much that I do not like wearing suits. In fact, I love wearing suits. I feel good in a suit. Many folks wear suits to church because they want to give God their very best and if that describes you, I applaud you for that. But I do not wear a suit most Sundays because I know that many of the men in my church do not even own a suit, and I want them to know that it is far more important that they be there to give God their very best than it is to be wearing their very best. When we start doing things because everyone else is doing them, instead of doing them to glorify God, we have crossed over from relationship to religion. Fasting is no different.

Thirdly, we should not fast to get something from God other than the deeper sense of His presence. Some people believe that if you just fast and pray long enough, God will get you that new car you need, or that better job, or that trophy wife. God is not some genie in a bottle that can be rubbed just the right way and have our three wishes granted. He cannot be manipulated into responding to any of our requests.

Ok, confession time. I have been guilty of doing nice things for my wife before in an effort to manipulate her in to giving me something that I want. I realize that I am probably the only person who has ever done that, NOT! But when Nan has had a really rough day—or the kids—or ministry has driven her right into a wall, my motives for doing nice things are much purer. I do things for her, not to gain anything, but just to please her and try to separate her from her cares.

When we fast just to be closer and separate ourselves to God, we please God because our motives are pure. I am not saying that we should not fast when we are struggling with something and desire God's wisdom. Those are exactly the times we should fast. I am only saying that we should not enter that fast already knowing the direction we want to go and then somehow try gaining God's blessing for going that direction.

So then, why should we fast?

The most obvious answer is found in the first word in our passage. Once again, just as in His command to give and to pray, Jesus begins by saying, *when* we fast, not if. Jesus expects us to fast. That is not just a cultural thing. It is as much an expectation as *when* you pray, *when* you give and *when* you drink of this cup. Those are not cultural idiosyncrasies; they are divine expectations. And the purpose behind that expectation is as to be drawn into a deeper sense of God's presence. I mentioned that passage in Matthew 9 where John's disciples asked Jesus why His disciples were not fasting. Jesus responded, "How can the guests of the bridegroom mourn while he is with them? The time will come when the bridegroom will be taken from them; then they will fast." (v. 15) He was simply saying that it is not necessary for His disciples to fast since they were as close to the Father as they were going to get. He was there with them, but a day would come when He would be taken away from them and then they would need to fast.

Until we are finally reunited wholly with God, we have a need to be in His presence and fasting fills that need drawing us into a deeper sense of His presence. In 2 Corinthians 12:2, Paul writes about that deep sense of God's presence when he said, "I know a man in Christ who fourteen years ago was caught up to the third heaven. Whether it was in the body or out of the body I do not know—God knows." Paul could not explain his experience in human terms, only that he knew that he was in some place other than the physical realm.

Have you ever noticed that much of what we do as church families is centered around food? We talk about the importance of the family dinner table and how much we enjoy the food fellowships that we have after service some Sundays. I love to meet with people over breakfast or lunch. And yes, some funeral dinners are to die for! (sorry). There is just something about how filling our stomachs with worldly pleasures such as hot fudge sundaes or juicy T-bones that opens our hearts and minds to a greater sense of communicating with the person or persons with whom we are eating. That is why many first dates often take place at a restaurant!

Removing ourselves from the physical dinner table enables us to fill our stomachs and our hearts with the things of God. Jesus said to the devil, "Man shall not live on bread alone, but on every word that comes from the mouth of God." (Matthew 4:4) He also said, "Blessed are those who hunger and thirst for righteousness, for they will be filled. (Matthew 5:6) Each of us has physiological needs such as food, water, shelter, and clothing. But we are also created with a spiritual need for God. We all have appetites for feasting on God, but *until we separate ourselves from the control of our earthly needs, our need for spiritual food gets misplaced, forgotten, and eventually dismissed.* If you do not have an appetite for God, it is probably because you are too controlled by your appetite for the world, and fasting frees us from that control so we can satisfy our spiritual appetites.

When I go on my three-day prayer and fast retreats, the first day is spent in reading and praying and trying to focus on why I am there, while the second day is spent trying to talk myself out of why I am there! I spend that whole second day focusing only on my hunger and the ole' devil is right there putting words in my mouth like, *this is stupid, it's pointless, it's unnecessary, there's a T-bone waiting right by the phone. All I need to do is call for room service.* If you have never fasted for more than a day, I can tell you that that second day is probably worse than you can imagine. But then, I wake up on that third morning and God is already at my side nudging me saying, *Randy, wake up, I want to show you something really cool* and I am in that *third heaven* with God and He is showing me things in His Word that I would never have seen on my own—life-changing things. One revelation that God shares with me in that third day is just how much power my flesh has over me when I am not disciplining myself through fasting. I have found that the devil uses my flesh to keep me in check, to keep my commitment to God at the superficial level. You see, if the devil cannot have my soul for his own, he goes after the next best thing, keeping me as far away from complete surrender to God as possible. For this reason alone, it is necessary to practice abstinence from fleshly pleasures such as eating.

Billy Graham shared the following story in his book, The Holy Spirit: Activating God's Power in Your Life:

> AN ESKIMO FISHERMAN came to town every Saturday afternoon. He always brought his two dogs with him. One was white and the other was black. He had taught them to fight on command. Every Saturday afternoon in the town square the people would gather and these two dogs would fight and the fisherman would take bets. On one Saturday, the black dog would win; another Saturday, the white dog would win—but the fisherman always won! His friends began to ask him how he did it. He said, 'I starve one and feed the other. The one I feed always wins because he is stronger.'[64](Graham, 1978, 92)

You see, in my experience with fasting, I had to spend time starving, or denying my flesh in order to allow God's Spirit to have complete control of me. That does not often come just by kneeling at my bedside and asking God to reveal His world to me. When Jesus and His close circle came down from the mountain after spending time with Moses and Elijah, they were confronted by the father of a demon-possessed boy and when the disciples asked, why they could not exorcize the demon, Jesus said, "*This kind can come out by nothing but prayer and fasting.*" (Mark 9:29, NKJV)

There are things that God wants to show us, but He can only do so when we have an appetite for it and fasting opens that passageway allowing us to feast on Him as He communicates with us, just as we communicate with loved ones around the dinner table.

John Piper writes in his book A Hunger for God,

> The greatest enemy of hunger for God is not poison but apple pie. It is not the banquet of the wicked that dulls our appetite for heaven, but endless nibbling at the table

[64] Graham, Billy. 1978. *The Holy Spirit: Activating God's Power in Your Life.* Waco: Word Publishing Co.

> of the world. It is not the X-rated video, but the prime-time dribble of triviality we drink in every night… If you don't feel strong desires for the manifestation of the glory of God, it is not because you have drunk deeply and are satisfied. It is because you have nibbled so long at the table of the world. Your soul is stuffed with small things, and there is no room for the great. God did not create you for this. There is an appetite for God. And it can be awakened. I invite you to turn from the dulling effects of food and the dangers of idolatry, and to say with some simple fast 'This much, O God, I want you. [65](Piper, 1997, 56)

Let me close with this classic illustration of how gold was purified in ancient days: The ore was placed in a great cauldron with fire underneath it; as it is heated up, the ore would melt and all the impurities would rise to the surface. The smelter (this is the guy doing the smelting) would then skim off the impurities, called *dross*. Then he would restoke the fire again and again and more and more of the impurities would rise to the top until the gold was pure. It is said that he knew that the gold was pure when he could see his reflection in the gold. God accomplishes the same thing in us whereby He heats us up through trials and adversity and then He scrapes off all of the dross, purifying us in the process until such time that He can see His reflection in us. Fasting is nothing more than allowing God to heat ourselves up whereby allowing Him to expedite that process of purification.

The goal in this chapter is not to twist your arm to persuade you to fast. It is simply to help you better understand the eternally rich rewards in doing so. The question is not, *do you have the stomach for fasting,* the question is *how badly do you want to fill the stomach you have for God?*

[65] Piper, John. 1997. *A Hunger for God.* Wheaton: Crossway

SECTION FOUR

THE KINGDOM AND THE TREASURES

I read about a letter sent to Ann Landers sometime back by a lady who was married to a tightwad who horded every penny he ever made and vowed to tuck twenty dollars of every paycheck away in his mattress. When he was taken ill and toward the end of his life, he said to his wife, *I want you to promise me one thing. I want you to promise me that when I'm dead, you will take my money from under the mattress and put it in my casket so that I can take it all with me.* She promised to fulfill his request and upon his death, she took all of the money out from under the mattress and deposited it all into their account. Then she went to the funeral home and as promised, put every penny he had saved into his coffin. She paid by check.

This bit of irony reminds us of the impact our treasures have on our behavior, but more important, it reminds us of Jesus' emphasis on how those treasures are to be handled. Over the course of the next several verses in Chapter 6, Jesus moves His focus once again to an issue that is near and dear to all of us, our priorities! It is here in these verses that we are brought face to face with reality and forced to answer the question, *what is truly important in our lives?* Throughout His sermon, *Jesus has been bringing together two parts of our lives: our spiritual self and our real self;* and He does that because for a Christian, there is no distinction between the two. Our spiritual self *is* our real self and now, having masterfully helped us to realize that in the previous portion of

His sermon, He moves into those things that are very personal to us and commands that we put feet to our faith in respect to them. He concludes this portion on our priorities (our treasures) with Matthew 6:33, "But seek first his kingdom and his righteousness, and all these things will be given to you as well." Read on!

SIXTEEN

Heavenly Hoarders

Do not store up for yourselves treasures on earth, where moths and vermin destroy, and where thieves break in and steal. But store up for yourselves treasures in heaven, where moths and vermin do not destroy, and where thieves do not break in and steal. For where your treasure is, there your heart will be also. (Matt. 6:19-21)

I mentioned that I love board games, but my all-time favorite board game is *Monopoly.* When I sit down to that game and have all this different colored money sitting in front of me and gazing at all of the different money-making opportunities from *Baltic* to *Boardwalk* something happens that just changes me. I turn from this little loving fuzz-ball into a jaguar that has not eaten in over a week and anyone who gets in my way is fair game. Nan will not play with me anymore because she complains that the game takes too long and I insist on playing till the winner is declared. She gets upset saying, *you always have to play until someone wins.* I am like, *uh, yeah… Isn't that the point?*

With that said, there is something worth noting here. *Monopoly* runs totally contrary to the teachings of Jesus. Jesus said, "Do not store up for yourselves treasures on earth." *Monopoly* is all about storing up treasures on earth. I think that at least to some extent, *Monopoly* is so popular because it reflects the mindset of this world: *work more to get more to have more to buy more.* And I think we do that because the world teaches us to measure our success by the size of bank accounts and the square footage of our homes. But just as He has been doing throughout His entire sermon, Jesus commands us to measure ourselves by a different standard, by storing up for ourselves treasures in heaven “where moth and rust do not destroy, and where thieves do not break in and steal. For where your treasure is, there your heart will be also.” (Matt. 6:20) So how should the Christian’s success be measured if not by those things that the world measures? The answer is found in Jesus’ teaching, those things that are in heaven, those things that have eternal value.

One way that disciples ought to measure their success is by the amount of time and effort they put into their serving. I realize that you are probably already thinking that this is just another pitch on a pastor’s part to get people engaged in serving and getting them off their holy derrieres, and well, it is. But only because what you do in church is a direct reflection of how you live out in the world, and ultimately, where your treasures are located. If you are serving God in church, it is a good bet that you are serving Him in your homes, neighborhoods and workplaces as well. You have heard it said many times that only about 20% of the people, do 80% of the work in the church, 100% of the time, but I cannot help but believe that this is some sort of invisible glass ceiling just waiting for the right congregation to come along and smash to smithereens. I refuse to accept the premise that your church or my church will never get more than one out of five people to commit to doing what Christ calls all of us to do, serve. Sometimes I think the local church cripples itself by buying into the premise that we will only ever get 20% of the people to step up and be the Church, by not pushing the other 80% to do likewise! Why should we not expect 100% of our membership to be actively involved in serving their church? I realize there are physical limitations with many people, but there are so many activities in the body that can be done and need to be done, such as prayer ministry, calling and card ministry, visitation, mentoring, even teaching. One of my dearest friends was an 86-year old who taught adult Sunday school every week and everyone wanted to be in her class. We had to move her classroom into the largest room in the fellowship building because it was the only place that could seat her entire class.

The ministering activities are the things that have eternal value. There is a young lady named Bridget at our church who grew up at Mary’s Chapel. Her grandparents helped build the church. One day, Bridget shared her testimony of when she was just a small child in Ms. Lois’ Sunday school class. She stated that sometimes, she would be the only one to show up for class and Ms. Lois would teach her like she was teaching an overcrowded classroom. She may not remember a single Bible lesson that Ms. Lois taught her, but you can bet that she remembers every single life-lesson Ms. Lois taught, because she lived it out in her own life and taught it to her own children and many others.

Vacation Bible School (VBS) is one of the most grueling weeks of the year at any church, but the day that we decide to discontinue VBS because of the effort involved is the day I go looking for another church! Every drop of perspiration that one servant sweats is another eternal seed that gets planted in the lives of these little ones and fulfills Jesus' commandment to *Go and make disciples!*

Another eternal measurement of success is found in the disciple's giving. The following is a true story that came out of the Titanic Disaster:

> On April 14, 1912, at 10:00 p.m. the Titanic crashed into an iceberg in the mid-Atlantic and four hours later sank. One woman in a lifeboat asked if she could go back to her room. She was given only three minutes to do so. She hurried down the corridors, already tilting dangerously, through the gambling room piled ankle-deep in money. In her room were her treasures waiting to be taken, but instead, she snatched up three oranges and hurried back to the boat. One hour before she would have naturally chosen diamonds over oranges, but in the face of death, values are seen more clearly.[66(Thompson, 2010, 24)]

Thirty minutes earlier, she would never have chosen even a whole crate of oranges over even her smallest of treasures. But the angel of death had come aboard the Titanic and instantly transformed all of life's values. *Priceless jewels became worthless and worthless fruit became priceless!*

As you gather with your church family this Sunday, stop and take notice of the magnificent building that you call home. If it is anything like mine, maybe the paneling is outdated and maybe the carpet is well-worn, or the pews have seen their better days. It is very possible that you can find

---

[66] Thompson, John L. 2010. *Urban Impact.* Eugene: Wipf and Stock Publishers

any number of things that need some tender loving care. Now, look around once more, but this time, look at it through the blood, sweat, and tears of those faithful Christians who gave everything they had to a common cause because they believed in something much bigger than themselves, something of eternal value. At my church, most of that generation has passed on to glory now, but I want to believe that there is a glorious cloud of witnesses up in heaven cheering and high-fiving each other every time our little ones gather for children's church, or we meet for worship, Sunday school, or Bible study. I cannot help but believe that every time God is honored by our worship, He looks over at that Mary's Chapel bunch in heaven who gave their all and honors them with His smile of approval for the sacrifices they made.

Every time you drop your offering in the plate, it is an investment in something much bigger than yourself and you can rest assured that you will see that offering again—in heaven! Every dollar you invest in God's Church will reap an eternity of reward. *You cannot out-give God, because He will just give you more so you have more to give.* Here is the real test. Stop reading right now, pull out your checkbook and look over the last 90 days. Then ask yourself this question, *Would I want Jesus to be my accountant?* The value of things in which we place the most importance is reflected in those bank registers.

There is a story floating around somewhere that John Maxwell, one of the world's top Christian experts on money, shared on tithing. The story goes something like this: When he was pasturing, a man from his church came to him at his office with a financial problem. He said, "I used to make $200 per week and I tithed my $20 faithfully. But now I'm making 10 times that… I'm having trouble turning loose of a $200 tithe. It doesn't seem fair, when most people don't have to give near that. What can I do? Maxwell pulled him to his knees and said, let's pray about it." Then he prayed, "Lord, my brother here is having trouble obeying you. His problem started when you began blessing Him so much financially. Lord, I pray you'll bring providential circumstances into his life that will reduce his salary back to where it used to be, so he can once again obey you*!*" The man jumped to his feet and said, "oh no, I can tithe, I can tithe*!*"

Finally, the disciple's success is measured by those they help get into heaven. There is nothing greater nor more satisfying in this life than to know that you helped open someone's heart to heaven, I know. I was present at all three of my children's births and the experience of a new life coming into this world is indescribable. That is as close as one can get to the experience of witnessing someone being born again.

Every time we stop long enough from trying to make money, or play with our toys to help someone through a crisis, to help mend a broken heart, to give a shoulder to cry on, to teach someone a biblical truth, or to lend a hand to someone in need, we are laying up for ourselves treasures in Heaven. I am not suggesting that everyone you try to help will make it there. We know different. I have some dear friends, Denny and Wendy who experienced that sometime back. They opened their hearts and their small auto garage business to a troubled young man just to give him a second chance and it ended badly. The young man took advantage of their Christian generosity and compassion and stole from their business. But don't you think that God has stored something very special for Denny and Wendy in heaven for their obedience to Him? When we truly believe that everything belongs to Him, we cannot be taken advantage of because it does not belong to us in the first place.

In my basement, there is a little room in which I keep many of my tools. I have tools that I have not used in over eight years when I first stored them there, yet I still hold on to them. One day I will find a good home for them where they will actually get used. Those tools have no value whatsoever because they are not used for anything. A tool is only of value if it is being used for its intended purpose. Likewise, *we are all tools for the kingdom of heaven,* but unless we are being used for our intended purpose, we have no eternal value. We were made for a kingdom purpose that has real kingdom value and God expects each of us to use what gifts and talents He has given us for that purpose. Every person with whom you come in contact is an opportunity from God to plant an eternal seed.

I mentioned my friend Marcus back in Chapter Six. Actually, Marcus is our Associate Pastor at Mary's Chapel. He and his wife Linda grew up at Mary's Chapel and then sometime later on in his adult years was called into the pastoral ministry. Marcus is a board member, Sunday school teacher, fill-in pastor and preacher, maintenance man, choir member and occasional fill-in worship leader. Linda also teaches Sunday school, children's church and is also a choir member, just to name a few of the responsibilities this couple has taken on. In my nine years as Pastor at Mary's Chapel, I have never known either of them to ever say no to anything that was asked of them and they are always the first to sign up to help or support with anything. I do not know of two more generous people than Marcus and Linda.

All of the little children of Mary's Chapel know Pastor Marcus as the *Quarter-Man.* Each Sunday, Marcus stands in the foyer and gives away at least one roll of quarters (sometimes more) to the children who pass through the front doors. It is wonderful to watch because no matter who is standing in the foyer (and there are several who gather there), when a child enters, the eyes immediately scan the foyer looking for Pastor Marcus. Marcus explained to me that when he was a child at Mary's Chapel, he often did not have even a penny to put into the offering plate as it was passed and as he stated, "I never want a single child to have nothing to put into the plate themselves."

A couple of years ago, the home of Marcus and Linda was broken into. The robbers got away with cash and valuables well into the thousands of dollars, including the bowls of quarters that Marcus used to give to the children. I remember being taken back by their response. Sure, they were disappointed and who could not feel personally violated after something like happen to them. But Marcus and Linda never skipped a beat. I never once heard a discouraging word and Christ's light continued to shine through them ever-so brightly.

Some months ago, it happened a second time! That's right, they were robbed once again while they were at church and I only found out about it when Marcus explained that he was on his way over to the church to change out the locks. It seems that this time, the robber(s) got away with his truck keys which also had the church keys on them. They had just lost thousands of dollars more in cash and jewelry and Marcus' greatest concern was for his church.

When I spoke with Marcus after this last incident, I got the same reply as I had gotten after the first, "It's only stuff and it all belongs to God anyway" and then he would end with that twangy country laugh that Marcus is famous for. Marcus and Linda are living examples of what it means to be *Heavenly Hoarders.* The things on this earth are only temporal. Everything that we have stored up here in our banks and basements will one day cease to exist—at least for us. But now, here is where the heavenly treasure comes in: A few weeks after the last break-in, I was asked to have Pastor Marcus and Linda come to the platform and without saying a word, all of the children in the church got up and formed a line and as they passed by, they fist-pumped (that is how Marcus presented them with their quarters) Pastor Marcus and gave him a quarter and to Ms. Linda, they gave homemade necklaces to replace the jewelry that was stolen. After that, every teenager and every adult in the church came to the front and showered both of them with more quarters and trinkets than they could possibly carry off themselves.

I am not sure how much the couple received in quarters, but I am sure it did not come close to the thousands of dollars they lost. And I am also sure that the home-made necklaces they received did not amount to much in terms of monetary value compared to Linda's precious jewelry that was stolen. But here is something else that I am sure of. One day they will soon forget the pain and disappointment of those break-ins and possibly even the valuables that were stolen during the break-ins. But I am absolutely 100% proof-positive that Pastor Marcus and Ms. Linda will NEVER forget the day when more than a hundred people whom they had impacted so willingly and wonderfully came forward to reward these heavenly hoarders with treasure that cannot be stolen or destroyed.

Like Marcus and Linda, on the surface, it would seem that Jesus' enemies got the best of him too. Jesus never owned a car, a home, or even clothes beyond what He was wearing (which were also stolen at the cross). All Jesus ever received in this world was betrayal, abandonment, and a horrible death on a Roman cross. By the world's standards, He was a complete failure in every sense. But His life was not focused on this world and His success was not measured by the world's standards. Jesus was also a Heavenly Hoarder and His treasure is found in every believer who trusts Him for their salvation. Consider stopping from advancing to the next chapter for just a moment and take an inventory of your journey. On what do you place great value in your life? Better yet, what does your checkbook and day planner say you place great value on in your life? By what standard of measurement do you measure your success!

SEVENTEEN

The Eye is the Lamp

The eye is the lamp of the body. If your eyes are healthy, your whole body will be full of light. But if your eyes are unhealthy, your whole body will be full of darkness. If then the light within you is darkness, how great is that darkness. (Matt. 6:22-23)

I love the sport of deer hunting! I took up the sport only after moving to north Alabama in 2009. I bought my first deer rifle, a *Remington .308,* from a dear friend of mine named James. He and his wife Jan allow me to hunt on their property each season for which I am grateful, because they are allowing me to keep my freezer full! I mention that because I want to tell you about my rifle scope which will introduce the next commandment of Jesus. My scope is not an expensive one, and one of the ways that I know that is by the fact that using it is worse than aiming with the naked eye at dawn or dusk. When I look through the lens, it is actually darker than if I were not using a scope at all and nothing is in focus. There are more expensive scopes that can adjust to and make up for the lack of light, but I am too cheap to buy one. I have sat in a stand waiting for the sun to come up while watching what I believed to be a deer in the field. However, I was unable to do anything about it because, although I could clearly see that there was an animal in the field, I could not determine if it was a deer or someone's cow. One day, I will break down and buy a stronger scope so that those with livestock who live nearby will be able to sleep at night during deer season!

In this chapter, we are looking at Jesus drawing a comparison between the human eye and a lamp. In our passage, Jesus speaks about the good eye and the bad eye and what affect each has on our bodies and our lives. Jesus says that, "if your eyes are unhealthy, your whole body will be full of darkness." If then the light within you is darkness, how great is that darkness. So, the first question that we should ask of this passage is what makes our eyes unhealthy besides a bb gun, rubber band, or poorly aimed cast of a fishing pole? Jesus says that whatever we allow into our eyes affects our whole body. The first thing that comes to most of our minds is TV shows and movies and while most who are reading this probably would never sit down to an X-rated film, far too many of us are more than willing to sit down to movies that come awfully close. In fact, according to Wikipedia, the *NC-17* movie rating was created in 1990 to replace the *X-Rating.*[67(Wikipedia)] I wonder if that change had anything to do with wanting to increase viewership with those who would NEVER go see an X-rated film… but I digress. And while most would never look at a girlie magazine, far too many have no problem with reading salacious novels that describe scenes in detail far worse than those magazines.

The problem with entertaining ourselves with those images and thoughts is that those same images and thoughts get burned into our psyche long after the actual image is gone. Let me illustrate. Pick something where you are right now and look at it for 5 seconds, then close your eyes. Chances are that you can still see that image in your mind, even in vivid detail. Our brains are amazing organs. You have heard of people who have photographic memories where they can study a complex wiring diagram for ten seconds and are then able to describe in detail what they saw. In truth, we all have photographic memories to an extent in that images that excite us, amaze us, or scare us, get seared into our minds.

I shared with you once before about a friend who I tried to help kick his problem with porn. You will remember that he was at his most vulnerable point when driving home from work passing the video store. I simply suggested that he change his route home—problem solved. But there was an even bigger problem that he had to deal with, one that he and he alone was going to have to work through with help from the Holy Spirit and sound spiritual guidance. The problem was that the saturation of those images burned into his psyche affected his relationship with his wife.

[67] Wikipedia. *Movie Ratings.* wikipedia.org/wiki/List_of_NC-17_rated_films

Jesus is telling us that when we allow darkness into our eyes, that darkness fills our whole bodies and by that, He includes our lives which includes the lives of those closest to us. And while there is always hope in redemption, through repentance, I believe that sin is a very slippery slope. Allow me to try and explain through a personal confession:

I can still remember the very first time I viewed pornography. I was probably thirteen years old playing out in a field near a friend's house and came across a *Playboy Magazine* that someone had thrown out there in the middle of the field. I remember vividly as though it was yesterday how my friend and I sat there and looked at all of these pictures for what seemed like hours. I remember it so well that here more than forty years later, I can take you back to that exact same spot where we sat (although I am sure the people who live there now wouldn't appreciate it since it is now an apartment complex). I can remember the first time I viewed pornography, but I cannot remember the second, third, fourth, or fifth time even though they were more recent than the first. Why do you think that is? For starters, that very first time, something brand new and shocking was seared into my mind, but the second, third and fourth time were not so shocking. Same pictures, same mind, but much less of an impact.

In Romans Chapter 1, Paul is also explaining the phenomena of the *slippery slope*. Let me set the stage first: Paul begins the chapter (after his greetings) with a bold statement about not being ashamed of the gospel for it is the power to save. Let's pick it up there:

> [16]For I am not ashamed of the gospel, because it is the power
> of God that brings salvation to everyone who believes: first
> to the Jew, then to the Gentile. [17]For in the gospel the
> righteousness of God is revealed—a righteousness that is
> by faith from first to last, just as it is written: 'The righteous
> will live by faith.' [18]The wrath of God is being revealed
> from heaven against all the godlessness and wickedness
> of people, who suppress the truth by their wickedness,
> [19]since what may be known about God is plain to them,
> because God has made it plain to them. [20]For since the
> creation of the world God's invisible qualities—his eternal
> power and divine nature—have been clearly seen, being

> understood from what has been made, so that people are without excuse.

Notice the references Paul makes to eyesight, or understanding. When someone tries to explain something to us and we finally understand, we usually respond by saying, *I SEE!* (coincidence? I think not). Paul is pointing out in these verses, especially in v. 20, that God has *revealed* enough of Himself, even in nature, that no one will be excused from the consequences of their disobedience and rejection. But here is where I am taking all of this, because in the remainder of the chapter, he lays out a progressive pattern of how sin *darkens* our hearts and slowly extinguishes the light that God has placed in us. Follow me:

> v. 24: "Therefore God gave them over in the sinful desires of their hearts to sexual impurity for the degrading of their bodies with one another."

The Greek word here for *desires* is the word, *epithuma* and in every New Testament use of this word, the writers refer to general desires of the heart, not necessarily bad and not necessarily of a sexual nature. For example, in Mark 4:19, Jesus uses the word in His parable of the sower to describe those things which we *desire* that choke out His word (bad), but in Luke 22:15, He speaks about His *desire* to eat the Passover meal with His disciples (good). To the unbelieving Jews in John 8:44, Jesus rebukes them saying, "you want to carry out your father's desires" (bad). And finally, in Philippians 1:23, Paul uses the word to describe his torn *desires* between being with the Lord and that of finishing his work here on earth (good). There are many uses of this word *epithuma* in the New Testament, but as I have satisfactorily proven here, its use is both general and non-moral in nature.

In v. 26, Paul moves on down the slippery slope and says, "Because of this, God gave them over to shameful lusts. Even their women exchanged natural sexual relations for unnatural ones."

The Greek word here is *pathos* and it describes *desire* of a specifically sexual nature. Unlike the previous word which is used many times, this word is only found in two other places in the New Testament, Colossians 3:5 and 1 Thessalonians 4:5, both of which are references to sexual sin.

Finally, in Romans 1:28, Paul says, "...so God gave them over to a depraved mind, so that they do what ought not to be done." The Greek word used here is *adokimos.* It means worthless, disqualified, failed, rejected, unfit (see 1 Corinthians 9:27, 2 Corinthians 13:5-7, 2 Timothy 3:8, Titus 1:16 and Hebrews 6:8).

It is my opinion then, that what Paul has laid out for us here is a natural (or unnatural as it be) progression of how sin darkens our senses to itself. And the more darkness we allow into our hearts through our lack of *focus* on the things of God (Colossians 3:2, Philippians 4:8), the more likely we are, not only to accept, but to embrace that next level down into the pits of hell where we are then *cast-away* (*adokimos*) by God.

Back to my hunting stories... There is another characteristic about rifle scopes that I was not made aware of until my second year of hunting. When I bought my rifle, I sighted it in about a month before the season started and had that thing sighted in on a quarter-sized bullseye at 50 yards. As a result, my freezer provided me with a near endless supply of tasty venison. At the end of the season, I cleaned it and gently put it back into its case and stored it in the closet. When I returned to the hunting fields the next season, on two back-to-back outings, I completely missed a deer at a fairly close range. I was very puzzled and my available freezer space was growing daily. I sought the wisdom from Tommy, an avid deer hunter at church. Tommy is a plethora of tree-stand wisdom whom I very wisely declared as my teacher and I his disciple. I shared my dilemma with Tommy and he informed me that scopes can come out of focus just by normal handling and should be re-sighted before each season. Because I was unaware of that little tidbit of knowledge, I failed to do my job in controlling the local deer population. Rest assured, I returned with a new vengeance the following year and made up for the mistakes of my past.

In speaking about good eyes, Jesus said, "The eye is the lamp of the body. If your eyes are healthy, your whole body will be full of light." *(Matt. 6:22)* The first rule we must learn in making and keeping our eyes healthy is that it does not happen automatically. Like my scope, it takes regular evaluation and maintenance to ensure that we stay focused on what is good, holy, and pure. Remember what Jesus' teaching is about in this segment—our treasures! It is great that you go to church most Sundays (unless there is a good game on), but what are you doing to keep your eyes healthy between Sundays?

When I am driving down Rascal Town Road (the country road I lived on while in Alabama), there are three fields that I always look into to check for deer and, to be honest, I have absolutely no clue why I do that. I do not have my rifle with me and I am pretty sure I have no intent of pulling my minivan off the road and running them down, yet I do it anyway. When I am driving down the road with Nan and I come to those spots, I stretch my neck looking for the deer and there appears to be some correlation between my eyes and my steering wheel, because I inevitably run off the road until Nan screams at the top of her lungs and I quickly snap back to attention as though I was in control the whole time. I know, you have never done that. Right? But here is my point: when I am looking straight ahead at what I should be looking at, I am good to go. Never is there a danger of running off the road; but take my eyes off for two seconds and I am all over the place. Any texters want to add to this discussion?

When we keep our sights on what we know to be right, there is never a danger of running off the road, or worse yet, crashing and burning all together. Staying in focus is a challenge for everyone. We must all admit that when we get busy, we get tired, or we just get consumed with life, we tend to lose our focus. But not to be out-done, when things are humming along for us without a care in the world, we also lose focus on what is truly important in life, and we stop "…seeking first His kingdom… ."

French Philosopher Pierre Teilhard de Chardin once said, *we aren't physical beings having a spiritual experience, we are spiritual beings having a physical experience.*[68](Chardin, Unk) The physical being within each of us will perish, but the spiritual being will last forever. We must focus on building up the spiritual being and let our physical being submit to God's Spirit in us (remember the lesson on *fasting*?). Jesus said in Luke 9:*23,* "If anyone desires to come after Me, let him deny himself, and take up his cross daily, and follow Me." He is saying that our focus ought to be on the cross and not on ourselves.

Everyone struggles with feeding their flesh; am I right? We have already

[68] Chardin, Pierre Teilhard de. Date Unk. *Brain Quote.* braintquote.com/quotes/quotes/p/pierreteil160888.html

covered over and over how there is an on-going battle for our attention (and our souls) between the kingdom of self and the kingdom of heaven. No one is immune to being selfish. Paul says that in the flesh dwells no good thing. Every day, we must face life from one of two perspectives: the here and now, or the eternal. Here is an apparent true story of how those two perspectives (self vs. heaven) cannot co-exist in the disciple:

> A certain tribe in Africa elects a new king every seven years but it invariably kills its old king. For seven years, the member of the tribe enjoying this high honor is provided with every luxury known to savage life. During these years, his authority is absolute, even to the power of life and death. For seven years, he rules, is honored and surfeited with possessions, but at the end he dies. Every member of the tribe is aware of this, for it is a custom of long standing; but there is never lacking an applicant for the post. For seven years of luxury and power men are willing to sacrifice the remainder of life's expectation. Scores and hundreds and thousands are willing to be bankrupt through eternity if they may only win their millions here.[69](Mitchell, 1922, 133)

If we lose sight of the cross, everything in the here and now will get out of focus. We will all be just like the guy who said, *I will build bigger barns* but did not realize that his time on this earth was up. The cross is where the flesh must die first if we are to become His disciples. The cross is still foolishness and is still a stumbling block to the unbeliever. Jesus says, "the eye is the lamp of the body and the healthy eye brings light into the whole body". The healthy eye represents someone who is single-focused on things of God.

Author Chuck Swindoll once shared a story about an actual experience one man had in the deep south. He says:

---

[69] Mitchell, William Samuel. 1921. *Elements of Personal Christianity.* New York: The Methodist Book Concern

> When I lived in Atlanta several years ago, I noticed in the Yellow Pages, in the listing of restaurants, an entry for a place called The Church of God Grill. The peculiar name aroused my curiosity and I dialed the number. A man answered with a cheery, 'Hello! Church of God Grill!' I asked how his restaurant had been given such an unusual name, and he told me: 'Well, we had a little mission down here, and we started selling chicken dinners after church on Sunday to help pay the bills. Well, people liked the chicken, and we did such a good business, that eventually we cut back on the church service. After a while, we just closed down the church altogether and kept on serving chicken dinners. We kept the name we started with, and that's Church of God Grill.[70](Swindoll, 1998, 214)

If my focus is money, I'll find ways to make more, invest more and spend more. If I am into playing sports, I will find ways to train harder, strategize better and play more often.

It is all about focus. Jesus began this lesson in v.19 when He said, "For where your treasure is, there your heart will be also". If your focus in on being a godly provider for your family, a godly parent, a godly husband or wife, it is going to happen. If your focus is on drawing closer to God and committing yourself to His teachings, it is going to happen. The truth of the matter is, we are all exactly as Christ-like as we choose to be, no more, no less. *We cannot say, I would like to become more like Christ and then have no ambition to set out to do* those things that will help us in achieving that goal. That is then not a goal, but a mere passing fancy, pipe dream and wishful thinking. Every morning you wake up, you are given a multitude of decisions to make. It is going to be a good day or it is going to be a bad day. I am going to live selfishly, I am going to live for Christ. I am going to choose to do what I know is wrong, I am going to choose to do what I know is right. Which eye has your focus? Is your healthy eye in charge of what enters your life, or is the bad eye calling the shots?

---

70 Swindoll, Charles. 1998. *Tale of the Tardy Oxcart.* Nashville: W. Publishing Group

EIGHTEEN

You Cannot Serve Two Masters

No one can serve two masters. Either you will hate the one and love the other, or you will be devoted to the one and despise the other. You cannot serve both God and money. (Matt.6:24)

A husband and wife were attending a county fair where, for twenty dollars a person, a man was giving rides in an old airplane. The couple wanted to go up but they thought twenty dollars a person was too expensive so they tried to negotiate a lower price. *We'll pay you twenty dollars for both of us,* they said to the pilot. *After all, we'll both have to squeeze into that tiny cockpit that was built for only one person.* The pilot refused to lower his fare, but he made a counter offer. He suggested, *Pay me the full price of twenty dollars each, and I'll take you up. If you don't say one word during the flight, I'll give you all your money back.* The couple agreed and got into the plane. Up they went and the pilot proceeded to perform every trick he knew, looping and whirling and flying upside down and lots more. Finally, when the plane had landed, the pilot said to the husband, *Congratulations! Here's your money back; you didn't say a single word.* To which the man replied, *Nope, but you almost got me when my wife fell out.*[71](Nicandro, 2006)

In this segment called "The kingdom and the Treasures," we have been looking at treasures from the kingdom of self vs. treasures from the kingdom of heaven. The passage before us in this chapter is the only portal

---

[71] Nicandro, Eddie. 2006. *Top Priority.* November 9, 2006 https://www.sermoncentral.com/sermons/top-priority-eddie-nicandro-sermon-on-commitment-to-christ-97740?ref=SermonSerps

that allows us to store up heavenly treasures and be single-minded in our focus. I stated previously that I believe God views our possessions as His greatest competitor and it is for this reason that I believe Jesus speaks more about this issue than even heaven or hell, by a large margin. *Attachment to money leads to detachment from God.*

Matthew 6:24 says, "No one can serve two masters. Either he will hate the one and love the other, or he will be devoted to the one and despise the other. You cannot serve both God and money." In the Greek, the word for money is mammon, which not only includes money, but all possessions. *Mammon* fights for control over our lives and it has many of the same characteristics of deity. It promises security, freedom and power. In the 1913 edition of the Catholic Encyclopedia, High Pope writes:

> During the Middle Ages, Mammon was commonly personified as the demon of wealth and greed. Thus Peter Lombard (II, dist. 6) says, "Riches are called by the name of a devil, namely Mammon, for Mammon is the name of a devil, by which name riches are called according to the Syrian tongue." [72](Pope, 1910)

In his famous poem Paradise Lost, John Milton writes of a very interesting (albeit lengthy) speech that the demon known as *Mammon* made to his superior, the devil, in which he tried to persuade the devil to change tactics in their battle against God. Here is that speech along with my translation interwoven:[73](Milton, 2005, 48-50)

> Either to dethrone the King of Heaven we war, if war be best, or to regain our own right lost. Him to unthrone we then may hope, when everlasting fate shall yield to fickle chance, and chaos judge the strife. The former, vain to hope, argues as vain the latter; for what place can be for us within Heaven's bound, unless Heaven's Lord supreme

---

[72] Pope, Hugh. 1910. *Mammon. The Catholic Encyclopedia. Vol. 9.* Jul 3, 1910. New York: Robert Appleton Company http://www.newadvent.org/cathen/09580b.htm>. https://en.wikisource.org/wiki/Catholic_Encyclopedia_(1913)/Mammon

[73] Milton, John. 2005. *Paradise Lost.* Indianapolis: Hackett Publishing

> we overpower? Suppose he should relent and publish grace to all, on promise made of new subjection; with what eyes could we stand in his presence humble, and receive strict laws imposed, to celebrate his throne with warbled hymns, and to his Godhead sing forced hallelujahs, while he lordly sits our envied sovereign, and his altar breathes ambrosial odors and ambrosial flowers, our servile offerings?

Mammon explains to Satan that this battle with *the King of Heaven* is futile and even if it wasn't, why would they want to be back in heaven anyway? Even if God were to extend grace to them, they would then be forced to sing *warbled hymns* and *forced hallelujahs.* Mammon continues:

> This must be our task in Heaven, this our delight. How wearisome eternity so spent in worship paid to whom we hate! Let us not then pursue, by force impossible, by leave obtained unacceptable, though in Heaven, our state of splendid vassalage; but rather seek our own good from ourselves, and from our own live to ourselves, though in this vast recess, free and to none accountable, preferring hard liberty before the easy yoke of servile pomp. Our greatness will appear then most conspicuous when great things of small, useful of hurtful, prosperous of adverse, we can create, and in what place soe'er thrive under evil, and work ease out of pain through labor and endurance. This deep world of darkness do we dread?

Mammon then pitches his idea to Satan insisting that they can *imitate* heaven here on earth and *seek our own good from ourselves... free and to none accountable.* He concludes:

> How oft amidst thick clouds and dark doth Heaven's all-ruling Sire choose to reside, his glory unobscured, and with the majesty of darkness round covers his throne, from whence deep thunders roar. Mustering their rage,

> and Heaven resembles Hell! As he our darkness, cannot we his light imitate when we please?

He states that since Jesus' Spirit (*Heaven's all-ruling Sire*) resides on earth in all of *His glory unobscured,* they should also imitate His light to draw others to them (*...for Satan himself masquerades as an angel of light,* 2 Corinthians 11:14). Mammon concludes:

> This desert soil wants not her hidden luster, gems and gold; nor want we skill or art from whence to raise magnificence; and what can Heaven show more? Our torments also may, in length of time, become our elements, these piercing fires as soft as now severe, our temper changed into their temper; which must needs remove the sensible of pain. All things invite to peaceful counsels, and the settled state of order, how in safety best we may compose our present evils, with regard of what we are and where, dismissing quite all thoughts of war. Ye have what I advise.

Mammon concludes his speech insisting that heaven cannot compare to the *magnificence* that they can muster here on earth. He goes on to say that over time, the bondage caused by such things as greed and lust will be their victim's *soft, tempered, peaceful and settled state of order.* In other words, it will be their victim's comfort, because it will be the only thing they know. This is the classic, *Frog in the Kettle* where the frog, basking in its warmth, does not even notice the water reaching boiling temperature.

It would appear that Satan took Mammon's advice, because it is exactly the effect that possessions have on the carnal heart. First of all, the things of God are foolishness to the unbeliever—things such as worship (1 Corinthians 2:14). And since they are foolish, having to engage in such forced activities out of duty, leaves the unbeliever at war with God and with himself. Then, because there is no peace either with God or with themselves, the unbeliever albeit unconsciously perhaps, sets up his own *kingdom* here on earth by means of acquiring possessions to give them the appearance of peace and contentment—not realizing that he is actually in bondage to himself and his possessions, because he must continue acquiring things in a futile attempt to find true peace and contentment. One day, every knee shall bow before God Almighty and that person who placed their faith in their things, will now find themselves naked before their Judge, *Heaven's all-ruling Sire.*

Jesus does not tell us in v. 24 that we cannot own nice things, or live in nice houses, or have comfortable incomes. But He does sternly warn us that to make those things the centerpiece of our lives, places us in bondage to them and blinds us to the things of God.

One day a farmer's cow gave birth to two calves, one solid and one spotted. He told his wife that he felt led to raise them and give the profit from one of them to the work of the Lord. She thought that was a great idea. She asked, which one goes to God? He said, *it doesn't matter.* A few days later he came in with a sad expression and said, *honey, I have bad news. What?* His wife responded, to which he replied, *The Lord's calf died!*[74]

John Stott put it this way, "We cannot maintain a life of extravagance and a good conscience simultaneously. One or the other has to be sacrificed. Either we keep our conscience and reduce our affluence by giving generously and helping those in need, or we keep our affluence and smother our conscience. We have to choose between God and money." [75](Stott, 1992,47)

One of the things that I teach young people in helping them establish a family budget is a lesson from Christian Financial Management Planner, Dave Ramsey. A budget helps us to become master over our money instead of slave to it. Francis Bacon once rightly said, "Money is a great servant, but a bad master." [76](Prentiss, 2020, 31)

In the military, there is line of authority called *chain of command.* The idea is that each person has one person to whom they report and take orders from. When you have more than one person to whom you answer and unless they are Siamese twins sharing the same brain, there will always be differences in leadership, which result in different priorities, resulting in different demands, and ultimately resulting in frustration. In the military, that kind of confusion can get people killed! This *chain of command* thing was not invented by the military, it was invented by God

---

[74] Lloyd-Jones, Martyn. Date Unk. *Humor. Sermon Illustrations*. sermonillustrations.com/a-z/g/giving.htm

[75] Stott, John. 1992. *Topical Memory System: Life Issues.* NavPress Software

[76] Prentiss, Demi. 2020. *Making Money Holy.* New York: Church Publishing

and He reminds us of that in Matthew 6:33. When Paul says in Romans 12:1 to offer ourselves as living sacrifices, that is a devotion that cannot be shared with anyone or anything. Whatever we give devotion to, that becomes our god. It may be money, toys, relationships, vanity, or any other number of things, that in and of themselves, are not evil, but become evil when we allow them the place in our hearts reserved only for God. When that happens, there begins an internal struggle that eventually will make its way out into our thought life and actions.

Jesus' entire sermon is a list of contrasts of values between the world and the kingdom. The world values money and possessions, while the kingdom values are stored in a safe in heaven. When Jesus says here in v. 24 that *"No one can serve two masters," it is not a command, but a statement of fact.* And when He says that either you will hate one and love the other, or be devoted to one and despise the other, He is making exactly the same point as He did in Luke 14:26 when He said, "If anyone comes to Me and does not hate his father and mother, wife and children, brothers and sisters, yes, and his own life also, he cannot be My disciple". He is not telling us that we must dishonor or disown our parents and families in order to be His disciple. He is telling us that unless we put Him first and love Him first, not only is our salvation at risk, but those other relationships are at risk as well. Jesus only wants us to be free from our possessions so that, we are wholly devoted to pursuing God's will for our lives.

Let me put this into real-life context that will probably step on a few toes. It is one thing to have no other choice but to work on Sunday. But when we choose to work on Sunday instead of leading our families to church, simply because the pay is much better, then we are going to begin to despise the things of God as a result of the guilt we feel from that internal struggle. As I stated above, there then becomes a war between that person and God as well as a raging war within them. Ok, now that some of you have just used my name with some pretty ugly adjectives in your mind, let me move on.

Last year, I lost my car keys and searched everywhere for them. The last place I remember having them was out behind the church property, sighting in my rifle with my son Austin getting ready for deer season. A friend of mine, Norman, lent me his metal detector and I was out there for two hours and found nothing. I guess I should have used that detector on my couch, because a couple of weeks later, I was moving the couch and found the keys down inside that thin liner under the couch. In 1980, a man who lived in a trailer park in Australia had just taken his new metal detector out for a test drive. He swept the ground looking for signs of hidden metal in his backyard. Never did he imagine that he would uncover a metal rock weighing 61 pounds. That rock turned out to be a massive hunk of gold. He sold the nugget to a casino in Las Vegas, appropriately called *The Golden Nugget.* The valuable rock was placed on display in the casino with some other very impressive gold nuggets. One of those rocks was called *The Hand of Faith,* because its shape resembled a hand. When one hears the word *faith,* not many people think of a gold rock, but isn't that exactly where many people have placed their faith, whether it is precious metal, jobs, bank accounts, or any other *mammon.* And Jeff Strite points out the irony in the fact that the ancient Israelites did exactly the same thing with a gold rock in the shape of a calf! [77](Strite, 2015)

I am reminded of a story about a man who wore a sandwich sign while walking down the street. On the front of the sign, it read, *I am a fool for Christ,* while on the other side, it read, *Whose fool are you?* It is noble to think that we are our own person and slave to no one, but it is also not realistic. Whatever has your devotion has your heart, and whatever has your heart is your master.

Let me end this chapter with the story of Mary, the sister of Lazarus and Martha. On the day Jesus made His triumphant entrance into the City of God (we call it Palm Sunday), He stopped by some old friends' house for dinner. As He sat there reclining and conversing with a house full of dinner guests, quite to the surprise of His disciples who were eating with Him, Mary broke open an expensive jar of perfume and proceeded to pour out the contents onto Jesus' feet anointing Him. Then she completed the act of devotion by drying His feet with her hair. You may recall, this was not the first time that Mary found herself at the feet of Jesus. It appears that she was quite at home, worshiping at the feet of her Master.

In Matthew's account, he states that all of the disciples were indignant about her wastefulness and proceeded to express their dissatisfaction with the Master. What we have here between His disciples and Mary is a stark contrast between masters being worshipped. For the disciples, their value

[77] Strite, Jeff. 2015. *The god of Gold.* February 22, 2015. sermoncentral.com

was placed on the contents of a bottle, while Mary placed her value on the One whom the bottle was emptied out on. Jesus once rebuked the Pharisees for placing more value on the gold in the temple, than on the temple itself (Matthew 23:16).

But here are two points from Mark's account that I want to make and are the reasons for my bringing up this story. In Mark 14:3, we read that she did not just open the jar, but that she broke open the jar. For Mary, there was no second guessing herself, no turning back. She knew that what God wanted from her was total devotion and her actions came out from of a heart of total devotion to her Master. The other point is found in v. 8 where Jesus rebukes the disciples saying "She did what she could". That is all that God asks of me and of you, to do all that we can. If God is truly able to change the world through one obedient servant whose devotion and focus is single-minded, would we not want that person to be us? God took a devoted young man named Joseph—turned slave—turned prisoner, who had only his heart to offer God and saved the entire world from starvation. God took a devoted young shepherd boy named David, who only had five small stones in his pocket and slayed a giant giving the Israelites the confidence in God to slay armies of giants. God took a devoted young boy who only had a lunch of fish and bread and left thousands of followers full and satisfied. God took a devoted young Pharisee, who only had zeal for Him to offer and through him, spread His Word throughout Asia and Europe. And He took a devoted young Air Force sergeant, who only had a desire to be used for the kingdom and called him into the full-time pastorate where he pastored a wonderful church in north Alabama and through that congregation, God is still changing the world for people in that community, helping them to find hope.

How about you? I am living proof that God is not in the habit of calling superman or superwoman to do His bidding. Rather, He is in the habit of only calling those who are willing to do all they can. The question is not *Are you able?* The question is *Are you willing?*

NINETEEN

Seek First the Kingdom of Heaven

Therefore, I tell you, do not worry about your life, what you will eat or drink; or about your body, what you will wear. Is not life more than food, and the body more than clothes? Look at the birds of the air; they do not sow or reap or store away in barns, and yet your heavenly Father feeds them. Are you not much more valuable than they? Can any one of you by worrying add a single hour to your life? "And why do you worry about clothes? See how the flowers of the field grow. They do not labor or spin. Yet I tell you that not even Solomon in all his splendor was dressed like one of these. If that is how God clothes the grass of the field, which is here today and tomorrow is thrown into the fire, will he not much more clothe you—you of little faith? So do not worry, saying, 'What shall we eat?' or 'What shall we drink?' or 'What shall we wear?' For the pagans run after all these things, and your heavenly Father knows that you need them. But seek first his kingdom and his righteousness, and all these things will be given to you as well. Therefore, do not worry about tomorrow, for tomorrow will worry about itself. Each day has enough trouble of its own. (Matt. 6:25-34)

I consider myself to be somewhat of a war buff. I am fascinated with people who are willing to give their lives for something much bigger than themselves. I admire both their courage and their sacrifice in the face of certain danger. Whenever I visit a precious friend named Willard who suffers from chronic pains and disabilities (as a result of his military service), our conversation often turns to his two tours in Vietnam in which he received two Purple Heart medals for bullet and mortar wounds. One of the things that amazes me most about people who served in that war specifically was the tactic known as *search and destroy* where they walk through jungles and tall elephant grass searching out the endless hiding places of the enemy. You have heard the phrase, *there's safety in numbers*—well, there is one person out on that patrol who is all alone by design and that person is known as the *Point Man.* For those who might not understand this position, let me share a portion from Steve Farrar's book, Point Men—written for men to help them lead their families:

> It's 1966. You are only eighteen. You are in the prime of your youth. You've got a driver's license, a girlfriend, and plenty of dreams. Your entire life is ahead of you. But through a strange series of circumstances you don't fully understand, suddenly your driver's license is useless, your girlfriend's picture is in your wallet, your dreams are on hold, and you are in a country thousands of miles from home. Welcome to Vietnam. On this day, you would give anything not to be here. For you are going out on patrol. You've been out on patrol before, but today is different, and that's why there is a knot inside your gut and an icy fear in your heart. Today is different because the patrol leader has appointed you to be "point man." In essence, you're the leader. Everyone else will fall in behind you. And as you move out to encounter the enemy, you realize that the survival of those seven men stepping cautiously behind you will depend on just one thing: your ability to lead.[78](Farrar, 1990, 14)

People's lives depended on the Point Man. Their buddies' wives and children depended on the Point Man. Steve points out that if you are out on patrol, the most important person in your life is not your wife, your children, or even your patrol leader, it is the point man. More on that at the conclusion of this chapter.

Today's commandment not to worry is probably the one commandment that I most struggle with. But when I say that I struggle, I am saying that

[78] Farrar, Steve. 1990. *Point Man.* Portland: Multnomah Press

I sometimes allow the things of this world such as the worries that come natural as a husband and father to wrongfully take center stage over God in my life. Worry, I believe, is responsible for strangling out more joy and zapping more energy than any other thing in our life. Author Glen Turner said about worrying: "Worrying is like a rocking chair, it gives you something to do, but it gets you nowhere."

[79](Turner, Date Unk) The word worry comes from the Old English word *wyrgan*, meaning *to strangle* and isn't that exactly what worry does? It strangles out every bit of joy that we have today, by worrying about what might very well never come tomorrow! Someone once said, *worrying is effective—the things I worry about almost never happen!* We read this passage about worrying, and most of us attribute this command to not worrying about material things such as food and clothing. But in fact, there are actually three aspects of our lives that Jesus is concerned with here. The first is those material things in v. 25 and following in which Jesus specifically mentions those necessities for life. We also understand this verse includes all of our material needs such as our homes, jobs, and families.

But Jesus also reflects a concern for how we use our time. In v. 27, He warns us against spinning our wheels and wasting what time He has given us by worrying. Not a moment of worry will add a millisecond to the length of our lives.

Finally, Jesus is concerned about our future when He warns us against worrying about our tomorrows in v. 34. In John 10:10, Jesus says, "I have come that they may have life, and have it to the full."

I enjoy watching the hit series, MASH on occasion. In that series, there is a scene that is depicted in several episodes reflecting *Hawkeye* and *B.J.* collapsing on their cots after 18 straight hours of surgery. No sooner do they get comfortable, they hear the whirling blades of helicopters approaching and *Radar's* voice coming over the loud speaker for all personnel to report to the OR.

I think that many of us can relate to that scene. I know that if you are a parent, you can picture the image vividly! It seems like there is never enough time to do all you need to do and no sooner do you catch your

[79] Turner, Glenn. Date Unk. *Brainy Quote.* brainyquote.com/quotes/quotes/g/glennturne108587.html

breath, your attention and energy is required by someone else? I have never heard anyone ever complain about having too many hours in the day unless it was my kids on Christmas Eve.

Virtually everything that you and I ever worry about, or will worry about, is wrapped up in v.v. 25, 27 and 34. Look at that popular connector word that begins v. 25, *therefore.* I always remind people that in Bible study, when one comes across the word *therefore,* you need to see what it is *there for.* This conjunction conjoins Jesus' thought on getting our priorities straight in v.v. 19-24 with this command not to worry about those things. Then, in v. 33, we come to this really big BUT, which can also be translated *instead.* It, too, is a conjunction that connects a previous thought to a preceding thought. "But [instead of worrying] seek first the kingdom and His righteousness and all these things will be added."

What things? Earthly things. I am going to be up front and declare that some of you are probably not going to want to hear what I am about to say and some of you will probably not even believe me, but here it goes anyway: *God does not care how much money you have!* God does not care that you are able to buy that new car, that great vacation, those designer jeans, or even that swimming pool to cool off with on a hot summer day. In spite of what *prosperity preachers* will tell you, God does not care about those things, but God does care that you have enough money to take care of your needs, a roof over your head, and clothes on your back. And what Jesus is telling us is that if we put our life in proper order and put Him first, He PROMISES to take care of our needs. This is not *Name it—Claim it* theology. That theology is in error because it is self-centered (kingdom of self). What I am talking about here is a promise that if you put all of your hope and trust in the Lord and seek Him first in all things, He PROMISES to handle those things of lesser importance.

Since everything in our life then (career, family, marriage, time management and future) depends on this one verse, let us take a closer look to make sure we understand it completely. The word *seek* can actually be found in the New Testament both in a negative context as well as positive. James says, "You want something but don't get it. You kill and covet [seek]." (James 4:2) Jesus tells us here in v. 33 that we are to *covet*, that is to desire and be jealous to make God first in our lives. How many of us *jealously* make God first in our lives? How many would rather worship God on

Sunday morning than worship your bass boats, golf clubs, or sunshine and swimming pools on Sunday morning?

The next word in v. 33 is the word, *first.* To be first means to have the best, the most prominent and the most important position and it is the same Greek word that Jesus used in the first and greatest commandment, to "love the Lord your God with all your heart, with all your soul, with all your mind, and with all your strength.' This is the first and greatest commandment." (Matthew 22:37-38) This is the word with which I struggle sometimes, but I will come back to that one in a minute. Let me first finish picking this verse apart.

The word *kingdom* is basileia and does not refer to a physical place or palace. Rather, it refers to God's rule and authority over our lives. Jesus says in John 18:36, that "My kingdom is not of this world". We are to covet His will first in our lives and pour out our lives into pursuing that will. Paul said in Acts 20:24, "I consider my life worth nothing to me; my only aim is to finish the race and complete the task the Lord Jesus has given me—the task of testifying to the good news of God's grace". To truly love Christ means to also have a desire to grow in Christ. It is through that spiritual growth that we learn to desire His will over our own. It is what we call being sanctified.

Finally, He says that not only are we to earnestly desire His will and rule over our lives before anything else, we are also to earnestly desire His righteousness before anything else in our lives. Jesus stated in His beatitude that a true disciple will hunger and thirst for righteousness, not self-righteousness, but a new righteousness, His righteousness.

Let me get back to that word that often trips me up. I confess to you that as a pastor of a little country church, I am often consumed by its success. Nan has rebuked me many times about turning off my phone in the evening and our church board has insisted that I keep my days off sacred and stay away from ministry. It is also for this reason that led me to the sabbatical from which I write these words. But the truth is even while I am away enjoying personal down time, reflection, and devotion, my thoughts often turn back to my church and the many struggles that my dear friends may be facing in their lives. As a husband, father and pastor, I am often guilty of worrying about things when instead, I should be putting God first and allowing Him do what only He can do.

Even while I write this, my thoughts are on my new friends Pastor Stan Griffin and his wife Emily. Stan is the pastor at the church Nan and I attended while on Sabbatical in Maine. Stan has a true evangelist's heart for the lost and will do anything to help change their world for them. A few nights before we left Maine, we had Stan and Emily over to the cabin for dinner and when I asked him about his time off, Stan admitted to me that it has been quite some time since he did not have to think about church, or his other job (Stan is bi-vocational). In fact, it had been quite a long time since they had even gotten away for a family vacation. In his last sermon that he preached before we left, Stan spoke about how people fill so much of their lives with *stuff* and how Satan has determined that if he cannot make us bad, he will just make us busy. I approached Stan after the service and told him that he was right on, but then I told him that he needed to take a dose of his own medicine! Now, I do not want anyone to misunderstand why I shared that, because Stan is a true man of God with a heart that is devoted to the kingdom of heaven, and I am not even remotely suggesting that Stan is consumed with worry. But from one pastor's heart to another, there is a very real danger of allowing ourselves to be consumed, even in building the kingdom, to the point where we are no good to anyone, not the least of which is our families and our congregations. Stan, I pray that you will take that wisdom (hard-learned) in the spirit that it is intended.

Jesus said that all the worrying in the world will not make a single lasting difference. I can do nothing for my family, or for anyone else that has any eternal value, outside of what I am given by my Father. So, if I am thinking about Nan, the kids, or the church more than I am of God, then I am cheating them of what God has for them. For example, one of a pastor's main functions is that of counseling people, but if I am more consumed with how "I" can help them instead of *seeking* intimacy with God, then I am merely shooting from the hip in trying to help that person.

That takes me back to *The Point Man.* When we allow God to take point, that is to be first in our marriages, our families, our careers, our churches and virtually every aspect of our lives, He is able to guide us through this enemy territory called the world, to get us through dangerous situations and traps used by our enemy to hinder, maim, and destroy us.

And when those fiery arrows start flying, our Point Man is there to take them for us to ensure our safe passage.

In Psalm 18:2, David calls God, *my shield*. God's protection over His people is limitless. There is no weapon, no matter how great or grand that the enemy can throw at us that God is not able to protect His faithful. It all comes down to the matter of choice. As He does throughout His entire sermon, Jesus has given us a choice between two options: we can spend our lives worrying as the world does about what we are going to eat, what we will wear, or how we will provide for and protect our families; or, we can put God first and make Him the single-most important Person in our lives, and entrust Him with our family's welfare, our physical bodies, and this ever-increasing immoral world in which we live. Let's put it another way; we can fight the world's temptations on our own and fail, or we can seek first His kingdom and His righteousness and allow Him to take the arrows of temptation and worry for us. God wants to be our *Point Man!*

Peter advises believers to, "Cast all your anxiety on him because he cares for you. (1 Peter 5:7) He is speaking about the same One who says, "Come to me all you who are weary and heavy burdened and I will give you rest. Take my yoke upon you and learn from me, for I am gentle and humble in heart and you will find rest for your souls. For my yoke is easy and my burden is light."(Matthew 11:28-30) A yoke is something farmers place on animals to keep them under their control while they are plowing the fields and the point Jesus is making is that we will all be under the control of something. Some will be under the control of sin, some habits, some desires and some worry. Jesus says here that if we want to have a more joy-filled life that lasts for an eternity, then we should allow Him to be our Point Man! He wants us to fall in behind Him and walk in His steps, not turning to the left, or to the right, but filing in behind Him as He moves us through enemy territory safely and free, free from those things that the devil uses to make us think we are in control, but actually keep us in bondage, things like worry.

Conclusion

As stated in the introduction, this segment is all about priorities—priorities of our time, our resources, our focus and most importantly, our hearts. The kingdom of self is consumed by all of those things, but the kingdom of self is a temporary kingdom. It will not last! In his revelation of the end of time, John writes, "Then I saw a new heaven and a new earth, for the first heaven and the first earth had passed away." (Revelation 21:1) Everything that we spend our focus on here on earth will one day cease to exist, but the kingdom of heaven will never cease to exist. It and all of Christ's disciples will go on for eternity.

The lovable monk, priest and reformer Martin Luther was never one to mince words—one of his many traits that often got him in trouble with Rome! Regarding Jesus' illustration of *the birds of the air*, Luther stated that they...

> ...put us to shame with their living example, so that we ought to be ashamed, and not venture to lift up our eyes if we hear a bird singing, that is proclaiming heavenward God's praise and our disgrace... Therefore, when you hear a nightingale, you hear the cutest preacher, who reminds you of this gospel, not with poor mere words, but with the living act and example... so that we, who are people endowed with reason, and besides have the Scriptures at hand, do not have so much wisdom as to imitate the birds, and must daily hear ourselves disgraced before God and the people, as often as we heard little birds sing.[80(]Luther, 1892, 340[)]

These are strong words of rebuke indeed. How can we so callously set aside the eternal riches for which God has beautifully created for all who put their faith in Him and instead, place our faith and our focus on earthly things which moths will eat, rust will rot and thieves will steal?

Martin Luther concludes his thoughts regarding the kingdom of self vs. the kingdom of heaven:

> That is the whole of it, and no one gets any more from it, and in a little while we must say good-bye to it all, and

---

80 Luther, Martin. 1892. *Commentary on The Sermon on the Mount*. Philidelphia: Lutheran Publication Society.

> we cannot prolong our life with it for a single hour when the time comes. Hence it is a poor, miserable, yes - a nasty, stinking kingdom… and shall I so shamefully reject and give up God and his kingdom, that I may take this dirty, deadly belly kingdom in preference to that divine, imperishable one that gives me eternal life, righteousness, peace joy and salvation? (Luther, 1892, 340)

Jesus compels us to seek first His kingdom and His righteousness, because He knows what is best for all of us. But this eternal blessedness will cost us. It will cost us money, possessions, friends, family, hardship, possibly our very lives even. But the rewards are heavenly, the rewards are eternal and the rewards are more precious than the finest rubies, silver and gold. Jesus will not be Savior unless He can also be Lord of our lives. Is He your Savior AND your Lord?

SECTION FIVE

THE KINGDOM AND THE WORLD

Monasticism was first practiced by Christians in the mid-Fourth Century, but the practice actually dates several hundred years before Christ in the eastern Buddhist religion. In Christianity, spiritual men would separate themselves from the world into *monasteries* for the primary purpose of studying the Scriptures. The word *monasticism* is derived from the Greek word, *monos,* which means *alone.* Some have suggested that the practice of monasticism at least contributed to the dawn of the *Dark Ages* in Fifth-Century Europe, because this communal lifestyle largely removed Europe's spiritual and learned men from society—taking with them, the light of Christ.

In these next 12 verses of Jesus' sermon, He turns His focus, at least in part, to the Christian's involvement with the world. If the local church is not focused on the world around it, it is *nothing more than a sanctuary for saints, negating its design as a hospital for the hopeless.* As we enter into the final chapter of Jesus' sermon, He begins instructing us on how we are to put feet to our faith in the world that He has created and in turn, bring heaven to earth. Paul stated that we are not to be conformed to the pattern of the world, but it was never Jesus' intent that we separate ourselves from the world physically. Rather, through our being transformed into His likeness, we are to shine His light into the world's darkness, leading others into a spiritual awakening through the revelation of His gospel.

TWENTY

Do Not Judge

Do not judge, or you too will be judged. For in the same way you judge others, you will be judged, and with the measure you use, it will be measured to you. "Why do you look at the speck of sawdust in your brother's eye and pay no attention to the plank in your own eye? How can you say to your brother, 'Let me take the speck out of your eye,' when all the time there is a plank in your own eye? You hypocrite, first take the plank out of your own eye, and then you will see clearly to remove the speck from your brother's eye. (Matt. 7:1-5)

I heard a story once of a man who boasted of a keen eye for artwork. One day he attended an art gallery with his wife and friends wanting to impress them; but forgetting his glasses and being nearsighted, he could hardly see his hand in front of his face. He figured he could wing it by making abstract comments and observations about some of the artwork, so he approached a frame and began criticizing it saying, *why would anyone want to paint something so hideously ugly? I mean, it may be a true rendering, but why waste your time painting such a disgusting subject?* At this, everyone was laughing by this time as his wife whispered into his ear, *John, it's a mirror!*

We begin a new segment called *The Kingdom and the World* and we begin this new segment with one of the most often quoted verses in Bible. Unfortunately, it is most often quoted incorrectly. Jesus said, "Do not judge, or you too will be judged." (v. 1). According to one website, Matthew 7:1 is considered to be "The mother of all Biblical misrepresentations."[81]

The irony is that most often, those who openly throw that verse around are themselves guilty of passing judgment. More times than not when this verse is quoted, it is done only to defend one's poor decisions and behaviors by taking the light off from themselves and placing it upon the one making the judgment. But now here is the problem: Jesus is not telling us that we should not use sound judgment, only to be sure that our motives are pure, because we will be judged in the same manner.

Every light-shining disciple has had this verse thrown into his face. When someone attacks you with these words of God, they are saying, *Mind your own business and I'll mind mine! You live by your rules and don't push your moral standards on me.* Sound familiar? I am sure that at least some of you reading this have had your own daughters bark something similar to you after you judged their boyfriend or date—*Honey, I'm just not sure that a boy named snake who can't leave the state and has a weekly appointment at the court house is the boy for you. I'm just saying.* And they reply, *judge not lest ye be judged.*

One of the most common places we see this sort of response today is on social media. Almost without fail, when someone takes a stand against destructive or immoral lifestyles in general, people come out of the word-works claiming they are *being judgmental, which Jesus absolutely condemns!* Well, they are right and they are wrong and so, in this chapter, I want to look at two things: what Jesus is not saying and what He is saying.

What Jesus is not saying:

To understand this passage, it is crucial that we go back to a passage that we spoke about earlier in the book. In Matthew 5:20, Jesus says, 'For I tell you that unless your righteousness surpasses that of the Pharisees and the teachers of the law, you will certainly not enter the kingdom of heaven." You will remember, I stated that understanding the true meaning of the

[81] Facebook. 2016. *The Top Ten Biblical Misquotes, Misunderstanding, and misuses: Are you guilty of any of these?* September 10, 2016. www.facebook.com/notes/the-fax-a-message-of-truth/the -top-ten-twisted-texts-of-truth/1064145213632895/

Sermon on the Mount is contingent upon understanding this single verse. The Pharisees' understanding of righteousness was based on how well they kept the letter of the law without placing any emphasis on what was in the heart. Their righteousness was an externally-based self-righteousness and Jesus was simply stating that to get to heaven, we must be in possession of a *new* righteousness that goes much deeper than that. As a result of their skewed understanding of righteousness then, there was an awful lot of judging going on in regards to people who did not live up to their expectations. We see that in story after story such as the Pharisee praying alongside of the sinner, the woman caught in adultery and Mary washing Jesus' feet with her tears. When you read Matthew 7:1-5 in context, it is clear that Jesus was commanding us not to judge with the same spirit as did the religious leadership of the day.

When Jesus says that we are not to judge, He is not talking about righteous judgment of open and obvious sin which we will cover later. He is talking about the cold and callous *holier than thou* attitude by which the Pharisees judged. They took nothing into consideration when passing judgment on others. For example, in Matthew 12 when Jesus' disciples picked wheat on the Sabbath, because they were hungry and had no food, the Pharisees condemned their actions to which Jesus responded that their most-esteemed King David did exactly the same thing when he was hungry and ate the temple bread, which was reserved for priests only.

How many times have we been judged by others before they knew all of the facts? How many times have we judged others before knowing all of the facts? Some call that *jumping to conclusions* or *judging a book by its cover.*

There is an old Indian saying: *Don't judge a man until you've walked a mile in his moccasins.* I get a chuckle out of comedian Steve Martin's version saying, "Never judge a man unless you've walked a mile in his shoes. Then you'll be a mile away and you'll have his shoes." I have met hundreds of people whom I have fought the carnal temptation to judge by the way they lived, spoke, or thought—all without having a clue as to the shoes they have worn out in their lifetime and that is what I believe Jesus is speaking against in our passage.

I heard a story about a newspaper reporter who was searching for a story about the laziness that appeared to exist in the South, as opposed to the fast-paced lifestyle in such places as New York City. He saw a man out in his field, sitting in a chair and hoeing his weeds and thought, this had to be the ultimate example of the laziness he was looking for. He rushed back to his car to start writing his story when he looked back and saw that the pant legs on the farmer hung down loose because he had no legs. That story goes to show the limits of what we sometimes see in other people. God once made the point that, "People look at the outward appearance, but the LORD looks at the heart." (1 Samuel 16:7)

Nan and I, while on sabbatical, went to see the movie, The Shack. There is a very powerful scene in which the main character *Mack,* bitter toward God for allowing his youngest daughter to be murdered, is given a life-lesson on the main problem with human judgment. Mack demanded justice from God against the person who murdered his little girl, and to help him with his understanding, "God" removes Himself from His *throne of judgment* and has Mack sit on the throne in His place. "God" then tells Mack that the first two people he must judge are his two other children. God reminds Mack of his children's disobedience and deceptive ways in their past and tells Mack that he must choose which one will go to hell and which will go to heaven. Mack refuses to choose, insisting they are both great kids, unlike the murderer of his youngest child. "God" then asks Mack, *what is good and what is evil?* In other words, what was asked is, *by whose standards do we define good and evil?*

That is a great question for each of us in understanding critical judgment. It was never God's intent for us to judge what is good and what is evil (see Genesis 2:17), but immediately after sin entered the world, Adam started judging and we have been guilty of it ever since. Look at what I am talking about:

> Then the eyes of both of them were opened, and they realized *[JUDGED]* they were naked; so they sewed fig leaves together and made coverings for themselves. Then the man and his wife heard the sound of the LORD God as he was walking in the garden in the cool of the day, and they hid *[JUDGED]* from the LORD God among the trees of the garden. But the LORD God called to the man, "Where are you?" He answered, "I heard you in the garden, and I was afraid *[JUDGED]* because I was naked; so, I

> hid." And he said, "Who told you that you were naked? Have you eaten from the tree that I commanded you not to eat from?" The man said, "The woman *[JUDGED]* you put here *[JUDGED]* with me—she gave me some fruit from the tree, and I ate it" (Genesis 3: 7-12).

There is only One Supreme Being who is able to judge and that is God alone, so when we judge, we are placing ourselves onto God's throne where we were never intended to sit!

Look at Jesus' illustration in v.v. 3-5:

> Why do you look at the speck of sawdust in your brother's eye and pay no attention to the plank in your own eye? How can you say to your brother, 'Let me take the speck out of your eye,' when all the time there is a plank in your own eye? You hypocrite, first take the plank out of your own eye, and then you will see clearly to remove the speck from your brother's eye.

Who ever said that God doesn't have a sense of humor? I think They were all sitting around their heavenly think-tank laughing when They came up with that one. What an incredibly effective and simple illustration to help us understand the hypocrisy in addressing other people's sins, when we are blinded by our own sins. And if I may step up on my soap box for just a moment, isn't that the single greatest problem that people out there in the world have with people in the church? We are very quick to help people address areas of their lives that need shoring up, but we seem to be a bit short-sighted when it comes to our own.

While Nan and I were *out* at Bar Harbor, Maine, touring a few days ago, we saw many lovely New England churches in our travels and snapped many pictures of them. Then each night, after returning to the cabin, we would load the pictures onto the computer and sit on the couch together and reminisce over each picture and place we visited. In one particular picture of a very beautiful church, there was a very large black mark on the otherwise pure white steeple. The mark looked to be about three feet long by nearly a foot wide and we didn't remember seeing the mark when

Nan snapped the picture. In fact, there was absolutely nothing out of place at this church. It looked just like someone had taken it out of a postcard. How could the keepers of that church allow such a hideous discrepancy on God's church to exist? It was then that we realized the mark was not on the steeple but on our windshield. It was a piece of mud measuring only about one-half inch long and she had taken the picture with this small, but unsightly, mud splatter directly in the center of the camera lens.

We must attack sin and help others to live pure lives for Christ. But we need to be careful that our ability to see our friends clearly and help them in purifying their lives is not hindered by the mud in our own eyes! Oswald Chambers said, "The average Christian is the most penetratingly critical individual, there is nothing of the likeness of Jesus Christ in about Him." He goes on to say that, the only reason that Christians are able to point out the *speck* in their brother or sister's eye is because they have a *plank* in their own; meaning, the reason the average Christian can point out sin in other Christian's lives, is because the one doing the judging, often has the same sin in their own heart. If he criticizes another for pride, there is often pride in his own heart. If he criticizes another for their hypocrisy, there is often hypocrisy in his own life. [82](Chambers, 2016, 78)

What Jesus was saying:

As is the case with Jesus' entire sermon, this is a tale of two extremes. In this absurd illustration of the speck and the plank, Jesus is not only warning us against being hypocritical in our judgment, He is also warning us, not to be permissive by not using any judgment. Look at that illustration one more time: Jesus says in v. 5 that after you have addressed the plank in your own eye, "then you will see clearly to remove the speck from your brother's eye." Call that what you will friends, but that is judgment! Jesus said, "Stop judging by mere appearances, but instead judge correctly." (John 7:24). He does not tell us to ignore the sin of our brothers and sisters, but rather, we are to help them to address and remove the sin in their lives.

The single-most neglected commandment in the church today is the commandment to hold one another accountable and help each other in

[82] Chambers, Oswald. 2016. *Studies in the Sermon on the Mount.* Dallas: Gideon House Books.

our pursuit of personal holiness. Church discipline is a must in any God-fearing and God-glorifying church. Jesus lays out the doctrine of church discipline in Matthew 18 and while it may not be a very popular doctrine, it is one that is wholly (and holy) necessary.

Jesus never intended that we ignore sin inside the body and permit anything and everything, because the sin of one person affects the whole body. That was His point with the parable of the yeast. A great example of church discipline is found in 1 Corinthians 5. Paul addresses a case of incest that is going on in the brotherhood and he just rips into the church, not only because they are tolerating sin, but because they are proud of themselves for their tolerance. Hmm, that'll preach in a lot of churches today won't it? Then in v.3 he says, "I have already passed judgment in the name of our Lord Jesus on the one who has been doing this. In essence, he is saying, "look, I already judged the sinner and now, I am judging you, the whole lot of you."

The most loving thing that one brother or sister can do for another is to help in ridding the things in their lives that separate them from God. "As iron sharpens iron, so one person sharpens another." (Proverbs 27:17) Here is another example of Jesus pointing out this very lesson:

In John 7, Jesus rebukes the Pharisees when they objected to His healing a man on the Sabbath by pointing out their hypocrisy to the law. The very next morning, Jesus is teaching the crowd when those same dejected Pharisees brought a woman to Him who had been caught in the act of adultery (not the guy, mind you), to try and get even for the tongue-lashing He gave them the day before. The law required that she die. She was caught in the act, and so there was never any doubt as to her guilt. But rather than jump to conclusions or judge the book by its cover, He began writing in the sand, which, as a side-bar, is one of my top ten questions when I get to heaven…*What were You writing?* I want to believe that He started writing the names of every sin they were guilty of, possibly even names of women that some of them had been in the company of—but I digress. What I want us to see is what Jesus did not do. He did not look down on the woman. He did not shun her, condemn her, or make her feel like she was somehow inferior to Him or anyone else. But neither did He justify her behavior. *He forgave her and then He judged her to stop sinning.*

Jesus can and will do the same thing for you. If you are serious about pursuing a life of personal holiness, God will open your eyes to those things which keep you from experiencing the fullness of His love and grace. When He does that, it is not to put you down, shun you, or make Himself superior to you. It is solely out of a sincere desire to help you experience abundant life. He wants you to trust Him enough to turn that *thing* over to Him allowing Him to come in and cleanse your heart. Then, just like the woman caught in adultery, He challenges you to leave that sin at the altar and live a life of holiness for Him.

TWENTY-ONE

Left Behind

Do not give dogs what is sacred; do not throw your pearls to pigs. If you do, they may trample them under their feet, and turn and tear you to pieces. (Matt. 7:6)

Something interesting happened sometime back while I was taking a shower. Usually, I have my shampoo there on the shower rack, but for some reason, it was not. It is all good however, because Nan often puts shampoo and conditioner in my shower that she has tried but does not like and so, they come to me. That's right, I get shampoo hand-me-downs! Now, since I cannot see clearly without my glasses, I could not make out which one was which, so I just grabbed one and hoped for the best. As I was lathering up, it had a strange scent of oatmeal, but I didn't think anything more about it. What I did not know was that she had just given each of the dogs a bath that morning… that's right! At least I will not have any issues with fleas or ticks and to make a cheesy segue into my topic, we should not give to man what is reserved for dogs any more than we should give to dogs that which was meant for us!

In the previous chapter, I wrote about two extremes of being judgmental. We looked at the critical and condemning spirit that Jesus warned us against having at one end of the spectrum and having an *anything goes* mentality at the other. Verse 6 actually belonged to that thought because I believe that the first five verses speak primarily to our judgment of other believers. I wished to devote more time to v. 6, which I believe speaks primarily, if not specifically of our judgment of unbelievers.

Matthew 7:6 reads, "Do not give dogs what is sacred; do not throw your pearls to pigs. If you do, they may trample them under their feet, and turn and tear you to pieces." To better understand this verse, we need to first understand, who the dogs and pigs are and second, what is holy or sacred to Jesus. I would suggest to you that we all know a few dogs and pigs in our lives. Now, before you start making a grocery list of who they are, let me caution you that first, the ones you are thinking about probably do not fit Jesus definition and second, someone just might be writing your name on their list as well, so be careful!

Let us try to figure out who the dogs and pigs are that Jesus speaks of. Nan and I are dog lovers and sometimes I wished we had just raised puppies instead of children because they are easier to train, not nearly as expensive, and they do not talk back. With that said, your cuddly little lap-puppy at home does not fit the context of the culture in which Jesus makes this statement. Dogs were not house-pets during Bible times. They were wild and vicious scavengers that traveled in packs in search of food. A better illustration for those who live in the likes of rural Alabama would be a pack of coyotes. And just so we are clear, there was also nothing good about pigs in Palestine either. Pigs were unclean animals and just touching them was enough to render a Jew unclean according to the law. Both of these animals were repulsive and viewed with contempt in Jesus' time. So, now that we have the same image as that of Jesus' audience as to His illustration, we can now begin to understand who the dogs and pigs are by understanding what is sacred or holy to Jesus.

If something is sacred to you, it is special to you, you have assigned it great value. Just like pearls, whatever this sacred thing is, it has great value. My dad's tools were sacred to him. He was a carpenter by trade and a pretty good mechanic as well, neither of which he passed on to me. I remember once when he walked in on me pounding a nail into my bedroom wall using his $50 *Snap-On* socket wrench. I thought he was going to come out of his skin and then take some of mine in his anger. That wrench was sacred to my dad and I was abusing it.

Jesus gives us a clue in this verse as to what is sacred when He speaks of not giving pearls to the pigs. In Matthew 13, we find several kingdom parables, using such things as seeds, yeast and hidden treasures to describe some common thing. Then in Matthew 13:45-46, He says, "Again, the kingdom of heaven is like a merchant looking for fine pearls. When he found one of great value, he went away and sold everything he had and bought it". He is saying that whatever this pearl is, we ought to be willing to give up everything we have, including our freedom or our lives, just to get it. The only thing that we ought to be willing to die for is God's Word and the gospel of Jesus Christ! We see this playing over and over in Muslim countries where people are voluntarily giving up their lives rather than reject their saving testimony of Jesus Christ.

In Revelation 1, John says that he was exiled on the island of Patmos and for what? "The word of God and the testimony of Jesus Christ." (1:9) In Revelation 20:4, he speaks about those who were beheaded, "because of their testimony for Jesus and because of the Word of God." It is the Word of God that is sacred to Jesus and it ought to be sacred to us. If you were to look at the front covers of your Bible, there is a good chance that it is called, *The Holy Bible, The sacred Bible.* Jesus rebuked the devil saying, "Man shall not live on bread alone, but on every word that comes from the mouth of God." (Matthew 4:4) And when Paul was imprisoned, the only thing that he wanted besides his cloak to keep warm was God's sacred Scriptures.

Now that we understand what was sacred, let us look again at who the dogs and pigs are. I like to follow a lot of smart people, read their commentaries, follow their blogs. I even email some of them when I struggle with a Bible text. Most of those smart people agree on one of two interpretations in regards to v.6, but I will be frank; one of those interpretations makes absolutely no sense to me whatsoever.

There are some who believe that Jesus is speaking of all unbelievers here and that belief seems to be fueled by His encounter with the Canaanite woman who sought healing for her demon-possessed daughter. Jesus replied to her request saying, "I was sent only to the lost sheep of Israel… It is not right to take the children's bread and toss it to the dogs." (Matthew 15:24, 26). Even Jesus called everyone outside of the seed of Abraham, a dog! But as I said, this interpretation makes no sense to me, since we are all called to carry out the Great Commission (*Go and make disciples*) to the whole world!

In fact, this belief of separating from the world entirely led to the practice of monasticism that I spoke about in my segment introduction. In the *monastic* lifestyle, learned and spiritual men separated themselves from society to study Scripture. Here is the problem with this practice: what happens in a room filled with lit candles, when one by one, all of the candles are removed? The room goes dark! As a result of these spiritual men removing themselves from society to seek a closer walk with Christ, they left a void in society where Christ's light was desperately needed.

The other camp believes that the dogs and pigs in this passage refer to those who are contemptable toward anything spiritual, those who are hostile and become aggressive at the mere mention of anything spiritual—faith—Jesus—church—God! These are the kinds of people that I suggest we all know. These are the dogs and pigs who are looking to tear apart the gospel and trample it under their feet. Jesus said in sending out the disciples with His gospel to take it back from anyone who was not worthy of it and shake the dust off their feet as they leave (Matthew 10:13-14). Every day, believers around the world are being abused by the dogs and pigs who, not only treat the gospel with scorn and contempt, but treat the messengers of that gospel in the same manner. Jesus warned that this was going to happen when He said, "If the world hates you, keep in mind that it hated me first." (John 15:18) He is saying that it is His testimony they are rejecting, not us! Paul said in 1 Corinthians 1:18 that the gospel of Jesus Christ is foolishness to the unbeliever, and so how do we respond to those who turn hostile against us? The same way He directed His disciples before sending them off, walk away and shake it off.

Here is how speaker and author, Andy Sochor, views this passage in his study on the Sermon on the Mount:

> The sad reality is that not everyone will respond positively to our help that we offer them in their spiritual lives. In Paul's letter to the Galatians, he wrote, 'So have I become your enemy by telling you the truth' (Galatians 4:16)? Though we might speak 'the truth in love' (Ephesians 4:15), many will not take it that way. They will reject the truth, attack us for 'judging' them, question our motives, and hate us despite our efforts to show them the path that leads to life. In our efforts to teach others, a time may come when we will have to 'shake the dust off [our] feet' and move on *(Matt. 10:14).* Failing to do this deprives others – those

> who could be receptive to the truth – of the help that we could provide. By continuing to try to teach those who have demonstrated a willful rejection to the truth, we are taking time away from potential opportunities to teach others who might be open to the truth. Furthermore, we have certain responsibilities that God has given us – family, work, church, etc. If we fail to follow Jesus' instruction to 'not give what is holy to dogs,' we may neglect our other responsibilities [83](Sochor, 2017, 92)

I can definitely relate to this last part about spending so much time with those who are not open to the gospel of Jesus Christ that I tend to neglect other duties, such as visiting with those saints who are sick and in need of pastoral care. I am even guilty of stealing my precious time (my pearls) away from my family and tossing to those who want nothing to do with hearing what Jesus is offering. That is just plain wrong!

But now, I want to share a third interpretation from the Bible of Randy. I am not saying that I do not buy into this previous interpretation, because I do. But I believe there is yet another pearl of great value hidden in here waiting for us to dig up, and let me illustrate my interpretation using a conversation I had with someone in jail. I had been meeting with this person for some eight months every week for Bible study. One day, when I went to see this person, he shared how upset he was about someone else in jail with him who was very close to him. This friend of his promised him over and over that he would attend the weekly service with him in jail, but when the time came, he would not get out of his bunk to go, claiming to be *too tired*. Over and over, my friend extended an invitation and over and over, his friend rejected and so, my friend was very upset with him. So, I asked my friend if that would have bothered him eight months earlier before he received the gospel. He understood my point and decided that grace was a more appropriate response than anger.

You see, he was judging his friend by Christian standards that his friend never possessed and if I can get personal for a moment, *we tend to do the exact same thing by judging the actions of others by the sacred standards*

---

[83] Sochor, Andy. 2017. *Sermon on the Mount: Instructions for Life.* Rockfield: Gospel Armory Publishing

that we have accepted as the norm. When we do that, we cannot help but have a critical spirit toward that person, because this entire passage (v.v. 1-6) is about critical spirits. I believe Jesus is telling us in this passage, at least in part, that we are not to judge unbelievers by our sacred standards, but to love them unconditionally, just as God loved us, "while we were yet sinners, Christ died for us." (Romans 5:8)

Once, while teaching some children, I used the illustration of *Humpty Dumpty* to explain the point of Romans 5:8. I asked one of them to break an egg (with Humpty's face drawn on it) into a bowl and asked for any volunteers to help put Humpty Dumpty back together again—no takers (I guess it was the thought of putting their fingers in raw and runny egg!). We were once all broken just like Humpty Dumpty and all the king's horses and all the king's men could not put us back together again either. That is where grace comes in. Grace did not wait until we got fixed to come and die for us, Grace came from heaven offered Himself as a sacrifice for sins at God's altar, and the very last words from His lips were *it is finished!* He did not say that His life was finished, or that His ministry was finished, or even that the judgment of the ones who killed him was finished, but the work that needed to be done so we could be fixed was finished! It was the saddest day in human history, but it was also history's finest hour and God's greatest work when He extended Grace to pay for the sins of the world and fix that which was broken.

I tend to think that Jesus would have us extend that same grace to unbelievers that He extended to us. We have a hard time wrapping our heads around this, but Jesus loved the king who beheaded His cousin John every bit as much as He loved John himself. And for the record, which of Jesus' disciples were living according to His *sacred* standards when He called them?

I am going to close with a story that I read from a blog about Samuel Colgate, founder of the *Colgate Company*. One day during a church revival, a prostitute came forward wanting to receive Christ as Savior. She was clearly broken-hearted and weeping uncontrollably. After the preacher led her through a prayer of salvation, she inquired about joining the church. The preacher hesitated in calling for a motion to accept her into membership, even after she pleaded saying she would, *gladly sit in the back corner.* Finally, in an effort to get his preacher out of a pickle, someone stood up and suggested that they postpone her request until a more appropriate time. At this, Samuel Colgate stood and said, dripping of sarcasm, "I guess we blundered when we prayed that the Lord would save sinners. We forgot to specify what kind. We'd better ask Him to forgive us for this oversight. The Holy Spirit has touched this woman and made her truly repentant, but apparently the Lord doesn't understand she isn't the type we want Him to rescue." Many in the congregation including the preacher blushed with shame. Another motion was made and the woman was unanimously received into the fellowship. [84](Burdine, Date Unk)

I am sure that there are some of you who are feeling the twang of the Holy Spirit for unfairly judging others by your sacred standards. Maybe you have been *sizing* them up to determine whether they are worthy of hearing the message of hope and salvation. Maybe you are determining whether that person was the right person for your church. Possibly, by your action or inaction, you have already determined them not worthy of your time and effort to give them a reason for the hope that you have. I guess that what I am asking you to do is search inside and ask yourself, "Who have I given up on and left behind?" Maybe it is a family member you are thinking about who keeps messing up their lives; or maybe it is a friend who after invite after invite, still does not seem to want to grasp the truth. Or possibly, it is even someone you consider to be an enemy. God wants you to know that it is His will that all should be saved and nobody left behind, not even that person whom you are thinking about right now. Do you believe that it was sheer coincidence that that person's name came to your mind just now? You need to know that God's grace not only extends to the far reaches of that *unworthy* person about whom you are thinking. His grace even extends out far enough to cover your judgmental heart. Stop what you are doing and seek God's forgiveness for your *unjust judgment* and then make it a point to extend that grace to your friend, family member, or enemy!

And since I am stirring up the pot for the Holy Spirit, I am guessing that someone reading this has also felt unworthy of Jesus' love and forgiveness for the things that you have done and the things that you are riddled over with guilt. Maybe you have felt *left behind* by those in the

---

[84] Burdine, Greg. Date Unk. *Greg Burdine's Blog.* https://gregburdine.wordpress.com/tag/samuel-colgate/

church who have judged you unjustly. Jesus says if you have the faith of a mustard seed, you can move mountains. Whatever mountain you are climbing today, know that with God, all things are possible and He can wash away your sins—your guilt—your shame and your pain in a blink of an eye, if you will only believe He can. *The Church is one body, one Spirit, one baptism and we will leave no one behind!*

TWENTY-TWO

I've Got the Check

Ask and it will be given to you; seek and you will find; knock and the door will be opened to you. For everyone who asks receives; the one who seeks finds; and to the one who knocks, the door will be opened. "Which of you, if your son asks for bread, will give him a stone? Or if he asks for a fish, will give him a snake? If you, then, though you are evil, know how to give good gifts to your children, how much more will your Father in heaven give good gifts to those who ask him! (Matt. 7:7-11)

One day, six-year-old Bobby asked his father for a puppy. 'Sorry, Bobby,' his father said, 'not now. But if you will pray really hard for two months, perhaps God will send you a baby brother.' Little Bobby prayed really hard for a month, but nothing happened so he quit praying. And he was very surprised a month later when a baby boy arrived at their home. As he was looking at the baby beside his mother, his proud daddy pulled back the covers a little to expose another baby, twin boys! His daddy asked. To which little Bobby replied, 'I sure am, but aren't you glad that I stopped praying when I did?' (Source Unknown)

In Chapter 13, we looked at how we should not pray as well as, how we ought to *prepare for prayer.* In this chapter, I want to focus instead on what expectations we should have from our prayer life. Ron Dunn spoke of a conversation he had with a missionary regarding a letter he had received from a little girl who was given a Sunday school class project to write a missionary. Evidently their teacher had told them that real live missionaries were very busy and might be unable to answer their letters, for the one he received said simply: 'Dear Rev. Smith, We are praying for you. We are not expecting an answer.'[85](Dunn, 2013, 167) That simple and innocent statement by that little girl describes the prayer life of many Christians. Most of us are faithful in our prayers, but we are not really looking for any response to them. In fact, most of us are either shocked when God does answer, or we just chock it up to coincidence!

Prayer is not about trying to manipulate God into doing something that He does not want to do. Prayer is about tapping into God's willingness and desire to lead us into asking for and receiving according to His will. In Matthew 7:7-11, we first have a commandment from Jesus (v. 7), followed by a promise (v. 8), followed by His power to fulfill that promise (v.v. 9-11). Let us look at each of these:

The Commandment:

In v. 7, Jesus commands us to "Ask and it will be given to you; seek and you will find; knock and the door will be opened to you."This may appear as three different forms of prayer and you may have even heard this preached or taught this way; but in fact, Jesus is only defining the different levels of persistence in the same prayer.

He first commands us to ask. Self-explanatory right? Let's say that you and I went out to lunch together and I asked you to buy. There was not a lot of effort on my part there and since I did not get a response from you, I suspect, there probably was not a lot of effort on your part to answer my request either. Jesus then commands us to get a little more serious and *seek.* Seeking is asking with action. So, after lunch, when the waitress brings the check, I motion for her to place the check at your end of the table. Once again, there is no effort on your part acknowledging, *I've got this!* Jesus then tells us to knock and the door will be opened and so now, I am going to go get in my car and take off, leaving you alone at the table… with the unpaid check! Now, that is a very brazen example and I am convinced that you probably will not be asking me out to lunch any time soon; but if we are praying in God's will, we should be asking in the confidence by which He commands us to ask. In Ephesians 3:12, Paul says we are to,

---

[85] Dunn, Ron. 2013, *Ron Dunn: His Life and Mission.* Nashville: B&H Publishing Group

"...approach God with freedom and confidence." The writer of Hebrews writes, "Therefore, brothers and sisters, since we have confidence to enter the Most Holy Place by the blood of Jesus... Let us hold unswervingly to the hope we profess, for he who promised is faithful." (Hebrews 10:19, 23) Finally, in 1 John 5:14, John says, "This is the confidence we have in approaching God: that if we ask anything according to his will, he hears us."

In looking at this commandment in the original Greek language, these are all present tense commandments, meaning that Jesus expects us to continually be asking, seeking and knocking. *Believing in prayer makes a difference in your life, but believing that God answers prayer, makes an even greater difference.* God does not ask us to pray, He commands it and not because He has some ego trip and wants us to beg, but because He has the answer and He wants us to trust that *He's got this!*

George Muller is a great example of someone who trusted God in prayer. Over the course of Muller's sixty-year orphan ministry, he cared for over 10,000 children without asking a single person for financial support. Not one single child under his entire care ever went to bed hungry, yet all of his support money came through prayer and then he simply waited for God to pick up the check. But George Muller did not simply ask; he asked, sought and knocked on God's door until God answered him and God not only answered him, He answered in abundance.

One of my favorite movies is Shawshank Redemption starring Morgan Freeman and Tim Robbins. Tim's character, an innocent convict in prison, writes to the state prison board asking them for funds to buy books for the prison library. Over and over again, he sent them letters and over and over again, the letters fell on deaf ears. One day, they finally sent him a few boxes of well-used books, but he kept writing. Many months and many request letters later, the prison received many boxes of books, records and other media along with a monthly financial promise in a personal letter stating that they now considered the matter closed!

That kind of persistence was the point of the parable of the persistent widow in Luke 18 asking the judge for justice. The judge, having been worn out by her endless barrage of requests, finally said, "yet because this widow keeps bothering me, I will see that she gets justice, so that she won't eventually come and attack me!" (v. 5) God wants us to wear Him out and what Jesus is teaching us here in v. 7, is to keep asking until God considers the matter closed. I have had many people ask me when they should stop praying for something. I answer them in all seriousness and sincerity if God had released them yet from their burden to pray. If God has not considered the matter closed, then we ought to keep asking, seeking, and knocking until He does!

The Promise:

In v. 8, Jesus qualifies His commandment in v. 7, stating that this promise goes out to everyone who asks in faith. "For everyone who asks receives; the one who seeks finds; and to the one who knocks, the door will be opened."An important warning should be expressed here: we must keep this promise in context, because taken out of context, this promise would actually contradict other Scriptures. In the Old Testament, God makes it clear that He hears only the prayers of those who are living holy lives (see 2 Chronicles 7:14). And just in case you think that is an Old Testament truth that no longer applies, James says the same thing, that the prayers of a *righteous* person are powerful and effective (James 5:16). Given that condition that God places on prayer, then Jesus says all of us are invited into the throne room of grace with our petitions.

The story is told of Missionary J. Russel Morse's return from the mission field, and was the guest of an American family. After his first night's sleep, his hosts asked how he had slept. He was rather embarrassed, but admitted that he was terribly cold all night long. They asked, *Didn't the electric blanket work?* Morse had never seen an electric blanket before! He did not realize that warmth and comfort were available at his fingertips. Once his eyes were opened to this power available to him, he had no more cold and sleepless nights. (Source Unknown)

The problem with many people is not that they do not know how to pray; they just do not realize the power they possess through prayer. It is like the fifth grade Sunday school class who was asked to go home and that night, go out in their back yards and count the stars in the sky as part of their next lesson. They each came back with various numbers. Some said 100—some said 1000—one even said a million. Finally, the teacher asked a little boy who had said nothing, "*How many stars did you count?*" He replied, *three.* The teacher asked *how did you only see three?* He said, *I guess we just have a small backyard.* Some of us just need a bigger backyard—of faith that is! [86](Shepherd, 2004) We need to believe that our big God is bigger than our biggest problems and then trust Him to pick up the check! Look at it another way, if what we are asking of Him actually brings Him honor and glory, why wouldn't He want to pick up the check?

The Motivation:

In v.v. 9-11, Jesus draws a word picture to describe for us God's unconditional love, and just as He does in all of His parables, He masters it here using the only thing in our lives that can even come close to His love for us, our love for our children.

Let me just make a couple of points here to help us better understand His word picture. The most common bread found during this time was the small round flat breads, probably resembling what we call pita bread today. They actually looked like round stones (see Matthew 4:3). And when He mentions giving a snake instead of fish, we might conjure up an image of our dads handing us a poisonous viper to bite us, but that would not fit the context of the picture He is trying to draw a familiar comparison for us. He is speaking about switching a cooked fish for a cooked snake, the fish being a clean animal and the snake being an unclean animal. We see that in v. 11 where even in our evil flesh, we would try and do good for our kids, hence a live poisonous snake does not fit the picture.

They say that the most endangered people in prison are those who cause harm to children, because even some of the vilest of people have a hard time excusing such actions against kids. Jesus says that, "if even in our evil flesh, we want the best for our kids, how much better is our Father in Heaven who is holy and in Him, there is no evil?"

God is motivated by His unconditional love for us and would never deny His children, which leads me to a point that I am sure could be contested, but I want you to at least entertain an idea here. Looking at the context of nearly this entire chapter, Jesus is speaking about one subject,

---

[86] Shepherd, Steve. 2004. *Friendship 101. Sermon Central.* https://www.sermoncentral.com/sermons/friendship-101-steve-shepherd-sermon-on-evangelism-how-to-72918?ref=SermonSerps

salvation and more specifically, choosing heaven over hell. In v.13, He compares the narrow gate to the wide gate, then the true prophet vs false prophets, disciples and builders. Each of these move our conscience directly toward making the single-most important decision in our life, heaven or hell! With that said, doesn't it fit that anyone asking God for forgiveness, will find forgiveness? God will not turn anyone away who earnestly seeks Him. Paul said, "If you declare with your mouth, 'Jesus is Lord,' and believe in your heart that God raised him from the dead, you will be saved. For it is with your heart that you believe and are justified, and it is with your mouth that you profess your faith and are saved." (Romans 10:9-10)

Let me close by sharing a testimonial that I once heard of a Korean layman who was invited to speak at his denomination's assembly:

Years ago, a Korean layman was invited to address the General Assembly of his denomination during one of the devotional periods. He said that he wasn't qualified to preach, but he wanted to present to the group a problem he was facing and ask for their advice.

'A year or two ago,' he began, 'I received a letter from a friend of mine in Seoul. He was a young dentist and wanted to establish himself in my city. He asked me to find a place suitable for his home and office combined. Now we had a great housing shortage, but I did all I could to help him. For three days, I searched my city. Finally, I found a place and wrote him about it I told him that the house was in bad condition. The wall surrounding the place was in disrepair there was a hole in the house wall, the roof leaked badly. The house was in a wretched neighborhood. Furthermore, the price was exorbitant.

In spite of my bad report, my friend sent me a telegram telling me to buy the house. A day or so later I received a check for several thousand yen as a down payment. So, I signed the papers and purchased the house. The down payment was made and the final payments were to be made in three days, at which time the old owner agreed to vacate the house. The final payments were made, but then the owner asked for a day or two more until he could find another house. I granted him this period of grace. But after a week he was still there. Two weeks, three weeks, a month, three months, six months have passed.

The man who sold the house has purchased new clothes for his family, and they are eating out at the best restaurants. He knows I am a Christian and that in Korea we Christians never go to court with other Christians and we try not to go to court with unbelievers. He laughs at me when I come.'

'Now, Fathers and Brothers,' the layman continued, 'my friend is greatly embarrassed because his capital is tied up in this house, and he is in a very difficult position. What am I to do?'

Several members of the General Assembly responded. One pointed out that the layman was not acting in his own behalf but as an agent. Another pointed out that he was obviously dealing with a man who was a thief at heart. All agreed that the speaker had a right to go to the authorities and ask for an eviction order. The speaker asked for a show of hands and all voted that he had a right to proceed legally.

Then the layman said, 'Thank you, Elders and Brothers, for the way you have considered my problem. Before I sit down, I would like to draw one conclusion. Nineteen hundred years ago, the Lord Jesus Christ came down from Heaven to purchase for Himself a dwelling place.' Then he put his hand on his heart. 'He bought this old shack. It was in a rundown condition. It was in a bad neighborhood. He bought me because He wanted to take possession and dwell in my heart. But I cling to my tenement and leave Him outside. Now if you say that I have the right to seek the help of the authorities to evict the man who is occupying my friend's house, what shall you and I say of ourselves when we deny the Lord Jesus the full possession of that for which He gave His own life?'

What a great question to ask of ourselves! How much of Jesus do we really want? When you asked Jesus into your heart to forgive you and save you, did you also ask Him to come in and take control of your life? And if you did ask Him to come in and take control, have you since refused to vacate the premises leaving Him standing out in the cold? Jesus said in Revelation 3:20, "Here I am! I stand at the door and knock. If anyone hears my voice and opens the door, I will come in and eat with that person, and they with me". Jesus is far more persistent in wanting to come in and have fellowship with us, than we are in inviting Him in. He will never stop knocking until we either open the door, or He returns to judge us. But when we open the door inviting Him into our lives, He does not enter grudgingly, but instead, He comes in, sits at the table with us and says, *I've got the check!*

TWENTY-THREE

Pay it Forward

So, in everything, do to others what you would have them do to you, for this sums up the Law and the Prophets. (Matt. 7:12)

There is a movie that came out a few years ago called Pay It Forward, in which a young boy Trevor and his class were challenged by their teacher to go out and find a way that would change the world. It took Trevor time to develop his idea, but it was this: do something good for three people that they cannot do for themselves, then each one of that three go and find three people to do the same for them—pay it forward! Before too long, there was a wave of people doing kind deeds for others expecting nothing in return, only to find three others and do something for them. Before long, news agencies from across several states were catching on to what was happening, but only a single reporter investigated to see where it all started.

The producers of that movie took a radical concept right out of the teachings of Jesus' Sermon on the Mount in what has been called, *The Golden Rule.* Matthew 7:12 says, "So, in everything, do to others what you would have them do to you, for this sums up the Law and the Prophets." In these 11 words, Jesus' entire radical movement of bringing heaven to earth is summed up. It was absolutely revolutionary and while you may be thinking that most other religions have the same sort of teaching, you would be correct, but you would also be incorrect. John MacArthur, Jr. writes:

> Every other form of this basic principle had been given in purely negative terms, and is found in the literature of almost every major religion and philosophical system. The Jewish rabbi Hillel said, 'What is hateful to yourself do not to someone else.' The book of Tobit in the Apocrypha teaches, 'What thou thyself hatest, to no man do.' The Jewish scholars in Alexandria who translated the Septuagint (Greek Old Testament) advised in a certain piece of correspondence, 'As you wish that no evil befall you, but to be a partaker of all good things, so you should act on the same principle toward your subjects and offenders.' Confucius taught, 'What you do not want done to yourself, do not do to others.' An ancient Greek king named Nicocles wrote, 'Do not do to others the things which make you angry when you experience them at the hands of other people.' The Greek philosopher Epictetus said, 'What you avoid suffering yourself, do not afflict on others.' The Stoics promoted the principle, 'What you do not want to be done to you, do not do to anyone else.' In every case the emphasis is negative. The principle is an important part of right human relations, but it falls short—far short—of God's perfect standard.[87](MacArthur, 1989. 328)

Yes, there are many religions that impress upon their followers not being mean to someone, but Jesus' commandment is unique in that it is the only one that commands us to go and find something kind to do. He says that whatever you would like done for you, you go and do. If you want to be appreciated, go and appreciate someone else. If you want to be accepted, go and accept someone else. If you want to be affirmed, go and affirm someone else. If you want to be forgiven, go and forgive someone else. If you are hurt, broken, or sad, go and find someone else who is hurting, broken, or sad and minister to them. Remember the teaching

---

[87] MacArthur, John. 1989. *Matthew 1-28 MacArthur New Testament Commentary Four Volume Set.* Chicago: Moody Publishers

in Chapter Ten about going the extra mile? Here is how another Bible commentary put it:

> The Golden Rule is concerned with true love and with positive, active behavior. It is more than not doing wrong (lying, stealing, cheating). It is more than just doing good (helping, caring, giving). It is looking, searching, and seeking for ways to do the good that you want others to do to you. It is seeking ways to treat others just as you want them to treat you.[88(Word Search Bible, 1989, 111)]

This teaching of going out and actually *going the extra mile* to show God's love to others is the essence of what sets the Christian religion apart from all other religions and the rest of the world. Dietrich Bonhoeffer calls this exceptionalism, "the quality whereby the better righteousness exceeds the righteousness of the scribes and Pharisees." [89(Bonhoeffer, 1937, 100)] In Matthew 5:47, Jesus concludes his description of a Christian saying, "And if you greet only your own people, what are you doing more than others? Do not even pagans do that?" The Greek word here for *doing more* is *perisson* meaning exceptional, unnecessary, peculiar and THIS is what *sums up the Law and the Prophets*!

Jesus has given us so many examples of the *exceptionalism* found in the golden rule. For example, when a young man asked him who his neighbor was that would come and be kind to him, Jesus told him to go and be the neighbor. When Jesus was grieving the loss of his dear cousin John and just wanted to be alone, He looked upon all of the hurting people and had compassion on them and ministered to them. This was truly a radical idea that did not fit into any Old Testament mold. That is why Jesus warned us that we cannot put new wine into old skins and new patches on old clothes—It can't be done! Back in Matthew 5:17, Jesus stated, "Do not think that I have come to abolish the Law or the Prophets; I have not come to abolish them but to fulfill them." These two verses (Matthew 5:17 and Matthew 7:12) create a sandwich and everything in between is how He fulfills the

---

[88] Word Search Bible. 1989. *The Preacher's Outline & Sermon Bible.* Chattanooga. *Leadership Ministries Worldwide*

[89] Bonhoeffer, Dietrich, 1937. *The Cost of Discipleship.* London: SCM Press

law and He uses us to accomplish it! Paul says in Romans 13, "Let no debt remain outstanding, except the continuing debt to love one another, for whoever loves others has fulfilled the law. The commandments, 'You shall not commit adultery,' 'You shall not murder' 'You shall not steal,' 'You shall not covet,' and whatever other command there may be, are summed up in this one command: 'Love your neighbor as yourself.' Love does no harm to a neighbor. Therefore, love is the fulfillment of the law" (v.v. 8-10). Matthew 7:12 *(The Golden Rule) is nothing more than a summation of everything that Jesus has taught us up to this point.*

I experienced my first real *Nor'easter* here at the cabin during our stay. The wind gusts were up to 50 MPH and up to 24 inches of snow fell on Maine and other parts of the northeast. As I sat in the living room being warmed by the fire, I watched the storm whipping up something fierce outside the window and I thought to myself, *Wow! Look at that wind!* I suddenly caught myself realizing what a silly thought that was. How can I possibly see wind? Wind is invisible. What I was watching were the effects of the wind—the snow whipping past the windows and the tree tops bowing to its force. The Greek word for wind is *pneuma.* It is also the same word used for *spirit* (Holy Spirit, *agio pneuma*). The Holy Spirit is not an invisible force like the Nor'easter. Rather He is the invisible God and is often only seen in the effects of His force—us!

Jesus wants us to get radical in the way we live. He wants us to think radical, He wants us to speak radical, He wants us to parent radical, teach, preach and live radical. *Every teaching from His sermon up to this point, has been a radical (perisson) teaching that is not possible without Christ.* Those who do not possess the Spirit of Christ and attempt these commandments will only fail in their efforts!

But for the disciple, these teachings are a must if we are to bring the kingdom of heaven to earth. Two men were walking along discussing God, eternity, and judgment. One of them stopped and said, "You know, there is a question I'd like to ask God." "What question?" his friend responds. "How could you let all the evil and despair and injustice occur in this world?" "Yeah, it doesn't make sense!" The first guy stopped, and with serious expression said, "But the question terrifies me!" "Terrifies you?

How could asking such a fundamental question terrify you?" "Well, I'm afraid God might ask me the same question." [90](Eberly, 2007)

We are all here for a reason and as I see it, there is only one reason why any of us are still here. That it is because God has a plan to bring His kingdom here to earth and He has purposed the Church to do it. Now, we can all be good little church people, amen one another and sing really pretty songs, or we can get off our holy cushions and get out there and be the Church that He calls us to be, but we cannot do both. I am not content being content and I believe that it is a sin to be good when you are called to be great. I want to be challenged, I want to be used, I want to be effective for the building of the kingdom, and I know that will never be possible as long as I am sitting around waiting for God to show up. I have news for you! God has shown up. He is waiting down the road at the hospital, at the jail, He is that neighbor no one really likes. He is all around us saying *come on in, the water's warm* and He is looking for anyone who will do anything for their King!

In 2 Samuel 23, David has been king now for forty years and he is coming to the end of his life. He has not had an easy go of it. From the time that he was first anointed, he has struggled through hard-ships and trials, some of it self-inflicted, some of it not. He has faced back-stabbers and back-biters and his kingdom seems to be falling apart around him. Everyone seems to be against him, everyone that is, except for a few loyal men called his mighty warriors. David's mighty warriors were extremely loyal and willing to do any righteous thing needed to ensure their king reigned. Each of these courageous warriors had a reputation of fierce devotion to their king.

One day, David and his army were fighting the Philistines and David was thirsty. It appears that he must have been deathly thirsty, because his mighty warriors overheard him begging for water, left the safety of the stronghold and broke through the front lines. They were completely surrounded and the only well near them was at Bethlehem behind enemy lines. So, they fought their way through the front lines just to get their king a simple glass of water. When they returned with the water, they gave David the water and he did the strangest thing. In 2 Sam 23:16, the author writes, "So the three mighty warriors broke through the Philistine lines, drew water

[90] Eberly, Mark. 2007. *Jesus Will Wreck Your Life.* Sermon Central. October 15, 2007. https://www.sermoncentral.com/sermons/jesus-will-wreck-your-life-mark-eberly-sermon-on-sermon-on-the-mount-112900

from the well near the gate of Bethlehem and carried it back to David. But he refused to drink it; instead, he poured it out before the LORD!"

Can you think of a more ungrateful, unthinkable and unforgiveable thing to do than to take that water and pour it out? That was water that his mighty warriors fought so hard for and risked so much for? Imagine being one of those servants as your king takes your offering and just dumps it out on the ground at your feet. None of this story would make any sense if not for those last three words, *before the Lord.* David was so moved by their sacrificial offering, that he knew no one was worthy of such an offering, but God. Only God deserved that level of devotion from David's mighty warriors and only God deserves that level of devotion from us.

It is not enough that we go to church on Sunday, Wednesday, or any other day of the week. It is not enough that we make sure to put God front and center on the Lord's Day. Jesus wants us to go out there every day looking for someone who we can love, who we can teach, who we can help and who we can hold. Why? Because that is exactly what we would want someone else to do for us. And if we are honest with ourselves, our first thought when we hear this verse is *what's in it for me. How does this benefit me?*

The movie, Pay it Forward, had such an impact on me because its ideals run completely contrary to the kingdom of self. The truth is in that young boy's project, and more importantly, in Jesus' Golden Rule, there is nothing in it for me and that is what makes us as Christians so *perisson*! We need to open our eyes to the hurting and the needs of people outside the Church, because that is exactly what I would want if I were walking in those shoes. In reference to doing good deeds, John Wesley said:

> Do all the good you can,
> By all the means you can,
> In all the ways you can,
> In all the places you can,
> At all the times you can,
> To all the people you can,
> As long as ever you can! [91](Wesley, 2008, 69)

---

[91] Wesley, John. 2008. *1001 Quotes, Illustrations, and Humorous Stories.* Grand Rapids: Baker Books

I mentioned Matthew 5:17 where Jesus states that He had come to fulfill the law. Jesus did not present a *new law*, but rather a *new covenant.* Jesus came to have relationship with us and to give *life* to God's law, to give it flesh and blood. He came to present to the world the miracle of grace and it is this grace that pours out into each and every disciple, that we might do likewise and pour out into others. We are the fulfillment of God's law!

Here is my challenge: what if every person reading this chapter right now were to go and find three people for whom you can do something nice, whether it is paying for someone's meal, fixing someone's flat, or carrying someone's groceries to their car for them? If you truly open your spiritual eyes, the Holy Spirit will show you more ways to be Christlike than you could possibly imagine. And if in the process of your doing that good deed, the opportunity presents itself, ask them to do the same for three others. Trevor's teacher challenged his class to find a way to change the world. Our Teacher challenges us to do the same thing. Imagine the power that we have in one simple act of random kindness for someone who is in need. God only knows what He can do through a few obedient servants who just want to be a blessing to someone else.

Conclusion

Through Jesus' teaching in these past 12 verses, we can only begin to appreciate the heart that He has for the lost in the world. There are many *Christians* who are content fulfilling their *spiritual duties,* checking off squares each week, that they might somehow achieve some spiritual promotion in God's eyes and the eyes of others. But Jesus' teaching is not some grocery list that needs to be filled out, that one might receive favor by God. I mentioned in the beginning of this book, that nowhere in His sermon does Jesus share the gospel of salvation, that was not the purpose of His sermon.

Rather, Jesus' teaching was nothing more than a description of what a true Christian looks like, thinks like and acts like. And nowhere, is the need for that true Christian to be more evident, than in the world in which we live. There are people dying every day to an eternal hell and we have all been placed here where we are, to save them! We will not do it by going to church, serving the church, paying our tithes, or sounding *churchy* in our speech. We can only be God's saving vessel, by being the Church to this lost and dying world.

I recently read an article that insists that millennials are leaving the church in droves, not because God's Word is no longer *sharper than a two-edged sword,* not because His Word no longer has the power to save, or that faith in Him can no longer move mountains. Millennials are no longer in the church, largely because they fail to see the Church in us!

SECTION SIX

THE KINGDOM AND THE DECISION

We have come to the final segment of the book, appropriately titled, *The Kingdom and the Decision.* Jesus is drawing near to concluding His sermon on the mountainside and as with any good sermon (this being the greatest ever preached) it leads the listener to a decision point—a fork in the road.

In these final seventeen verses, Jesus lays out and makes the point, not once, not twice, not even three times—but Jesus puts forth the reality four times that there are only two ways to travel into eternity: His way of the kingdom of heaven, or the devil's way of the kingdom of self. There is no other business to be conducted, no more lessons to teach and no other loose ends to tie. It comes down to decision time. Will you seek first God and His kingdom, or will you take the much wider path toward eternal destruction? Will you seek to know the truth, or will you instead, desire to be fed the lies of the great deceiver? Will you build your foundation on the Rock of Ages, or will you settle for the sands of time which will wash away in the storms of life?

Jesus said, "I am the way, the truth, and the life. No one comes to the Father except through Me." (John 14:6) He leaves us with no doubt that there is not an easier path, but He also leaves us with no doubt that His way is the only way that leads to life eternal and abundant. If you are still on the fence, if you still have not surrendered your all to the Alpha and Omega, the Beginning and the End, may I ask you to do something before reading these last four chapters? Will you please humble yourself now, go to your knees, and ask God to reveal Truth to you as you make your way through these final seventeen verses? I am one hundred percent certain that when you are sincere in seeking and knowing Truth, God will reveal the Truth of His Son, Jesus Christ, to you. May God bless you in your reading and in your study.

TWENTY-FOUR

The Road That Leads to Life

Enter through the narrow gate. For wide is the gate and broad is the road that leads to destruction, and many enter through it. But small is the gate and narrow the road that leads to life, and only a few find it. (Matt. 7:13-14)

Time is precious! I wonder if you are like me, where every-so-often, you figure out where you are on death's slide-scale—you know, that scale in our heads where we figure out where we are in terms of life-expectancy! I remember when I was in my twenties and thirties, I used to think to myself, *dude, you're not even close to 50% yet...no worries.* Then, all of the sudden, someone greased my slide and now it is suddenly way over here in the senior citizen section and I am like, *wait a minute...where did this middle part go? How did this happen? I didn't even get a t-shirt!*

I now think more about dying than I did in my twenties, but I also now think a lot more about living, than I did then. And it is that abundant life that Jesus promises me and provides me that causes me to try to make the most of every day. I never want to go a day without making Nan smile. I never want to go a day without telling at least one of my kids that I love them and miss them. And I never want to go a day without being kind to someone who does not deserve kindness, and hugging on the necks of those who do.

At some point in my life, this ride ends and regardless of what my *slide-scale* says, it may be much sooner than I think. It may be this year, this month, this week, or even before I finish writing this book. I think that is the point Jesus is trying to make in Matthew 7:13-14. I do not believe that it is coincidence that He makes mention of this crossroad before us immediately after teaching us *The Golden Rule.* I think that among other things, He is telling us to get our affairs in order and that the most important thing we ought to be focusing on is to love people as we would want to be loved. That is exactly what Peter said, "The end of all things is near. Therefore, be alert and of sober mind so that you may pray. Above all, love each other deeply, because love covers over a multitude of sins. Offer hospitality to one another without grumbling." (1 Peter 4:7-9).

If you were told that you had seven days to live, how would you spend your final week on earth? Have you ever really contemplated what would change in your life with such short time left? How would your priorities change? Would you be consumed with working over-time? In this passage, Jesus tells us there are only two roads to travel in life: the road that is widely traveled by the world and the little iddy-biddy path that gets a lot less traffic. But, in making that decision, He also shares with us the sobering truth that the one which is well-traveled leads to destruction, while the iddy-biddy path leads to life.

It has been estimated that only about 20% of Adult American Christians live a life according to God's will. So, the flip side of that is, 80% of Adult American Christians are telling God that although they believe in Him, He is just not important enough to them to want to live according to His Word. (Note: Please understand that the word Christian in these statistics refers to those who only identify themselves as Christian, not to those whose calling and election are sure with God.)

The following statistic just astounds me: according to *The Barna Group*, 64% of adult American Christians said, "truth is always relative to the person and their situation. The perspective was even more lopsided among teenagers, 83% of whom said moral truth depends on the circumstances, and only 6% of whom said moral truth is absolute." [92](Barna, 2002) In other words, two-thirds of all adult American Christians and more than four of every five teenage American Christians believe that morality is based on their unique situation! Most Christians have joined the non-Christian culture in believing that we set our own standards, because God is not capable of establishing realistic guidelines for us to live by. God's

[92] Barna Group 2002. *Americans Are Most Likely to Base Truth on Feelings.* February 12, 2002 barna.com/research/Americans-are-most-likely-to-base-truth-on-feelings/

Word is no longer applicable to many Christians and is only something we grab off the shelf on Sunday morning and dust off on our way out the door. Sure, it looks good sitting on the coffee table when someone comes over, but its writings are foreign to our way of life. During the 2016 presidential election, I was blown away by something Democratic Vice-Presidential Candidate Senator Tim Kaine said during the Vice-Presidential Debate with then Gov. Mike Pence. When asked about the issue of same-sex marriage, Senator Kaine, who considers himself to be a *devout Catholic,* said he acknowledged that his "unconditional support for marriage equality is at odds with the current doctrine of the church I still attend. But I think that's going to change, too!" [93](Kaine, 2016)

There is an old adage that states, every road leads to Rome, and unfortunately, the world has made the same claim about heaven. But what is worse is that many Christians have bought into it. Jesus said, "I am the way and the truth and the life. No one comes to the Father except through me." (John 14:6). He does not leave any grey areas for us to figure out for ourselves. Over and over in the book of Acts, Luke refers to the fledgling church as *The Way.* God made it clear that Jesus is the only way to heaven and there is not another.

In his book, Answers to Life's Toughest Questions, a very dear friend and brother in the Lord, Dr. Ray Hundley wrote about this growing belief in and the acceptance and embracing of *universalism.* He specifically wrote about one *mega-church* pastor and writer within this universalist movement and points out the very real danger of this false teaching:

> Rob Bell founded Mars Hill Bible Church in Grandville Michigan, which now has an average Sunday attendance of ten thousand people. He has published seven books and was chosen as one of Time Magazine's 2011 'most influential people in the world.' His book, 'Love Wins,' has caused a great deal of controversy among evangelicals who see it as a denial of the biblical doctrine of hell and a blatant espousal of universalism.

[93] Kaine, Tim. 2016. Catholic Church Will Evolve On Same-Sex Marriage. September 10, 2016. americamagazine.org/content/dispatches/tim-kaine-catholic-church-will-evolve-same-sex-marriage

Dr. Hundley, goes on to share a quote from Bell's book:

> It has been clearly communicated to many that this belief [that Christians will spend eternity in heaven, while the rest of humanity will spend it in hell] is a central truth of the Christian faith and to reject it is, in essence, to reject Jesus. This is misguided and toxic and ultimately subverts the contagious spread of Jesus' message of love, peace, forgiveness, and joy that our world desperately needs to hear. And so this book.

Dr. Hundley then quotes five points from Bell's book which are in agreement with universalism beliefs:

1. It cannot be true, that God created millions of people over tens of thousands of years who are going to spend eternity in anguish.
2. It is not true that if a person has a personal relationship with God through Jesus, they will be saved from hell and judgment. The phrase 'personal relationship' is found nowhere in the Bible, so it cannot possibly be the heart of the Christian faith.
3. Heaven is not a state separate from the world; heaven is this earth changed to conform to God's will. When we help people with their physical problems, we, in effect, bring heaven to earth.
4. Hell is not a place of eternal punishment and separation; it is a place of refining and pruning so that people can finally repent and be welcomed into full fellowship with God and others.
5. It is not necessary to accept the Christian faith to be saved. Many people find God through other religions, or no religion at all, and enter God's kingdom without ever knowing Jesus' name or the gospel story at all.[94](Hundley, 2013)

With beliefs such as the ones Mr. Bell espouses, is it any wonder that he and many others like him are able to fill an auditorium with thousands

[94] Hundley. Raymond C.. 2013. *Answers to Life's Toughest Questions.* Lexington. InterVarsity Press

of people? But if I may use another old adage that my mom always used on me: *If he jumps off of a bridge, are you going to jump also?*

You see, as I have been attesting to over and over, Jesus spent all this time on that mountainside sharing with His audience the contrast between two truths: the way of the world (kingdom of self) and the way of the Lord (kingdom of heaven). And as wonderful and liberating as those beliefs mentioned above might seem to people, they come straight from the kingdom of self's book of rules and regulations that God is too good of a God to send anyone to hell and/or we are too good to be sent there! The Pharisees preached a false doctrine that one could be saved through their own efforts (kingdom of self) and Jesus spent the whole afternoon helping His disciples to understand just how dangerous their beliefs were. Now, here in Chapter 7, He begins wrapping up His sermon by saying we have but two ways, two teachers, two builders and two foundations, but only one way, one Teacher, one Builder and one Foundation will lead to eternal life. The other way might seem good, seem easier, seem more logical and less costly, but in the end, it only leads to destruction.

We want things fast, easy, and trouble-free, whether we are talking about our next meal or our next marriage. So, is it any wonder that we also want fast, easy, and trouble-free salvation? The rich young ruler said to Jesus that he wanted salvation. I am sure that he thought that by being a man of stature and wealth, it would be fast, easy, and trouble-free for him to attain it. But Jesus told him to go and sell everything he had and give all of his money to the poor. Then He said, "…and you will have treasure in heaven. Then come, follow me." (Luke 18:22) The man went away saddened because he did not want to get out of the fast lane.

Jesus never said that His way was going to be easy, fast, or problem free, but He did say that the reward for taking His way is eternal life. The fast-lane, on the other hand as they say, is paved with good intentions and temptations, but its end only leads to destruction. Voltaire was a French philosopher, famous for his attacks on the church. Toward the end of his life, he wrote, *I wish I had never been born*. Lord Byron lived a life of luxury and pleasure, never wanting for anything, yet toward the end of his life, he wrote *The worm, the canker, and the grief are mine alone.* American millionaire and ninth richest man in America, Jay Gould stated from his death bed, *I suppose I am the most miserable man on earth.* And finally, Lord

Beaconsfield, who was a man of prominence, position, prosperity, and personal friend to the British royal family, wrote in his old age, *Youth is a mistake; manhood, a struggle; old age, a regret.* [95](Journey, 2013, 170) What do all of these men have in common? They all are wealthy, all prominent members of high society, all unbelievers and all filled with regret and sorrow. I can say without any doubt that I have never heard a truly born-again Christian ever enter into their next life with regrets about having lived for Christ in this one.

In our passage, Jesus offers us two ways to die and by default, two ways to live. He is telling us that there are but two roads, His way to heaven, or Satan's highway to hell. There are no do-overs and as He is wrapping up His sermon, Jesus wants everyone to understand that there are only two ways from which to choose, and what we do now with our lives determines which road we have chosen. That bottle might look good now, until you wake up one day and your family has gone. Those drugs might look good right now and even help to take away some distant pain, until such time your whole life is centered on finding your next fix. That affair might look good right now, until it all blows up in your face and your family is torn apart and your reputation shattered. The fast-lane seems enticing and exciting right now, but a time will come and even sooner than your slide-scale suggests where you will be made to give account for the choices you made. And you might say as Jesus predicts you will in Matthew 7:22, that you lived your whole life for His kingdom, to which Jesus will say, *I never knew you. Away from me, you evildoers!*

Let me end this chapter by sharing a story that I once heard about raccoons. Apparently, raccoons go through a meta-physical change at about two years of age, after which they have been known to attack their owner. Since a thirty-pound raccoon can be equal to a hundred-pound dog in a scrap, a zoo keeper felt compelled to mention the change coming to a pet raccoon owned by a young lady named Julie. Julie listened politely as he explained the coming danger. He never forgot her response, *It will be different for me…* Then she smiled, adding, *Why, Bandit would never hurt me.* Julie underwent plastic surgery just three months later for facial lacerations sustained when her adult raccoon attacked her for no apparent

---

[95] Journey, Tina. 2013. *I Am Tina: A recorded and transcribed journal.* Victoria B.C.: FriesenPress

reason. [96](Richmond, 2010) All too often, the temptations of the fast lane come dressed in pretty and playful disguises and so we play with it. How often we find ourselves saying, *Oh It will be different for me.*

Warnings are important. As the watchman for our church, I have been sounding the alarm and blowing the trumpet of God's Warning. If the smoke detector in your house goes off, it is a warning that something needs to be given attention. If the lights on your car's dash come on, it is a warning that something needs to be given attention. If your child's temperature spikes, it is a warning that something needs to be given attention. I hear people all of the time who insist they are in a safe place with God and that, because God is a loving God and knows the works they have done, they know they are heaven-bound. If that is your thought, I want to ask you one question: where do you find that in the Bible? Many people, when asked about their salvation, like to point back to a time when they surrendered their lives to Christ and asked Him into their lives. But as I read the Bible, I find no place in it where a person's salvation is proven by looking at some past experience. Salvation is proven only by the fruit they are bearing in their lives today.

Many people who attend church are ignoring the Bible's warnings, warnings straight from the mouth of the very One in whom they claim to place their trust for their eternity. Time is precious and time is short. We really are not here on this earth for very long. We are like that light bulb that burns out when we go to turn the switch on. One day it will eventually happen and it may be without prior notice. So, how will you make the most of the time you have left on earth? We can make the most of the time we have by making the most of our walk with God.

[96] Richmond, Gary. 2010. *Sin is Like a Raccoon Sermon Central.* https://www.sermoncentral.com/sermon-illustrations/77884/christian-disciplines-by-rodelio-mallari?ref=TextIllustrationSerps

TWENTY-FIVE

The Wolves Amongst Us

Watch out for false prophets. They come to you in sheep's clothing, but inwardly they are ferocious wolves. By their fruit you will recognize them. Do people pick grapes from thorn bushes, or figs from thistles? Likewise, every good tree bears good fruit, but a bad tree bears bad fruit. A good tree cannot bear bad fruit, and a bad tree cannot bear good fruit. Every tree that does not bear good fruit is cut down and thrown into the fire. Thus, by their fruit you will recognize them (Matt. 7:15-20).

Wolves get a pretty bad rap from both Hollywood and writers of fairy tales. Dating back to 1941, when Lon Chaney Jr. brought the first werewolf to the big screen, America has had a fascination with wolves. But wolves' reputations date back long before that. In the 1840's, the first story of the *Three Little Pigs* hit the book stands and even long before that, a story came out of Europe about a young lady who left her home to deliver some food to her sickly grandmother. Of course, I am speaking of Little Red Riding Hood.

Although wolves have always gotten a bad rap from movies and fairy tales, it is not necessarily without cause. Wolves are known to be vicious hunters that will sometimes kill just for the sport of killing. Ranchers often testify that although they might find one sheep eaten, it is not uncommon to find ten others with their throats ripped out, but otherwise, completely intact. Wolves are also experts in stealth and concealment. For an unsuspecting sheep, its most prized victim, when the wolf finally reveals itself, it is much too late for the sheep!

Sheep, on the other hand, are very simple creatures. There is not a lot there to figure out. They are led to pasture where they gorge themselves until they either blow up, or are removed from the food source. They pay no attention to their surroundings and it is not uncommon for them to wander off totally brainless to the world around them. Their only focus is on filling their stomachs. I believe that sheep rank about one step above that of the turkey in brains. But for sheep, their greatest downfall is their selfishness. They have a flock mentality which instinctively leads them as far toward the center of the flock as possible, giving them the best chances of survival against a predator. But because of this *everyone for himself* mentality, the weak, sick, and young are left on the outside.

Jesus' lesson in Matthew 7:15-20 is about false teachers, those whom I would call wolves! The Rabbi makes it clear in the opening verses of Matthew 24, that as the end of this age draws closer, more and more *wolves* will emerge. We are seeing that occurring throughout the world. Sometime ago, a charismatic pastor headed to a small area in South America with about 1000 followers. Jim Jones claimed to be the Messiah and coaxed 918 of those followers into committing suicide. How could so many people be deceived by one person? And since that time, cult leaders (a.k.a. wolves) have come out of the wood works searching for their unsuspecting prey.

Since the massacre at Jonestown, Joseph Di Mambro and the Solar Temple claimed seventy-four lives, Heaven's Gate's leader Marshall Applewhite and thirty-nine followers killed themselves waiting for a spaceship and the Branch Davidians' David Koresh led eighty followers to their deaths, many of them children. There are literally thousands of known cults around the world, but there is one prime common denominator among these leaders. They all claimed to be a form of messiah, or an apostle of the true Messiah. Once again, how can so many be deceived? Jesus' own warnings of Matthew 24:4-5 says ta*ke heed that no one deceives you. For many will come in My name, saying, 'I am the Christ,' and will deceive many.*

I am reminded of a story that the author of The American Sniper, Chris Kyle's dad reportedly shared with his kids.

> There are three types of people in this world: sheep, wolves, and sheepdogs. Some people prefer to believe that evil doesn't exist in the world, and if it ever darkened their

> doorstep, they wouldn't know how to protect themselves. Those are the sheep. Then you've got predators who use violence to prey on the weak. They're the wolves. And then there are those blessed with the gift of aggression, an overpowering need to protect the flock. These men are the rare breed who live to confront the wolf. They are the sheepdog. [97](Kyle, 2014)

It is my desire to make sheepdogs of everyone reading this, and the only way we can do that is by heeding Christ's teachings and looking toward the sky for His glorious reappearing. So for the remainder of this chapter, I want to share a personal experience I had with a wolf, so that you can understand what to look for and know how you are to respond.

On April 2, 2008, a revival began in Lakeland Florida, about 90 minutes from where I was on staff at Bradenton First Church of the Nazarene. The revival, led by Canadian Pentecostal Evangelist Todd Bentley, was only supposed to last five days, but it wound up lasting six months as thousands flocked, hearing of the miraculous signs and healings that were taking place.

I heard reports and incredible stories from numerous members of my own church who had gone to experience this movement. Even members of our own staff were astounded by the amazing things that were taking place there. I would be lying to you if I said that I was not at least a bit curious, but because of a sickening feeling in my stomach that something was not right, I steered clear. But also, out of concern for the members of our flock that we were charged with protecting, I began listening to Bentley's sermons on *God TV* as they were all being recorded and then broadcast on the internet. I would love to tell you that what I witnessed was the manifestation of pure evil on the stage, breathing fire and eyes of blood red, but that would not be true. What I actually witnessed was a man who looked as though he had been touched by the hand of God with anointed messages of faith, hope, and love. He spoke with authority and with great knowledge of the Scriptures and people responded rushing the platform wanting to be touched by this *man of God*. I watched as people came up with crutches and wheelchairs, and as he ordered them to remove

[97] Kyle, Wayne. 2014. *American Sniper IMDb Quotes*. imdb.com/title/tt2179136/quotes

the crutches and get up from their wheelchairs they did! I witnessed time after time, people coming to him with diseases and ailments and then being *slain in the Spirit* as he laid his hands on them, all the while, the multitude of people broke out in chanting prayers and songs of praise.

I continued to follow this *miracle worker* on the internet as he spoke night after night. It is believed that a million or more people from over 100 different nations attended these revival meetings with millions more viewing over the internet. It was even getting nightly coverage on both the local and national news stations. I actually began thinking to myself, *maybe I am wrong here. Maybe there is something to all of this. Maybe God truly is reviving the hearts of people through this holy man.* Then I started listening to a couple of sermons a day that had been previously taped and after seemingly hours of listening and doubting my own eerie suspicions, something took place at one of the meetings that opened my eyes like saucers. There was an altar call! Now, I know what you are thinking, *of course there was an altar call, because it was a revival and people are brought to a place where they must face their sin and deal with it.* But see, that is where I found the core of my uneasiness.

In Bentley's altar call, three words were conspicuously missing: sin, confession and repentance. How can I be revived if I am not brought to a place of brokenness first? How can I be made alive again when I am not brought to a place where I first realize I am dead? There was no attempt of any kind to lead the sinners to grace by acknowledging that they are sinners and forced to deal with that first! Then I got curious. Maybe that was a fluke, maybe he just forgot part of his message; after all, it happens to me all the time and my poor audio-visual technician Drake is left up there in the sound booth as lost as a duck in the desert trying to figure out where I am going. So I went back and re-listened to those other sermons I had already heard and although there was much about holiness, forgiveness, love, heaven, healing and hope, the issue of sin and repentance never came up! In all of the messages I had listened to, I never once heard Bentley refer to someone's need to turn his or her life around in order for change to take place. I was immediately reminded of Jeremiah's rebuke of Judah's false prophets. He said in Lamentations 2:14, *The visions of your prophets were false and worthless; they did not expose your sin to ward off your captivity. The prophecies they gave you were false and misleading.* You see, all of the false prophets of Judah were telling the people that all is well, that nothing needs to change, right up to the time that Nebuchadnezzar's army plowed through their front gates.

About a month after I finished my *investigation* and informed other members of our staff to get the word out, Bentley was noticeably absent from the nightly revival meetings with no explanation. I looked on the internet to find out why, and I found a statement from one of his organization's board members. It read, *Todd Bentley has entered into an unhealthy relationship on an emotional level with a female member of his staff and that he would refrain from all public ministry for a season to receive counsel in his personal life.* In fact, Bentley was tied up in court, seeking a divorce from his wife. The Lakeland Revival quickly died.

There are many Bentleys in the church today, many of whom are well-dressed, well-educated and well-versed in Scripture. They are very effective at showing you around the Bible without actually stopping long enough to allow you to examine it for yourself. It is like the *Wizard of Oz* scene where the *Great and Powerful Oz* tells Dorothy to pay no attention to the man behind the curtain.

When I go to the supermarket, I like to feel the produce before I buy it. I like my avocados to be a bit soft and my *Gala* apples to be as firm as possible. The religious charlatans want to you buy what they are selling without first feeling the fruit. And that is exactly how Jesus tells us that we can learn to be the sheepdogs instead of the sheep, by examining the fruit. Jesus finished his warning about false teachers saying, *Therefore, by their fruits you will know them.*

Look at their fruit! A bad tree bears bad fruit. Look into their personal lives, look into their work ethic, look into the lives of those with whom they associate, but mostly, study the Scriptures for yourself! Never, ever take anyone's word as gospel, except the very words about Whom and by Whom the gospel is written. Paul said in Galatians 1:8-9, "But even if we, or an angel from heaven, preach any other gospel to you than what we have preached to you, let him be accursed. As we have said before, so now I say again, if anyone preaches any other gospel to you than what you have received, let him be accursed."

It seems Paul had some insight about some of those who would follow him. In Acts 20:29, he said, "I know that after I leave, savage wolves will come in among you and will not spare the flock." I would argue that any pastor who does not speak the truth in love does not love his flock, but only loves what he can gain from his flock. Once he has gained all that he can, he departs leaving behind pain, disappointment, loss of faith and even broken relationships. One preacher said it this way, *they (those false teachers or preachers) would be covered in the blood of their flock but not the blood of the Lamb.* There was a day when you would go to church and learn about sin, you would confess that sin, seek forgiveness for that sin and Jesus would look at you and say *what sin.* Today, people go to church, hear a wolf deliver a great feel-good message and they walk away saying *what sin*? Paul prophesied to his disciple Timothy about this desire of the world to be drawn to *feel-good* teaching saying, "For the time will come when they will not endure sound doctrine; but wanting to have their ears tickled, they will accumulate for themselves teachers in accordance to their own desires, and will turn away their ears from the truth and will turn aside to myths." (2 Timothy 4:3-4)

Nan and I went to visit our daughter Emily and her husband Andy some time ago. They had just moved from Raleigh to Charlotte North Carolina and we were celebrating the building of their first home. They had not been there long and still had not found a church they would call home, but they had attended a rather large church and seemed to like it well enough. We knew we were in trouble when the ushers handed out ear plugs as we entered. After the *very lively* music, the pastor, a young *cutting-edge* charismatic speaker, shared a message via video. It seems he was out of town that Sunday, but had prepared something in advance for his flock.

After we left the service, we said good-bye to our precious kids and headed home. As we drove along, neither of us really said anything about the service and so I finally broke the ice. I asked Nan to research the pastor and found out that he was drawing a very robust paycheck for his ministry and that he lived in a \$1.7M, 16,000 square foot mansion! We were both taken back by these revelations, which fueled a rather long conversation about the exorbitant salaries of some pastors. Listen, I do not have an aversion to money. I am just like the next guy who likes to have nice things and live comfortably and Paul says that churches ought to pay their pastors a living wage so they are not side-tracked from their ministry. But Scripture also tells us that pastors ought to live modestly and live humbly.

It is my opinion that many pastors need to modify their lifestyles and live more humbly.

Someone recently posted a picture of Joel Olsteen's mansion and made the comment that maybe it is time to tax churches. I responded, *No! It is time pastors start focusing on their calling instead of their cash.* Dietrich Bonhoeffer stated it this way: "Maybe he [false prophet] hopes his intellectual ability or his success as a prophet will bring him power and influence, money and fame. His ambitions are set on the world, not on Jesus Christ... He may even be unconscious himself of what he is doing. The devil can give him every encouragement and at the same time keep him in the dark about his own motives." [98](Bonhoeffer, 1948, 212-213) Someday, these wolves will meet the Lamb of the Scriptures and they will be rewarded for what they have done to the Lord's flock and the sheep, though lost for eternity, shall finally be avenged.

Each year during Pastor Appreciation Month, my wonderful church recognizes Nan's and my ministry with wonderful and thoughtful gifts. This past year, the children got together and painted a canvass sign for my office wall that I am most proud of. It reads: *Pastor, only because hardcore devil stomping ninja isn't an official job title.* If my only fault (Ha! Don't I wish!) was that I shared with my congregation the truth without watering it down, or sugar-coating it trying to increase the number of my flock (or my paycheck), I will go on into glory with my head held high!

In ancient China, gem merchants often took on apprentices to study the craft of selecting, cutting and selling rare stones. One young man came to a master craftsman requesting to become an apprentice. The craftsman agreed and asked him to come back the next day. The following day, the apprentice arrived and was given a ruby and told to sit in the corner and hold it. Throughout the day, that was all he did. He did the same thing the next day, and the next... After a couple of weeks, the apprentice complained and asked why he was being treated this way. Without saying a word, the master placed a red stone in the young man's hand at which the apprentice quickly stated, *That's not a ruby!* He had learned to know the authentic from the fake by constant exposure to the real thing. [99](Strite, 2002)

---

[98] Bonhoeffer, Dietrich. 1948. *The Cost of Discipleship*. London: SCM Press

[99] Strite, Jeff. 2002. *Owooooo... I Mean Baaa. Sermon Central.* https://www.sermoncentral.com/sermons/owooooo-i-mean-baaa-jeff-strite-sermon-on-sermon-on-the-mount-51286

Do you want to learn how to be the sheepdog instead of the sheep? Learn this—Study Jesus! Jesus says that His sheep know His voice. Younger sheep in the flock do not yet recognize their master's voice, and so they follow the older ones who do, and they do what the older ones do. Do not be caught unaware. Do not be fooled into believing that anything can be proven in Scripture. Study the real deal every day and when that ole smelly stanky swanky wolf shows up, you will be ready!

TWENTY-SIX

Twistianity

Not everyone who says to me, 'Lord, Lord,' will enter the kingdom of heaven, but only the one who does the will of my Father who is in heaven. Many will say to me on that day, 'Lord, Lord, did we not prophesy in your name and in your name drive out demons, and in your name perform many miracles?' Then I will tell them plainly, 'I never knew you. Away from me, you evildoers! (Matt. 7:21-23)

Mickey Cohen was an infamous member of the Jewish-mob in the early 1920's. He began his life of crime bootlegging during the days of prohibition. His life of crime finally came to an end in the 1960s when he became a resident guest at Hotel Alcatraz.

One of Cohen's men, Jim Vaus, a wire-tapper for the mob, became a Christian while attending a tent meeting of a young unknown evangelist named Billy Graham, in 1949. Cohen could not help but notice a big difference in Vaus, especially when Vaus decided to leave his life of crime and serve the Lord as both evangelist and youth leader. As a result, Cohen's own interest in Christianity led him to seek out an audience with Billy Graham and apparently, decided to give his life to the Lord also. But unlike his friend Vaus, nothing at all changed in Cohen's life. He continued to be the same ruthless gangster that he always had been. When his friend confronted him with the inconsistency, Cohen said, No one had told him that he would have to give up his work or his friends. After all, there were

Christian football players, Christian cowboys, Christian politicians; why not a Christian gangster?[100] (Goettsche, 2001, 248)

According to the website, Christian Standpoint, a Twistian is defined as: *One who manipulates Christianity to justify un-Christian personal, political, or cultural biases.* (Galaska, 2010) Twistians are people who profess Christ as their Savior, but their belief has no effect on their lives, and they are often guilty of *twisting* God's Word to suit their own lifestyle. A great example of this are those who are in bondage in homosexual lifestyles. They attempt to explain that anti-homosexual Scriptures in both the Old and New Testaments do not apply to monogamous homosexual relationships. These, and many others like them, refuse to submit their lives to Christ's commandments, but instead, they twist the gospel in a manner that suits their sinful lifestyle. These professing Christians are what is known as twistians and the truth is, there are many twistians in the Church today: twistian adulterers, twistian racists, twistian cohabitators, twistian addicts and twistian drunks—just to name a few!

One thing that I would like to point out is that as a reader progresses through Jesus' whole sermon, he cannot help but to see a rise in the intensity of Jesus' words. Going back at least as far as Matthew 7:13, Jesus really takes the reader to task saying, *look, in the end, unless you choose My way, you are not going to make it to heaven.* It is crunch time in Jesus' sermon and He is delivering His knock-out punch. In Matthew 7:21-23, that punch gets only harder! He says that when He returns, there will be some people who expect to join Him in His glorious appearing, but He will say to them, "I never knew you. Away from me, you evildoers!" Can you even begin to imagine those words being directed your way from our Savior's lips?

Thankfully, we are all safe, aren't we? I mean after all, we are honoring God by our presence in church, aren't we? Thankfully, we have our ticket to ride stamped and sealed, evident by the fact that we go to church three times a week, give 10% of our NET income and we even serve as usher, teacher, deacon, or elder! I mean we are all good people—right? There is no way that God is going to turn us away—in fact, I bet He cannot wait

[100] Goettsche, Bruce. 2001. *Faith Lessons: Lessons in Faith from Genesis.* Vienna: Xulon Press
Galaska, Chet. 2010. *Christian Standpoint: Twistians.* September 14, 2010. christianstand point.blogspot.com/2010/09/twistians.html.

till we get there, because we will make heaven that much sweeter and brighter—right? I can prove that we are all going to heaven. I can still remember the day I said that special prayer, that *Sinner's Prayer.* That sealed it tighter than a Navy submarine!

I am going to say something that may come across as divisive between denominations, but I hope you will understand when I explain. There is a belief that suggests *once saved, always saved* and I believe it is one of the most deceptive weapons the devil has. Sometime back, I got into one of many theological discussions with my dear friend and brother in the Lord, Jeff, following a Bible study. We started talking about the deceptive schemes of the devil and specifically, we were speaking about those who were deceived by this false doctrine. Once again, please do not misunderstand my intent here; it is not to create divisiveness. I know many good and godly pastors who are faithful to the Scriptures and are wonderful servants, but it is my belief that they are themselves deceived by this doctrine that they preach to their flock.

In keeping with the sheepdog theme from the previous chapter, I have an incredible responsibility as a pastor to speak out against deceptions. The devil's greatest weapon is deception, and he wants nothing more than for people to have a false sense of their eternal security. I do not think there are too many people who would not love for this doctrine to be true, but as Jeff and I discussed that night, we would probably have to rip out about thirty percent of the New Testament in order to justify that belief because there is a wheelbarrow full of Scripture that contradicts it. How many people who bought into that false doctrine will stand before our Savior and hear those heart-wrenching, soul-sacrificing words, *I never knew you. Away from me?*

Did you know that the hardest language on earth to learn is English? That is largely because so many words have so many different meanings. For example, according to a website called Stack Exchange, the word with the most meanings in the English dictionary is the word *set* with 464 different meanings. That word is followed by the word *run* with a 396 and *go* with 368.[101(Stack, 2011)] Then, there are words that are so confusing that it is no wonder they want to do away with English as being our first language. Someone rightly noted there is no butter in buttermilk, no egg in

[101] Stack Exchange Network. 2011. *Words With Most Meanings.* english.stackexchange.com/questions/42480/words-with-most-meanings

eggplant, no ham in a hamburger and no apple in a pineapple. Quicksand works very slowly and boxing rings are square!

But those are not the only confusing words. Another very confusing word is the word, *Christian*. This word means different things to different people. If you were to ask several people, *what is a Christian,* you would probably get several answers. Some would say, *A Christian is someone who goes to church every Sunday,* or, *someone who is actually a church member.* Then others might say, *A Christian is a person who tries to do what is right,* while still others might say, *A Christian is someone who has been baptized.* I think it is safe to say that the more people you ask, the more differing answers you would get.

Fortunately, we do not have to rely on your answers or mine to that question, because we have it straight from God and isn't His definition the only one that matters to us anyway? So then, how would God define a Christian? Well, let us take another look at Jesus' words and see if we cannot figure this thing out. He says:

> Not everyone who says to me, 'Lord, Lord,' will enter the kingdom of heaven, but only the one who does the will of my Father who is in heaven. [22]Many will say to me on that day, 'Lord, Lord, did we not prophesy in your name and in your name drive out demons, and in your name perform many miracles?' [23]Then I will tell them plainly, 'I never knew you. Away from me, you evildoers (Matthew 7:21-23).

First of all, in v. 22, Jesus is speaking about those who *prophesy,* that is to say, those who proclaim God's Word. Each time a pastor, preacher, or evangelist stands in the pulpit, he or she is prophesying some truth to you that God has already revealed to all of us in Scripture. However, Jesus says that not everyone who stands up and shares His Word with others will get into heaven. It is not enough to tell others about Jesus. Jesus, Himself, warned His disciples to steer clear of the Pharisees prophesying saying, "but do not do what they do, for they do not practice what they preach." (Matthew 23:3) He made it clear that their preaching was not going to get those false prophets into heaven. They, instead, will hear those haunting seven words, "I never knew you. Away from me".

Then Jesus says in v. 22 that those who drive out demons in His name are not safe either. I am reminded of the passage in Acts 19 where some Jews tried to copy Paul in chasing out demons using Jesus' name and in v. 15, the evil spirit said, Jesus I know, and Paul I know about, but who are you? Then the evil spirit proceeded to give the men a whooping they would not soon forget. "I never knew you. Away from me."

Finally, He speaks about those who are doing miracles, or works in His name. I think most here have probably had to wrestle with this one at some point before. Paul said plainly in Ephesians 2:8-9, "For it is by grace you have been saved, through faith—and this is not from yourselves, it is the gift of God— not by works, so that no one can boast." Jesus makes it clear that good works will not get us into heaven. Instead, good works are the fruit (evidence) of our salvation (James 2:14-17). So, if you are counting on your resume of deeds, be prepared to hear those same dreaded words, "I never knew you. Away from me."

Since telling people about God, my efforts to free people from their demons and my many good works will not save me from those dastardly seven words. What will? Let us back up one verse and we will find something that you may have just glossed over in your reading. Verse 21 reads, "Not everyone that says to me 'Lord, Lord' shall enter the kingdom of heaven, <u>but he that does the will of My Father in heaven".</u> Well, that really clears things up for us, now doesn't it (sarcasm intended)? Actually, it does, because it gives us a place to begin to search out *The Standard* by which we will be judged for all of eternity. We only need now to understand God's will and in John 6:40, Jesus provides that little important piece of information saying, "For my Father's will is that everyone who looks to the Son and believes in him shall have eternal life, and I will raise them up at the last day."

Being a Christian is not about what you say, what you do, who you are, or even what you believe. Being a Christian is about Who you believe in. That word *believe* in John 6:40 is the same word that is found in the most recognized verse in the entire Bible, John 3:16. It is not a head belief (*I know who Jesus is)*, but a heart belief (*I know Jesus as my personal Savior*). The Bible says that even the demons know that Jesus is the Son of God, but they do not trust in Him for their salvation. This word *belief* means to trust, to lean on, to place your hope in. Salvation is not about a what; it is about a Who.

There are many people who believe in the *twistian* faith, a warped belief that they can remain in a sinful lifestyle their entire lives and still be a Christian. But with only a cursory examination of the Scriptures, they could only conclude that they (Scriptures) condemn their sinful behavior. When a person's nature has truly been born-again by the Spirit of Christ, he is no longer a slave to sin. Paul said, "Therefore, if anyone is in Christ, he is a new creation. The old has passed away; behold, the new has come." (2 Corinthians 5:17)

Of twistians like Mickey Cohen, Jesus said, *I never knew you. Away from me* and that is exactly where Martin Luther found himself, long after believing that he was forgiven and saved. Recognized as a leading figure of the Protestant Reformation, Martin Luther was considered to be a rising star in the Roman Catholic priesthood, an astute doctor of theology and an esteemed professor of religion. Yet, after becoming disenchanted with many of the policies and practices within the Catholic Church, he began searching the Scriptures for himself. When he opened the book of Romans, he was struck with six small words that Paul used to open with in Chapter 1, *The righteous will live by faith* (v. 17). Everything in which he had placed his faith (kingdom of self), came crashing down around him and he realized that he did not know Christ personally, but was rather, trusting in himself for his salvation. William Barclay stated in his commentary on Matthew:

> There are two great permanent truths within this passage There is only one way in which a man's sincerity can be proved, and that is by his practice. Fine words can never be a substitute for fine deeds. There is only one proof of love, and that proof is obedience. There is no point in saying that we love a person, and then doing things which break that person's heart. When we were young maybe, we sometimes used to say to our mothers, 'Mother, I love you.' And maybe mother sometimes smiled a little wistfully and said, 'I wish you would show it a little more in the way you

> behave.' So often we confess God with our lips and deny him with our lives. It is not difficult to recite a creed, but it is difficult to live the Christian life. Faith without practice is a contradiction in terms, and love without obedience is an impossibility. [102](Barclay, 1956-1959)

Barclay stated that "There is only one proof of love, and that proof is obedience." Those are great words, but William Barclay was not the first to say them. Jesus repeated them over and over again to His disciples:

> John 14:15: If you love me, keep my commands
> John 14:21: Whoever has my commands and keeps them is the one who loves me
> John 14:23: Anyone who loves me will obey my teaching
> *John 15:10: If you keep my commands, you will remain in my love*

Jesus made it crystal clear that true love for Him will result in obedience to His Word, not twisting it, ignoring it, or pleading ignorance to it. Bonhoeffer explained the difference between a Christian and a twistian this way:

> The man who says 'Lord, Lord'—means the man who puts forward a claim on the ground that he has said it—the doer—is the man of humble obedience. The first is the one who justifies himself through his confession [of faith], and the second, the doer, the obedient man who builds.[103](Bonhoeffer, 1948, 215)

I heard a story about a thirty-one-year-old woman in Massachusetts who learned she had cancer. She was treated and they were in hope that all would be well. She got married, became pregnant, but the cancer reoccurred and shortly afterwards she died. The reason she died is that

---

[102] Barclay, William. 1956-1959. *Barclay's Daily Study Bible: Matthew 7.* https://www.studylight.org/commentaries/dsb/matthew-7.html

[103] Bonhoffer, Dietrich. 1948, *The Cost of Discipleship*, London: SCM Press

she refused treatment and therapy until after the baby was born. Once the baby was born, it was too late for treatment. She died in her baby's place. She saved it by dying for it.

Paul said, "If you declare with your mouth, 'Jesus is Lord,' and believe in your heart that God raised him from the dead, you will be saved. For it is with your heart that you believe and are justified, and it is with your mouth that you profess your faith and are saved." (Romans 10:9-10) There is no other way to heaven! The Bible says that Jesus came to earth to take our sins to the cross and our Father raised Him again three days later. All that is required of us is to accept His payment for our sin and trust in Him alone for our salvation. To everyone else who comes to Him, those seven dreaded words will ring in their ears for all eternity, *I never knew you. Away from me.*

TWENTY-SEVEN

The Wise Builder

Therefore, everyone who hears these words of mine and puts them into practice is like a wise man who built his house on the rock. The rain came down, the streams rose, and the winds blew and beat against that house; yet it did not fall, because it had its foundation on the rock. But everyone who hears these words of mine and does not put them into practice is like a foolish man who built his house on sand. The rain came down, the streams rose, and the winds blew and beat against that house, and it fell with a great crash." When Jesus had finished saying these things, the crowds were amazed at his teaching, because he taught as one who had authority, and not as their teachers of the law. (Matt. 7:24-29)

I have reminded you many times of Jesus' stern warning in Matthew 5:20, where He says that unless our righteousness surpasses that of the Pharisees, we will never enter into the kingdom of God. That passage, I believe, is the thesis for His entire sermon.

I mentioned previously that there is an increased level of intensity in Jesus' words, and now He concludes His sermon with a very straightforward declaration that there are only two ways to go, His way or the *hell way*. In this final passage of Jesus' sermon, He speaks about building houses, something that as a carpenter's Son, He most certainly knew something about. The integrity of any structure depends upon three things: the wisdom of the one building it, the materials used, and the foundation itself. If you were to use the very best of materials, but lacked the know-how of putting those materials all together, it might look like something I built and it would not last. Likewise, if you were to use inferior materials, no matter how well you built it, it also would not last.

If we were to skim back over these three chapters we've been looking at, we can see that Jesus first provides us with wisdom by focusing on our attitude and how we view the blueprints. In Chapter 5, He lays down the proper attitude of the Christian in the beatitudes and follows that up with a proper understanding of His Word—*You've heard it said, but I tell you...* Then, in Chapter 6, He begins providing all of the materials we need to enable us to have that proper attitude and Scriptural worldview. As He sat on that mountainside teaching, He has been providing for His disciples (that would be us), all we need in order to build and preparing us for our task. Now, He is commanding us to get out there and start building!

At least as far back as Paul's journeys, man has been trying to broaden the gospel and insist that there is more than one way to get to heaven. As the day of His return approaches, more and more false prophets appear to share with us a "*different gospel*" as Paul calls it.

The world would have you believe that you have a myriad of choices to choose from to get to heaven, whether it be Islam, Buddhism, Mormonism, Jehovah's Witness, Confucianism, Hinduism, Shintoism, Native American spirituality, Wicca, or any other belief system that denies the deity of Jesus Christ and the sovereignty of the Triune God. In Chapter 15 (fasting), I mentioned that we are a people of multiple choices from which to choose and that is certainly the case in the world with the buffet of religions to suit our liking. But God does not see it that way. According to the Author of the Bible, there are not many ways, but only two–Christ's way which leads to life and everything else which lead only to death. Neal Anderson states in his book, The Bondage Breaker, that the devil's greatest trick is deception.[104](Anderson, 1990, 248) If he can deceive you, he can defeat you. Deception worked in the Garden of Eden, and it has been working ever since.

There was a man on trial for murder in Oklahoma. Evidence of his guilt was overwhelming, but there was no corpse. In his lawyer's closing statement, knowing that his client would probably be convicted, he resorted to a trick. *Ladies and gentlemen of the jury, I have a surprise for you*

---

[104] Anderson, Neil. 1990. *The Bondage Breaker*. Eugene: Harvest House Publishers. Eugene

all, the lawyer said as he looked at his watch. *Within one minute, the person presumed dead in this case will walk into this courtroom.* He looked toward the courtroom door. The jurors, somewhat stunned, all looked on eagerly. A minute passed. Nothing happened. Finally, the lawyer said, *Actually, I made up the previous statement. But you all looked on with anticipation. I, therefore, put it to you that there is reasonable doubt in this case as to whether anyone was killed and insist that you return a verdict of not guilty.* The jury, clearly confused, retired to deliberate. A few minutes later, the jury returned and pronounced a verdict of guilty. *But how?* inquired the lawyer. *You must have had some doubt; I saw all of you stare at the door.* The jury foreman answered, *Oh, we did look. But your client didn't!*" [105](Snyder, 2001) If you know the truth, you cannot be deceived into believing a lie. *Jesus removed from the devil all power and authority over us at the cross.* The only thing that he has to use against us is deception, but Satan uses it well, because there are many Christians who are leading defeated and ineffective lives.

God said in Deuteronomy 30:19, "This day I call the heavens and the earth as witnesses against you that I have set before you life and death, blessings and curses. Now choose life, so that you and your children may live". Let me make an appeal to the *logical* side of your brain for a moment: If our God, who loves us, will not override our right to choose and force blessings on us, then He certainly will not allow Satan to force his will on us either. The devil cannot put death and cursing on you unless you permit him to by your own free will. So, who then would ever choose death and cursing over life and blessings? Only a person who is deceived.

I read a story about a farmer who decided to buy a chain saw. The man at the local hardware store guaranteed that he could cut down as many as 15 trees in a single day. A week later, a very unhappy farmer came back to report that the power saw must be faulty—it averaged only three trees a day. The salesman grabbed the saw, pulled the cord and the saw promptly went Bzzzzzzzz. *Hey*, demanded the startled farmer, *what's that noise?* There are many Christians who are content living defeated lives because they do not realize how much power is found in the truth.

---

[105] Snyder, Eric. 2001. *A Defendant on Trial for Murder. Sermon Central.* October 22, 2001. https://www.sermoncentral.com/sermon-illustrations/4324/faith-by-eric-snyder?ref=TextIllustrationSerps

In this final passage of Jesus' sermon, there are some similarities between the two builders, but one major difference. The first similarity is that both men were building a house. Jesus does not say that the man building his house on the sand was a lazy sloth. He was probably every bit as determined, meticulous and hard-working as the other man. He probably got up very early in the morning and worked till the sun went down. By all intents and purposes, his house was probably every bit as beautiful and sturdy as the other man's house. He had the know-how and used only the very best of materials. The only difference was the foundation on which he built.

There are many people who mistake busyness for godliness. There are many people who are busy building their houses of ministry thinking that their service will warrant them entry into heaven, but their foundation is superficial; it is fluid like sand, moving and shifting to suit their lifestyles.

On Oct. 17,1989, a massive 6.9 earthquake struck the San Francisco area and caused an estimated $6 Billion and killed sixty-three people. Some buildings and highways collapsed like a house of cards, while other structures such as the Golden Gate Bridge sustained very little damage. The Golden Gate Bridge sits directly on top of the San Andreas fault, yet it was literally untouched, because the entire weight of the bridge rests on the two towers deeply embedded into the rock beneath the sea. Some of you may remember seeing pictures of the highways in San Francisco that just collapsed like playing cards. These roads were built on land that had been filled in. They all looked the same until the time of testing had come!

Jesus points out in v. 24 that He is actually speaking about our handling of His Word when He speaks about buildings and foundations. He ends His entire sermon with a warning. It is as if He is saying, *look, I have given you everything you need to live holy lives. I've explained what a real disciple looks like, how he thinks and what he must to do to obtain eternal life.* Then, here in this final passage, He says that you have two choices—you are at a crossroads—you can live with the truth, or you can die with the lie, because as Jesus points out, there is still one more similarity between the believer and the unbeliever and it is the main point of His message here. In v.v. 25 and 27, He points out the fact that both the believer and the unbeliever will face storms, but it is only the one who trusts and obeys who will weather the storm.

God uses many storms that come in a variety of ways to help us strengthen our faith in Him. Centuries ago when ship-builders built ships with giant masts, they would go into the forest and find the strongest tree. Then they would clear out all the trees around it and leave that one tree standing, leaving it exposed to the wind and storms. As the tree continued to grow, it would gain strength, the kind of strength it would need to be able to stand up in the storms at sea. Those trees would never gain the strength they needed to weather those hurricane winds at sea if they had not been exposed to the storms. They gained their strength from the storms.

We will all face storms, it is not a matter of if. The only variable is how well we prepare for the storms that will come. Jesus points out in v. 24 that it is not enough to come to church, that it is not enough to read the Bible, that it is not enough to go to Bible study, Sunday school, or small group. The wise person will also apply His word to their lives—the foolish person will not!

On May 10, 1996, eight people died on Mount Everest after a wicked blizzard caught the party by surprise. Neal Beidleman survived the expedition. Those who had died paid $65,000 for their chance to climb the world's highest peak. When interviewed about what went wrong, Beidleman said, "Tragedies and disasters . . . are not the result of a single decision, a single event, or a single mistake. They are the culmination of things in your life. Something happens and it becomes a catalyst for all the things you've had at risk."[106](McCasland, 2020)

The things at risk in our lives today can overwhelm us when the storms come. As believers, the Rock of Ages as the Foundation of our faith, gives us safe passage through the storms. In Chapter Three, we are reminded that not a single commandment in Jesus' sermon will be possible for those who do not possess His Spirit to obey them. Then I gave an invitation to accept Jesus Christ as your personal Savior. If you are not yet a believer, you need to know that the greatest storm you will ever face is judgment by a holy God, and you, my friend, cannot and will not stand on your own merit before a holy God. Your anchor will give way and you will slip into the eternal abyss.

---

106 McCasland, David C.. 2020. *The Storm: Our Daily Bread.* odb.org/2003/11/11/the-storm.

If you are a believer and you are withered, worn, and weary from the crashing waves of life, be encouraged today by the words to a song written by Edward Note nearly 200 years ago:

My hope is built on nothing less
than Jesus' blood and righteousness.
I dare not trust the sweetest frame,
but wholly lean on Jesus' name.

Refrain:
On Christ the solid rock I stand,
all other ground is sinking sand;
all other ground is sinking sand.

When Darkness veils his lovely face,
I rest on his unchanging grace.
In every high and stormy gale,
my anchor holds within the veil.
(Refrain)

His oath, his covenant, his blood
supports me in the whelming flood.
When all around my soul gives way,
he then is all my hope and stay.
(Refrain)

When he shall come with trumpet sound,
O may I then in him be found!
Dressed in his righteousness alone,
faultless to stand before the throne!
(Refrain).[107(]Mote, 1834[)]

I have a dear friend in the ministry named Randy Duncan. In fact, Pastor Randy and his wife Robin were directly involved in Nan and my being led to a saving relationship with Jesus Christ, and for that we will

[107] Mote, Edward. 1834. *My House is Built on Nothing Less*

be eternally grateful. One Sunday, as Randy was preaching, he shared an experience that related to his topic. He explained that as he was driving down the road, he was beside another gentleman, tapping on his steering wheel as though he was performing a drum solo and moving his head from side to side singing along to music. Randy immediately began station-surfing on the radio trying to find the station the guy might have been listening to. I am not sure if Randy ever found the station (and that is not important) but he made the point that the man was obviously *marching to the beat of a different drummer,* and that was the point of Randy's sermon.

As followers of Christ, it is not enough to call ourselves Christians. It is not enough to go to church on Sunday, read our Bibles, or serve in His kingdom. Jesus' entire message that day on the mountainside was that as true believers—disciples—Christians, we are to *march to the beat of a different Drummer.* In other words, we are not only to sound the part, or look the part, we are to BE the part! And that is not something we can achieve any way other than by surrendering our all in all to Jesus, making Him not only Savior of our lives, but Lord of our lives.

It is my sincerest of prayers that this book has been and will continue to be a blessing to you in your journey. I pray that it helped you in some small way to better understand what it means to be a true, heaven-bound Christian, who is sold out for Jesus. Allow me to end this book with the Apostle John's own testimony describing God's promise that awaits all those who are:

> Then I saw 'a new heaven and a new earth,' for the first heaven and the first earth had passed away, and there was no longer any sea. I saw the Holy City, the new Jerusalem, coming down out of heaven from God, prepared as a bride beautifully dressed for her husband. And I heard a loud voice from the throne saying, 'Look! God's dwelling place is now among the people, and he will dwell with them. They will be his people, and God himself will be with them and be their God. He will wipe every tear from their eyes. There will be no more death or mourning or crying or pain, for the old order of things has passed away.'

> He who was seated on the throne said, 'I am making everything new!' (Revelation 21:1-5a).
>
> Then the angel showed me the river of the water of life, as clear as crystal, flowing from the throne of God and of the Lamb down the middle of the great street of the city. On each side of the river stood the tree of life, bearing twelve crops of fruit, yielding its fruit every month. And the leaves of the tree are for the healing of the nations. No longer will there be any curse. The throne of God and of the Lamb will be in the city, and his servants will serve him. They will see his face, and his name will be on their foreheads. There will be no more night. They will not need the light of a lamp or the light of the sun, for the Lord God will give them light. And they will reign for ever and ever (Revelation 22:1-5).

May the King of the kingdom of heaven find us all faithful!

CONCLUSION

We saw at the end of Matthew 4, in a very short time Jesus had gained quite a following since returning from His rendezvous with the devil in the desert. In Matthew Chapters 5-7, Jesus preached, what is inarguably, the greatest sermon of all time, the Sermon on the Mount.

As Jesus and his disciples traveled along looking for places to preach the kingdom of heaven, Jesus went up to the mountainside where He began to teach the Scriptures in a manner they had never been taught before. Unlike the teaching of the scribes, He taught with power and authority. In fact, the final two verses of Matthew 7 describe the impact He had on His audience when Matthew recorded, "When Jesus had finished saying these things, the crowds were amazed at his teaching, because he taught as one who had authority, and not as their teachers of the law."

As we learned in Chapter one of this book, there were uneducated blue- collar workers, learned professionals, believers and skeptics, Jews and Arabs, artsy and military. It was literally a smorgasbord of humanity gathered there for one reason: to listen to what this holy One had to say.

But then, in the opening verses of Matthew 8, we see Jesus come down from the mountain, and there was a crowd of Jews, Gentiles and Arabs following right behind Him. They did not seem to get enough of this holy Man, so they followed Him, and just as if He had planned it, the very first person they met was a man with leprosy (Matthew 8:2). In the societal pecking order of these ancient Palestinian villagers, there was only one group of people who were below sinners and Gentiles; those were the lepers. Even the tax collectors, whom they loathed, were not forced to live well outside of the village!

For a moment I want you to put yourself into a leper's shoes in ancient Palestine. Imagine waking up one morning and as you stumble out of bed, your eyes are half-closed as you stub your toe on Jr.'s toy camel. Your four kids, ages two, five, six and nine are already awake and getting ready for school. Your wife is busy in the kitchen stirring up some breakfast so everyone can sit down and eat together before going their own way. For you, it means getting your catch of fish from the night before out to the market place before it opens. Later this evening, you will team up with your buddies on the shore and head back out for another long, cold and dangerous night on the water.

It is the same routine every morning. By the time you make your way to the family eating table, your wife and your four children are already seated waiting for you to come and say the blessing over the food. It is the same routine, but this day would be different—this day would be drastically different! As you sit down, your precious wife looks at you and tears immediately begin welling up in her eyes and running down her cheeks. You are deeply puzzled by her reaction, until she finally shares with you that you have a strange mark on your cheek. You reach up to touch it, and it indeed is that scaly lesion that is often the first sign of the disease—leprosy!

Your thoughts immediately turn to the five people staring at you. The nine-year-old begins to cry, because she knows what is going on. She has seen this happen before with her friend's parents at school. The six-year-old catches on and he, too, begins to weep. Finally, the little ones begin crying out of the shear fear of seeing mommy crying. Who will take care of them? Who will provide for them? Who will be a daddy to his sons, his little girls? Who will watch after his precious wife knowing that by day's end, he will be forced to live in a new place, miles outside the village, in a compound with signs all around it warning passers-by not to enter.

Knowing how quickly the disease spreads, you quickly gather what clothes you can carry while your wife puts some food inside of an animal skin satchel. You dare not even kiss your precious little children or reach out to wipe their tears, because the disease is so contagious. You step outside your home, turn to see your family weeping uncontrollably and you begin shouting, *UNCLEAN, UNCLEAN,* as required by the law and you make your way to the priest, where he will examine you and determine what you already knew and dreaded.

Let me ask you a question as I conclude this book on the greatest sermon ever preached: Do you actually believe it was a coincidence that the Rabbi, His disciples, and the rest of His audience would come face to face with the most ostracized, rejected, and dejected of society immediately after He told them what it meant to be a Christian? Do you actually believe that it was shear happenstance that this sea of humanity would come face to face with their deepest biases only moments after hearing Christ's teaching about putting hands and feet to God's Word?

This leper, possibly a family man like I described, waited at the foot of the mountain, not daring to climb up the mountain and have to declare himself *UNCLEAN*, only to be mocked, spat at and possibly even beaten for interrupting their worship service. He waited patiently until Jesus made His way down and then seized his one-and-only chance of being made whole again. Notice how humble this man is. He does not just holler out wanting to be healed, as did those whom Jesus often encountered. The man, acknowledging Jesus' position as One to be worshipped, immediately drops to his knees in worship and says, *Lord, if you are willing, you can make me clean.* And now look at Jesus' response: *I am willing. Be clean!*

I cannot think of a better object lesson to illustrate His teaching from the mountain than for this crowd of people to see God's love up close and personal. The Jews amongst them have been learning under the local rabbis all their lives, the importance of maintaining the law, because it is the law. Jesus said, "I have come to breathe life into God's Word, to give it hands and feet, to give it heart, to give it passion".

This scene in the opening verses of Matthew 8 was orchestrated and ordained by God Himself to give His disciples, both those on the mountainside and those reading this book, a living example of the Sermon on the Mount in flesh and blood. We live in a world with a myriad of different cultures, races, generations, backgrounds and beliefs. And if we the Church are to love them as Christ commands us—that is, if we are to follow in the steps of our Rabbi and *fulfill the law,* we must be willing to step outside of our cultural norms—our likes and dislikes—our biases and prejudices and our comfort zones and be the hands and feet of Jesus Christ in this lost, hurting, and dying world. May we all walk in the footsteps of our Rabbi and be found faithful in following Him—God Bless You!

ABOUT THE AUTHOR

Randy French is an Ordained Elder and retired Pastor with the Church of the Nazarene. He is a former Children and Family Pastor, Executive Pastor, and Senior Pastor. Randy is also retired from the U.S. Air Force. Currently, Randy and his wife Nannette reside in Calais Maine where Randy works in the mental health industry, while Nannette works in the physical health industry

Printed in the United States
By Bookmasters